Designing App with Spring Boot 2.2 and React JS

Step-by-step guide to design and develop intuitive full stack web applications.

by
Dinesh Rajput

FIRST EDITION 2019

Copyright © BPB Publications, India

ISBN: 978-93-88511-643

Distributors:

BPB PUBLICATIONS
20, Ansari Road, Darya Ganj
New Delhi-110002
Ph: 23254990/23254991

DECCAN AGENCIES
4-3-329, Bank Street,
Hyderabad-500195
Ph: 24756967/24756400

MICRO MEDIA
Shop No. 5, Mahendra Chambers,
150 DN Rd. Next to Capital Cinema,
V.T. (C.S.T.) Station, MUMBAI-400 001
Ph: 22078296/22078297

BPB BOOK CENTRE
376 Old Lajpat Rai Market,
Delhi-110006
Ph: 23861747

Published by Manish Jain for BPB Publications, 20 Ansari Road, Darya Ganj, New Delhi-110002 and Printed by him at Repro India Ltd, Mumbai

Dedication

To my country, India.

My grandpas, the late Mr. Arjun Singh and the late Mr. Durjan Lal Rajput.
To all readers of DineshOnJava and my books.

To my mother, Indira Devi, and my father, Shrikrashan, for their sacrifices and for
exemplifying the power of determination.

To my kids, Arnav and Rushika, and my wife, Anamika, for being my loving
partner throughout my life journey.

About the Author

 **Dinesh Rajput** is the founder of https://www.dineshonjava.com, a blog for Spring and Java techies. He is a Spring enthusiast and a Pivotal Certified Spring Professional. He has written several bestselling IT books Like Spring 5 Design Patterns and Mastering Spring Boot 2.0. **Mastering Spring Boot 2.0 is the Amazon #1 best-selling book on Java**. He has more than 10 years of experience on various aspects of Spring and cloud-native development, such as REST APIs and Microservice Architecture.

He is currently working as an architect at a leading company. He has worked as a tech lead at Bennett, Coleman & Co. Ltd, and Paytm.

He holds a Master's degree in Computer Engineering from JSS Academy of Technical Education, Noida, and lives in Noida with his family.

His Website: https://www.dineshonjava.com
His Blog: https://www.dineshonjava.com&https://www.dineshrajput.com
His Linked in Profile: https://www.linkedin.com/in/rajputdinesh/

Acknowledgements

I would like to start my acknowledgement with the following quote:

*"There is nothing unachievable in the world if you have one thing **'let us try'**."*

I would like to start by thanking Mr. Manish Jain for giving me an opportunity to write this book. I would like to express my gratitude to the BPB Publications team. It started with Vinay and Anugraha, my acquisition editors, who patiently worked with me. Along the way, my development editor challenged me to become a better author. I would like to thank Subha Nadar, my technical editor, who gavea technical shape to the book and constantly checked my work and ensured the overall quality of the examples and the code I produced.

I would like to thank my family for their love and support. To my wife Anamika, you have been my best friend and the love of my life. I would also like to thank my kids, Arnav and Rushika. You both make me a better father as well as a better author and more importantly, a better person.

Finally, I would like to thank the Dinesh on java readers who bought this book early and shared their valuable feedback. I hope that you enjoy this book as much as I enjoyed writing it. Thank you!

Preface

Designing Applications with Spring Boot 2.2 and React JS is for all Java developers who want to learn Spring Boot and React JS in the enterprise full stack applications. Therefore, enterprise Java and Spring developers will find this book useful in understanding REST architectural design patterns using Spring Boot 2.2,how React JS helps in the development of front-end applications, how to create reusable UI components, and they will appreciate the examples presented in this book. Using Spring Boot, you can solve common design problems of the REST ful applications. Before reading this book, readers should have basic knowledge of Core Java, Spring Core Framework, REST basics, and JavaScript.

Spring Boot 2.2 has been newly launched by Pivotal with the reactive programming and cloud. Spring Boot 2.2 introduces many new features and enhancements from its previous version. We will discuss Spring Boot and its essential key components in this book. Designing Applications with Spring Boot 2.2 and React JS is a full stack development book that will give you in-depth insight into Spring Boot for backend application development and React JS for front-end application development.

The great part of today's Spring Boot is that many companies have already adopted it as a primary framework for the development of backend applications, especially for the REST APIs using the microservices architecture. For Spring Boot, no external enterprise servers are needed to start working with them. React JS is also a very popular JS framework used for the development of front-end applications.

The goal of writing this book is to discuss a full stack application using Spring Boot and React JS and the common designs used behind the REST ful applications. Here, the author has also outlined some best practices to understand the React JS components life cycle.

The book contains 10 chapters, which cover everything from the development of a full stack application to the deployment of the front-end and backend applications by either using virtual machines or containers such as Docker.

Designing Applications with Spring Boot 2.2 and React JSis divided into three parts. The first part introduces you to the essentials of the Spring Boot 2.2 framework and you will learn how to create and secure REST APIs. The second part explains the steps for the development of front-end applications in React JS and discusses React features and its advantages. The third part expands on that by showing how to deploy the backend and front-end applications in the PaaS platform and finally, the fourth part explains how to deploy application container technologies such as Docker.

What you need for this book

This book can be read without a computer or laptop at hand, in which case you need nothing more than the book itself. However, to follow the examples in the book, you need Java 8, which you can download from *http://www.oracle.com/technetwork/java/javase/downloads/jdk8-downloads-2133151.html*, and you will also need your favorite IDE.I have used the Software Spring Tool Suite; download the latest version of Spring Tool Suite (STS) from *https://spring.io/tools/sts/*all according to your OS. Java 8 and STS work on a variety of platforms: Windows, MacOS and Linux.

Downloading the code bundle and colored images:

Please follow the link to download the
Code Bundle and the *Colored Images* of the book:

https://rebrand.ly/b3bf0

Errata

We take immense pride in our work at BPB Publications and follow best practices to ensure the accuracy of our content to provide with an indulging reading experience to our subscribers. Our readers are our mirrors, and we use their inputs to reflect and improve upon human errors if any, occurred during the publishing processes involved. To let us maintain the quality and help us reach out to any readers who might be having difficulties due to any unforeseen errors, please write to us at :

errata@bpbonline.com

Your support, suggestions and feedbacks are highly appreciated by the BPB Publications' Family.

Table of Contents

CHAPTER 1

Getting Started with Spring Boot 2.2

Spring Boot is a tricky framework to understand. In this chapter, we will discuss Spring Boot 2.2 and the underlying important concepts like starter projects, auto-configuration, and starter parents. We will also discuss how Spring Boot makes software development easy. As a bonus, I will discuss the story behind the success of Spring Boot. This chapter will cover a demo application with Spring Boot and create a REST service.

In this chapter, we will cover the following topics:

- Introduction to Spring Boot 2.2
- Essential key components
    - o Starters
    - o Auto-configuration
    - o The Spring Boot CLI
    - o The Spring Boot Actuator
- System requirements and setting up the Spring Boot workspace
- Creating a Spring Boot application
- Introduction to Spring Boot DevTools

Introduction to Spring Boot 2.2

Spring Boot is one of the most popular frameworks used to develop software for any enterprise application. It is useful to develop a modern cloud-based distributed system such as microservices-based application. Spring Boot was one of the very major projects of the Pivotal team and it was launched in 2013.

Spring Boot makes it easy to create standalone, production-grade Spring-based applications that you can run. We take an opinionated view of the Spring platform and third-party libraries so that you can get started with minimum fuss. Most Spring Boot applications need very little Spring configuration.

Spring Boot is built on top of the existing Spring framework. So basically, it is not a separate framework, but it is similar to the existing Spring framework with some features. It's a collection of ready-made things to just pick and use without taking any overhead configuration.

The primary goals of the Spring Boot are as follows:

- Spring Boot provides faster Spring application development

- Eliminate a lot of configurations from the application development and provide a new strategy for application development with minimal fuss.

- You just focus on the application functionality rather than investing a lot of time in meta-configuration.

- Spring Boot is a very opinionated framework out-of-the-box. It never forces to use auto-configuration for any module. We can easily override 100% configuration for any module if requirements start to diverge from the defaults.

- Spring Boot does not generate code for you. It provides auto-configuration based on the module's libraries available on the classpath of the application.

- Apart from the auto-configurations, Spring Boot also provides a range of non-functional features that are common to large classes of projects (such as embedded servers, security, metrics, health checks, and externalized configuration).

- Spring Boot reduces friction of project dependency management in the spring application. As we know that the dependency management and deciding versions of depending libraries are very hectic work for any software engineer.

- Spring Boot allows you to create a Java application such as JAR and WAR artifact.

The Spring team is continuously working on the Spring framework and provides very interesting features till now. Spring Boot is one of the main projects of the Spring team. Spring Boot is not a separate framework or code generation library. It is a Spring framework by heart that means Spring Boot is on top of the Spring framework with some auto-configuration for modules based on the libraries available on the classpath of the Spring application. Let's see the following diagram:

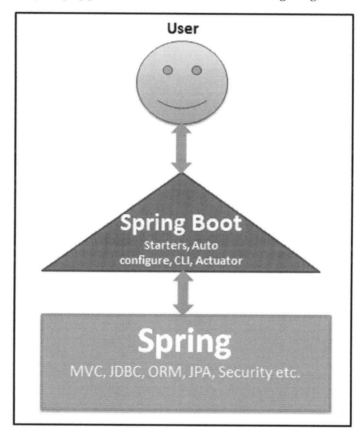

Figure 1.1: The Spring Boot framework representation

In the preceding diagram, you can see the Spring Boot framework on the top of the Spring framework with all the modules such as Spring MVC, Security, JDBC, ORM, Batch, JPA, and so on. Internally, Spring Boot uses the Spring framework to provide core functionality of Spring such as bean creation, providing bean's scopes, etc. Let's suppose you want to develop an application with Spring MVC and Spring Security, so you just need to add the libraries of these modules to the classpath of the application. You do not need to add configurations of Spring MVC and Spring Security to your application. Spring Boot adds this configuration by default in your application based on the libraries available in the classpath of the application. You can still override the default configuration of these modules. Spring Boot never forces you to use the default configuration. Further, let's discuss the key components of Spring Boot in the next section.

Essential key components of Spring Boot

Spring Boot simplifies the Spring application development, so some magical components are behind this. The four essential key components of Spring Boot are as follows:

- Spring Boot Starters
- Auto-configuration
- Spring Boot CLI
- Spring Boot Actuator

Let's discuss these key components in detail.

Spring Boot Starters

Starters in Spring Boot are like small Spring projects for each module with all the required configurations such as Spring Web MVC, Spring JDBC, ORM, JPA, Security, Spring Batch, and so on.

According to the Spring Boot documentation, *Starters are a set of convenient dependency descriptors that you can include in your application. You get a one-stop-shop for all Spring and related technologies that you need, without having to hunt through sample code and copy-paste loads of dependency descriptors.*

In your Spring Boot application, add the starters of the respective modules to the classpath of your application and Spring Boot will ensure that all dependencies and transitive dependencies of the modules is using Maven or Gradle.

Let's suppose you want to develop a REST web application to expose RESTful web services. For this REST application, you need to add the Spring web MVC module to your REST web application by including the springboot-starter-web dependency in your project using Maven build, as shown in the following code:

```
<dependency>
  <groupId>org.springframework.boot</groupId>
  <artifactId>spring-boot-starter-web</artifactId>
</dependency>
```

You can also add the same springboot-starter-web dependency to your project using a Gradle build as shown in the following code:

```
dependencies {
 implementation 'org.springframework.boot:spring-boot-starter-web'

  ...

}
```

The preceding Maven and Gradle dependencies configuration for the Spring web MVC module resolves the following transitive dependencies:

- spring-web-*.jar

- spring-webmvc-*.jar

- tomcat-*.jar

- jackson-databind-*.jar

Similarly, you can add the other modules to the same application such as ORM, Security, Spring Test, Spring Data JPA, and so on by including respective starters of these modules as follows:

- spring-boot-starter-test: This is used to write unit and integration tests.

- spring-boot-starter-security: This is used for authentication and authorization using Spring Security.

- spring-boot-starter-data-jpa: This uses Spring Data JPA with Hibernate.

- spring-boot-starter-cache: This is used to enable the Spring framework's caching support.

- spring-boot-starter-data-rest: This is used to expose simple REST services using Spring Data REST.

Spring Boot provides a lot of starters in the Spring Boot project under the org. springframework.boot group.

The version of the starters in the Spring Boot application is managed by the Spring Boot starter parent POM in the Maven build application. The parent starters in the POM file are as follows:

```
<parent>
 <groupId>org.springframework.boot</groupId>
 <artifactId>spring-boot-starter-parent</artifactId>
 <version>2.2.0.BUILD-SNAPSHOT</version>
 <relativePath/> <!-- lookup parent from repository -->
</parent>
```

The preceding Spring Boot Starter parent POM manages the versions of the all child modules in the project. And also, it manages the default Maven build plugins in the Spring Boot application.

Let's discuss another magical key component of the Spring Boot framework.

The Spring Boot auto-configuration

The Spring Boot auto-configuration is one of the most essential key features of Spring Boot. Spring Boot detects the libraries in the classpath when the application starts. Spring Boot automatically configures the beans in the Spring application context to enable the Spring's module.

In the previous section, we added the Spring web MVC starter to our Spring application. In this case, Spring Boot will automatically configure the beans in the Spring application context to enable Spring MVC. It will also configure the embedded Tomcat server in the Spring application context. This means the Spring Boot auto-configuration does all work related to the configuration, for you to just write your business functionality code.

> **If you forget a dependency for a specific module, Spring Boot cannot configure this module.**

We will discuss more about the Spring Boot auto-configuration in the next *Chapter 2: Customizing Auto-Configuration*. Further, let's see another component of Spring Boot in the next section.

The Spring Boot CLI

The Spring Boot framework has a command-line interface used to create a Spring application quickly using some commands provided by Spring Boot. You can use Groovy scripts to create very fast Spring applications and the Spring Boot CLI allows you to run the Groovy scripts on the CLI. Spring Boot support Groovy language to create a Spring application with almost zero boilerplate code compared to Java.

The Spring Boot documentation says:

You don't need to use the CLI to work with Spring Boot but it's definitely the quickest way to get a Spring application off the ground.

The Spring Boot CLI can be downloaded from the official site of the Spring framework:

• https://repo.spring.io/snapshot/org/springframework/boot/spring-boot-cli/2.2.0.BUILD-SNAPSHOT/spring-boot-cli-2.2.0.BUILD-SNAPSHOT-bin.zip

- https://repo.spring.io/snapshot/org/springframework/boot/spring-boot-cli/2.2.0.BUILD-SNAPSHOT/spring-boot-cli-2.2.0.BUILD-SNAPSHOT-bin.tar.gz

Starters, dependencies and auto-configuration can be easily added to the Spring application using the Spring Boot CLI. The Spring Boot CLI allows you to focus only on writing your application-specific code. Let's see the following Groovy script:

```
@RestController
class HelloController {
 @GetMapping("/")
  String hello() {
  return "Hello World!!!"
 }
}
```

Let's save the above Groovy file as app.groovy in a directory and you can run this file on the Spring Boot CLI using the following command:

$ spring run app.groovy

The preceding Groovy script is not only a simple controller class but it is also a whole application, and you can also run this application and access it from http://localhost:8080/. You can see the output Hello World in the browser.

Hello World!!!

Figure 1.2: Groovy application output in the browser

This means the Spring Boot CLI is a smart tool because you do not need to add any dependencies to build files such as Maven's pom.xml or Gradle's build.gradle. There is no import required in the Groovy script.

The Spring Boot CLI detects the following:

- Dependencies and libraries using classes being used in the application.
- Auto-configuration based on the classes in the application.

Let's move on to another key component of Spring Boot's building blocks. This is a Spring Boot Actuator that gives us insight about running a Spring Boot application.

Spring Boot Actuator

We discussed the three key components of Spring Boot to simplify the Spring development. But a final key component of Spring Boot is Actuator. It provides post-production grade features. You can monitor application health, metrics, and other monitoring features using Spring Boot Actuator in the production. It provides HTTP endpoints to monitor your Spring application during the production.

The Actuator provides some of the following benefits:

- The Actuator provides various metrics such as memory usage, web requests, garbage collection, and data source usage.

- It gives all details about the configured beans in the Spring application context.

- You can get all details about the Spring Boot auto-configuration using the Actuator.

- Also, you can get other configurations such as environment variables, system properties, configuration properties, and command-line arguments.

- It provides a trace of recent HTTP requests handled by your application.

- It also gives information about the current state of the threads in the Spring Boot application.

We discussed all the four essential key components of Spring Boot. These components work to simplify the Spring development.

Let's move on to the next section and discuss system requirements for the Spring Boot 2.2.0 based Spring application and set up the Spring Boot workspace.

System requirements and setting up a workspace

Spring Boot 2.2.0 recently released the framework with advanced features which we will discuss later in this chapter. The minimum system requirement for Spring Boot 2.2.0 is as follows:

- Spring Boot 2.2.0 requires Java 8 and is compatible up to Java 11.

- This version 2.2.0 of Spring Boot has the Spring framework version 5.1.4.RELEASE.

- It provides build support for the following build tools:

Build Tool	Version
Maven	3.3+
Gradle	4.4.4 or 4+

- Spring Boot 2.2.0 provides support for the following embedded servlet containers:

Name	Servlet Version
Tomcat 9.0	4.0
Jetty 9.4	3.1
Undertow 2.0	4.0

The minimum requirement of the servlet container for Spring Boot 2.2.0 application is Servlet 3.1+. Let's set up the Spring Boot in your machine.

Setting up the Spring Boot workspace

Before we set up Spring Boot in your machine, please ensure your Java version in your machine with the following command:

$ java -version

You can use Spring Boot as a classical Java development tool. There is no specific tool or libraries integration required for Spring Boot. You need to include the spring-boot-*.jar files in the classpath of your application. You can use any IDE for the Spring Boot development (But I personally like to use Spring Tools Suits). Let's see the following ways to set up the workspace for the Spring Boot application:

- Using the Maven installation for Spring Boot
- Using the Gradle installation for Spring Boot

Now, we will explore how to set up a Spring Boot application with Maven and Gradle in detail.

Using the Maven installation for Spring Boot

Spring Boot 2.2.0 is compatible with Maven 3.3+. If your machine does not have it, let's install it. You will find the installation instructions at https://maven.apache.org/. Also, ensure your Java 8+ and you will find it at https://www.oracle.com/technetwork/java/javase/downloads/index.html.

Spring Boot uses the Maven dependencies with groupId as org.springframework.boot and your Maven configuration file POM inherits the Spring dependency version management and Maven plugin to create executable JARs from the parent project with artifcatId as spring-boot-starter-parent. Let's see the following Maven dependency pom.xml file:

```
<?xml version="1.0" encoding="UTF-8"?>
<project xmlns="http://maven.apache.org/POM/4.0.0" xmlns:xsi="http://www.w3.org/2001/
XMLSchema-instance"
 xsi:schemaLocation="http://maven.apache.org/POM/4.0.0 http://maven.apache.org/xsd/
maven-4.0.0.xsd">
 <modelVersion>4.0.0</modelVersion>

    <!-- Inherit defaults from Spring Boot -->
     <parent>
  <groupId>org.springframework.boot</groupId>
  <artifactId>spring-boot-starter-parent</artifactId>
  <version>2.2.0.RELEASE</version>
  <relativePath/> <!-- lookup parent from repository -->
 </parent>

    <groupId>com.dineshonjava</groupId>
 <artifactId>myproject</artifactId>
 <version>0.0.1-SNAPSHOT</version>
 <name>myproject</name>
 <description>Demo project for Spring Boot</description>

<properties>
 <java.version>1.8</java.version>
</properties>

    <!-- Add typical dependencies for a web application -->
<dependencies>
 <dependency>
  <groupId>org.springframework.boot</groupId>
  <artifactId>spring-boot-starter-web</artifactId>
 </dependency>

 <dependency>
```

```xml
      <groupId>org.springframework.boot</groupId>
      <artifactId>spring-boot-starter-test</artifactId>
      <scope>test</scope>
    </dependency>
  </dependencies>

     <!-- Package as an executable jar -->
    <build>
     <plugins>
      <plugin>
       <groupId>org.springframework.boot</groupId>
       <artifactId>spring-boot-maven-plugin</artifactId>
      </plugin>
     </plugins>
    </build>
</project>
```

The preceding pom.xml file has the bare minimum requirement for the Spring Boot 2.2 application with the Spring MVC web module. Let's discuss another way of Spring Boot installation that is Gradle setup for the Spring Boot application.

Using the Gradle installation

Spring Boot 2.2.0 is compatible with Gradle 4.4+. If your machine does not have it, let's install it. You will find the installation instructions at https://gradle.org/. But it requires Java 8+ for both installations either with Maven or Gradle. Now let's see the following dependencies for the Spring Boot with groupId as org.springframework.boot:

```
buildscript {
 ext {
  springBootVersion = '2.2.0.RELEASE'
 }
 repositories {
  mavenCentral()
 }
 dependencies {
  classpath("org.springframework.boot:spring-boot-gradle-plugin:${springBootVersion}")
 }
}
```

```
apply plugin: 'java'
apply plugin: 'org.springframework.boot'
apply plugin: 'io.spring.dependency-management'

group = 'com.dineshonjava
version = '0.0.1-SNAPSHOT'
sourceCompatibility = '1.8'

repositories {
  mavenCentral()
}

dependencies {
  implementation 'org.springframework.boot:spring-boot-starter-web'
  testImplementation 'org.springframework.boot:spring-boot-starter-test'
}
```

The preceding build.gradle file has the bare minimum requirement for the Spring Boot 2.2 application with the Spring MVC web module. After setting up the Spring Boot workspace either with Maven or Gradle, let's create a Spring Boot application and see how to set up the project structure using Spring Boot Initializr in the next section.

Creating a Spring Boot application

In this section, we will create a simple Hello World REST web application using some of Spring Boot's key features. In this REST application, we will create a simple REST service that will return the Hello World message on request. We will use Maven to build this project.

Let's create a project for this simple example. Spring Boot allows us to create the Spring Boot application project structure using the Spring Boot Initializr. The Spring Boot Initializr provides solutions to all problems related to set up work, and it creates a more traditional Java project structure.

You can use the Spring Initializr to create a skeleton Spring project structure. It is both a browser-based web application and a REST API. You can use it in the following ways:

- The Spring Initializr can be used from the web interface at https://start. spring.io/.

- The Spring Initializr can be used from the command line using the curl command.

- The Spring Initializr can be used from the command line using the Spring Boot command-line interface.

- You can use the Spring Initializr by creating a new project with Spring Tool Suite.

- You can use the Spring Initializr by creating a new project with IntelliJ IDEA.

- You can use the Spring Initializr by creating a new project with NetBeans.

We have seen several ways to use the Spring Initializr to create a Spring Boot application skeleton, but in this chapter, we are not going to discuss all of them. My favourite IDE is **Spring Tool Suite (STS)**; I will use it in this book throughout chapters. Let's start from the Spring Initializr using the web interface at https:// start.spring.io/.

Initializing a Spring project with a web interface

A web application hosted at https://start.spring.io/ by the Spring team can be used to create a Spring Boot application. It is one of the simplest ways to use the Spring Initializr. You can choose the project build tool either from Maven or Gradle. Also, it has the option to choose languages either from Java, Kotlin, and Groovy. Finally, we have the version of Spring Boot.

Let's see the following screenshot of how the home page looks like:

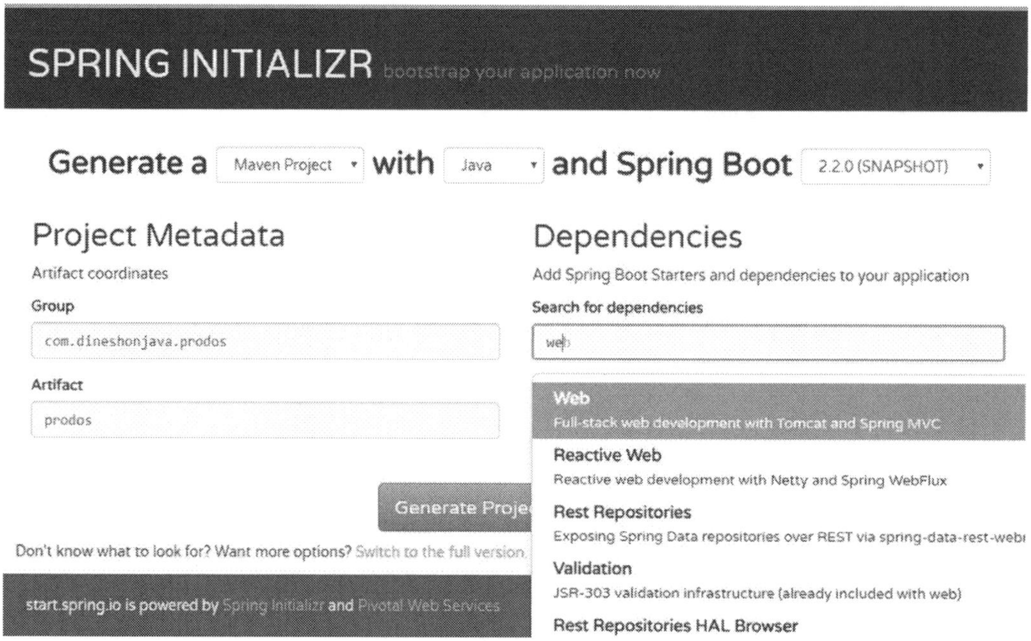

Figure 1.3: The Spring Initializr web interface

In the preceding screenshot, there are a lot of options to choose from to create a Spring Boot application, which are as follows:

- Project build tools, Maven and Gradle

- Programming languages (currently supported languages are Java, Kotlin, and Groovy)

- Spring Boot version

- On the left-hand side, there is a **Project Metadata** section. You can provide project metadata such as group ID, artifact ID, packaging, java version, and so on.

- On the right-hand side, there is an application **Dependencies** section; you can select dependencies from here.

Let's select dependencies for Spring Web MVC. Just type web and select, and then click on the **Generate Project** button. It will create a Spring Boot application project skeleton.

Initializing a Spring project with the STS IDE

The Spring Tool Suite is one of my favourite IDEs for Java development. It is also popular among many Java developers and used to create Spring-based application. You can install it from http://spring.io/tools/.

Let's see the following screenshot to display the menu structure:

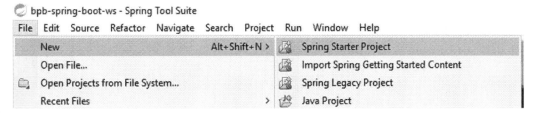

Figure 1.4: Starting a new project in STS with the Spring Starter project

After selecting **Spring Starter Project**, a new window appears, as shown in the following screenshot:

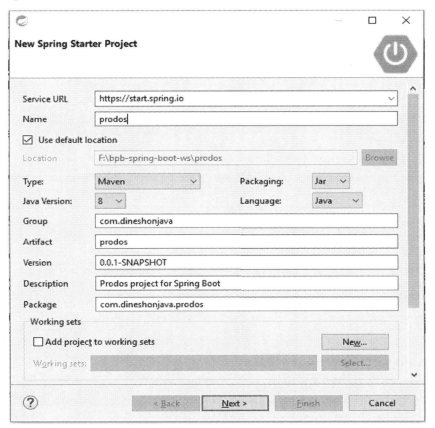

Figure 1.5: Specify project information

As you can see in the preceding screenshot, the first page asks you to fill the project information such as project name, project build tool, packaging, language, group, artifact, and other essential information and then click on **Next**.

In the next page of the wizard, you can select Maven dependencies to be added to your Spring project, as shown in the following screenshot:

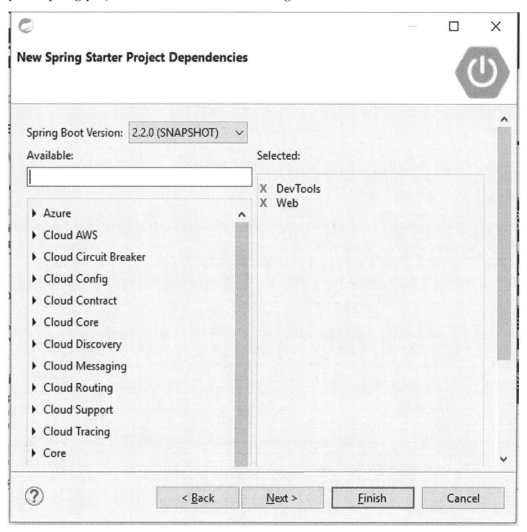

Figure 1.6: Choosing starters dependencies

Let's select the version of Spring Boot based on your application architecture. In our case, we selected the Spring Boot 2.2.0 version. After choosing a version of Spring Boot, let's check the desired project dependencies for your application. For the Prodos application, I have chosen web starter as of now.

Again, click on the **Next** button. Another dialogue box appears in the wizard as shown in the following screenshot:

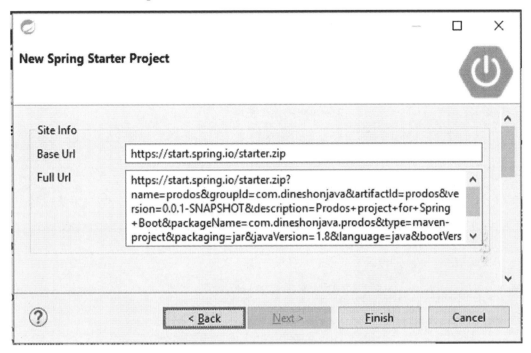

Figure 1.7: Starting a project using the Spring Initializr

In the next screen, you can see that the project wizard makes a call to the Spring Initializr at http://start.spring.io to create the project. So, let's click on the **Finish** button.

After clicking on the **Finish** button, your project will be downloaded from the Spring Initializr and loaded into your defined workspace. Initially, the final step will take some time due to load project dependencies. After loading all the required dependencies in your project, you will be ready to code your business logic. But, first take a look at the imported project structure in the STS, as shown in the following screenshot:

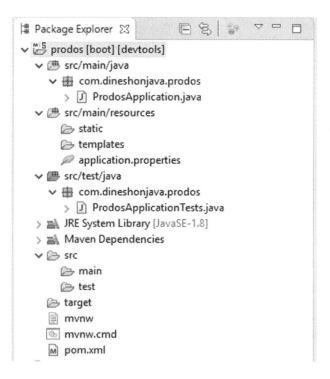

Figure 1.8: Generated Spring Boot project structure

The web interface of the Spring Initializr also creates the same project structure as a ZIP file. You have extract it into the desired workspace and import it as the Maven project into the STS IDE.

In the preceding screenshot of the project structure of the Spring Boot application, there are a couple of files and directories that are generated. These files are placed under some specific directory based on the Maven or Gradle build tool. The application source code is placed under /src/main/java and the test code file is placed under src/test/java, and other non-java files are placed under src/main/resources. The following files are automatically generated:

- pom.xml: This is a build tool file for Maven used to build specification.

- mvnw.cmd and mvnw.cmd: These are wrapper script files for Maven, and you can use these script wrapper files to build your Spring Boot project even if you do not have the build tool Maven installed on your machine.

- ProdosApplication.java: This bootstraps your Spring Boot project. It is the main application file (a class with a main() method) of your Spring Boot application.

- application.properties: This is an empty configuration file. You can specify configuration properties to as you see fit.

- static: This is an empty folder. You can place any static content such as images, stylesheets, JavaScript, and so on. This content is served to the browser.

- templates: This folder is used to place template files that will be used as the UI and render content on the browser.

- ProdosApplicationTests.java: This is an empty JUnit test class file used to ensure the Spring application context is loaded successfully. But you can write more JUnit test cases.

Let's move on deeper into the file generated by the Spring Initializr.

The Spring Boot application launcher file

The Spring Initializr creates the main application class file as the application bootstrap file to launch the Spring Boot application. Let's see the following code of this file:

```
package com.dineshonjava.prodos;

import org.springframework.boot.SpringApplication;
import org.springframework.boot.autoconfigure.SpringBootApplication;

@SpringBootApplication
public class ProdosApplication {

  public static void main(String[] args) {
    SpringApplication.run(ProdosApplication.class, args);
  }

}
```

In the preceding application class file, there are a few lines of code but these lines have a very powerful functionality of Spring Boot. Let's discuss this in detail:

- @SpringBootApplication: The main class of the application is annotated with this annotation. This annotation works when the application is launched to scan recursively for Spring components inside this package and register them. The @SpringBootApplication annotation also enables the Spring Boot auto-configuration. The auto-configuration is a process used to create the beans automatically based on the classpath settings, property settings, and other factors. The @SpringBootApplication annotation is not a simple annotation. It is a composite application annotation. It combines three other annotations as follows:

      o   @SpringBootConfiguration: This annotation indicates that this class is a configuration class in the Spring application. You can also add other configuration files to this class as per requirement. This annotation is a specific form of the @Configuration annotation.

      o   @EnableAuto-configuration: This annotation enables the Spring Boot automatic configuration in the Spring Boot application. It automatically loads all related configuration files based on classpath settings.

      o   @ComponentScan: This annotation enables component scanning in the Spring application. You can use the @Component, @Controller, @Service, and other stereotype annotations to change a class to component in Spring. The component classes are automatically discovered by the Spring application context.

- main(): This is another powerful piece of code of the main() method in the main application class file. This method will be run when the JAR file is executed.

- SpringApplication.run(): This method is called by the main() method. This method is available in the SpringApplication class; it is responsible for creating the Spring application context. This method has two arguments, a configuration class and the command-line argument.

We discussed the main application file; it does not need to be changed in the application. Some applications have more than one Bootstrap class. In this case, it is better to create separate configuration files, especially for non-auto-configure files.

Let's dive deeper into another file, that is, a testing file.

Testing the application file

As we know that testing is one of the most important parts of software development. The Spring Initializr creates a simple testing file for you in your Spring application:

```
import org.junit.Test;
import org.junit.runner.RunWith;
import org.springframework.boot.test.context.SpringBootTest;
import org.springframework.test.context.junit4.SpringRunner;


@RunWith(SpringRunner.class)
@SpringBootTest
public class ProdosApplicationTests {
```

```
@Test
public void contextLoads() {
}


}
```

This is a default generated test class file in the Spring Boot application. This class is almost empty; it only performs to test whether the Spring application context is loaded successfully or not. In this class, you can add your own test cases for the application functionalities:

- @RunWith(SpringRunner.class): This annotation annotates the main application test class. The @RunWith annotation is not a Spring annotation, it is a JUnit annotation. But it needs a runner class that guides JUnit in running a test.

- SpringRunner: This is a Spring-provided test runner. It provides the creation of a Spring application context that the test will run against.

- @SpringBootTest: This annotation is also used on the application test class. This annotation tells JUnit to bootstrap the test with the Spring Boot features such as auto-configuration, beans creations, and so on.

> **SpringRunner is an alias for SpringJUnit4ClassRunner and was introduced in Spring 4.3 to remove the association with a specific version of JUnit (for example, JUnit 4).**

We have seen all code provided by the Spring Initializr at this point. You can also see the build file generated by the Spring Initializr as follows.

The build specification file

This file is generated according to the selected build tool. I have selected Maven as a build tool for this application. That is why the pom.xml file is created with all selected dependencies of the starters and Spring Boot Maven plugins:

```xml
<?xml version="1.0" encoding="UTF-8"?>
<project xmlns="http://maven.apache.org/POM/4.0.0" xmlns:xsi="http://www.w3.org/2001/
XMLSchema-instance"
  xsi:schemaLocation="http://maven.apache.org/POM/4.0.0 http://maven.apache.org/xsd/
maven-4.0.0.xsd">
  <modelVersion>4.0.0</modelVersion>


<!--Spring Boot parent dependency->
  <parent>
```

```xml
      <groupId>org.springframework.boot</groupId>
      <artifactId>spring-boot-starter-parent</artifactId>
          <!—Spring Boot version→
      <version>2.2.0.RELEASE</version>
      <relativePath/> <!-- lookup parent from repository -->
    </parent>

  <!—JAR packaging information→
   <groupId>com.dineshonjava</groupId>
   <artifactId>prodos</artifactId>
   <version>0.0.1-SNAPSHOT</version>
   <name>prodos</name>
   <description>Prodos project for Spring Boot</description>

  <!—Java version→
   <properties>
    <java.version>1.8</java.version>
   </properties>

  <!—Starter dependencies→
   <dependencies>
    <dependency>
      <groupId>org.springframework.boot</groupId>
      <artifactId>spring-boot-starter-web</artifactId>
    </dependency>

    <dependency>
      <groupId>org.springframework.boot</groupId>
      <artifactId>spring-boot-devtools</artifactId>
      <scope>runtime</scope>
    </dependency>
    <dependency>
      <groupId>org.springframework.boot</groupId>
      <artifactId>spring-boot-starter-test</artifactId>
      <scope>test</scope>
    </dependency>
   </dependencies>
```

```
<!—Spring Boot plugin→
 <build>
  <plugins>
   <plugin>
    <groupId>org.springframework.boot</groupId>
    <artifactId>spring-boot-maven-plugin</artifactId>
   </plugin>
  </plugins>
 </build>
</project>
```

The preceding Maven configuration file has starter dependencies and Spring Boot plugins. The starter dependencies resolve all transitive dependencies related to the module. Starter dependencies provide the following benefits:

- It is very simple and easy to manage because you do not need to manage all related libraries to a module.

- You do not need to care about the library versions. You can rely on the version provided the Spring Boot parent dependency.

- Each starter dependency denotes a capability it provides, so you do not need to care about the list of individual libraries used in a specific capability.

There are many more benefits of using Spring Boot's starter dependencies. Let's see some important points related to the Spring Boot plugin:

- This plugin provides the Maven goal to your project. The Maven goals are used to run your project using Maven.

- This plugin also ensures all related libraries in the classpath are used in the executable JAR file.

- This plugin also creates a manifest file in the JAR file to provide the information about the main class file inside the executable JAR file.

We discussed the pom.xml file and also discussed the default generated code either for the main application class file or application test class file. Now, let's create a controller class file for your application as per your business requirement, but this is a very simple REST application, so we will create simple controller class for a Hello World message.

Implementing a REST controller

Here, we will create a simple application file that is a REST controller file. We know that Spring MVC is one of the key modules of the Spring framework and controller is a heart of Spring MVC. The controller is nothing but a class to handle requests and responds with some information.

In our case, I have created a REST controller class with a single request handler method as shown in the following code:

```
package com.dineshonjava.prodos;

import org.springframework.web.bind.annotation.GetMapping;
import org.springframework.web.bind.annotation.RestController;

/**
* @author Dinesh.Rajput
*
*/
@RestController
public class HomeController {

  @GetMapping("/")
  String home(){
    return "Hello World!!!";
  }
}
```

The preceding RestController (HomeController) has a small piece of code as of now. Let's discuss some details about this small controller file:

- @RestController: This annotation indicates that this is the rest controller class and its result writes into the response body and does not render a view.

- @GetMapping: This annotation indicates that this is a request handler method and it is a shorthand annotation for @RequestMapping(method = RequestMethod.GET).

- home(): This returns a greeting message.

We need to see the HomeController class and its home() request handler method. Let's see the test class for this controller.

Writing a test for the controller

We have written a Rest controller to handle the request and return 'Hello World' as a response message. Now, you're almost ready to run your first Spring Boot application and see the output. But first, let's write another file that is a test file for the controller as shown in the following code:

```
package com.dineshonjava.prodos;

import static org.hamcrest.Matchers.containsString;
import static
org.springframework.test.web.servlet.request.MockMvcRequestBuilders.get;
import static
org.springframework.test.web.servlet.result.MockMvcResultMatchers.content;
import static
org.springframework.test.web.servlet.result.MockMvcResultMatchers.status;

import org.junit.Test;
import org.junit.runner.RunWith;
import org.springframework.beans.factory.annotation.Autowired;
import org.springframework.boot.test.autoconfigure.web.servlet.WebMvcTest;
import org.springframework.test.context.junit4.SpringRunner;
import org.springframework.test.web.servlet.MockMvc;

/**
 * @author Dinesh.Rajput
 *
 */

@RunWith(SpringRunner.class)
@WebMvcTest(HomeController.class)
public class HomeControllerTest {

  @Autowired
  private MockMvc mockMvc;

  @Test
  public void testHome() throws Exception {
    mockMvc.perform(get("/"))
```

```
      .andExpect(status().isOk())
      .andExpect(content().string(
        containsString("Hello World")));
    }
  }
```

The preceding HomeControllerTest class is a testing class for the HomeController controller. This class differs slightly from the ProdosApplicationTests class with regards to configurations such as annotations. In this test file, we are using the @WebMvcTest annotation instead of @SpringBootTest. Let's see the used components, which are as follows:

- @WebMvcTest: This annotation is a special test annotation to test the Spring MVC flow. It enables a server and mocks the mechanics of the Spring MVC. This annotation also registers the associated controller in Spring MVC so that you can use this controller to serve requests against it. In our case, we have registered HomeController in Spring MVC so that you can throw requests against it.

- MockMvc: This class is injected with the test controller class and provides a MockMvc object for the test to drive the mock.

- testHome(): This class defines the test case you want to perform against the testHome() method of the controller class. This method starts with the MockMvc object to perform an HTTP GET request for mapping (/). Let's see the following expectations for this request:

  o   The server must respond with the HTTP status 200 (OK).

  o   The return response message should contain the text 'Hello World'.

You can run this test class as the JUnit test run. If the MockMvc object performs the request to those expectations, and if all expectations are met, the test passes. If expectations are not met, the test fails:

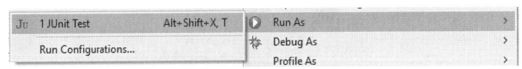

Figure 1.9: Run as the JUnit test

The written test should pass if everything is fine. It shows a green colour bar that indicates a passing test as shown in the following screenshot:

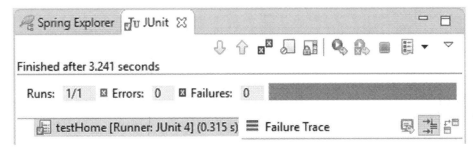

Figure 1.10: JUnit test console output

As you can see in the preceding screenshot, the test is passed successfully. After writing test cases for HomeController of the Prodos application and also after verifying the test cases, if all things are going well, then let's run your application to test the actual data using a browser or any REST client.

Let's run your Spring Boot application in the STS IDE as a Spring Boot application with an embedded server by selecting **Run As | Spring Boot App** from the **Run** menu as follows:

Figure 1.11: Run as Spring Boot App

Let's run your Spring Boot application and observe the logs on the console as follows:

Figure 1.12: Spring Boot console output

We know that we have used the spring-boot-starter-parent POM. It provides a useful run goal, and you can use it to start the Spring Boot application using the following Maven command:

mvn spring-boot:run

You can run the preceding command and see the following output on the console screen:

Figure 1.13: Console output of Maven run command

In the preceding console logs, you can see the following:

- The Spring Boot banner at the top of the logs with the Spring Boot version.

- You can customize the Spring Boot banner by adding banner.txt or banner.png and putting this file into the src/main/resources/ folder.

- By default, our application runs with the embedded Tomcat server with port 8080.

- But you can customize the server port by adding the server.port property to the application.properties file using the following command:

    server.port=8181

Let's verify it on the system browser where it will look as follows:

Hello World!!!

Figure 1.14: The Spring Boot application output in a browser

The preceding screenshot displays the 'Hello World' message responded by the Rest controller of our Spring Boot application.

Introducing Spring Boot DevTools

In the POM file, I have added a specific Maven dependency as follows:

```
<dependency>
 <groupId>org.springframework.boot</groupId>
 <artifactId>spring-boot-devtools</artifactId>
 <scope>runtime</scope>
</dependency>
```

The preceding Maven dependency adds Spring Boot DevTools to your application. As the name suggest, DevTools provides some handy development tools to the Spring developers. The tools are as follows:

- If you make any change in the code, it automatically restarts your application.

- If you make any changes to browser-related resources such as templates, JavaScript, CSS, and so on, it automatically refreshes the browser to detect new changes.

- It automatically disables the caches of the template in the development environment.

- It also provides the H2 Console for the H2 database, if you use it in your application.

The Spring Boot DevTools is smart enough; it disables itself when you deploy your application with the production settings. It only enables with the development settings. It works with all IDEs such as Spring Tool Suite, IntelliJ IDEA, and so on.

Conclusion

In this chapter, we discussed Spring Boot and its essential key components. We saw four essential keys components such as Spring Boot auto-configuration, Spring Boot starters, Spring Boot CLI, and Spring Boot Actuator.

We learned how Spring Boot makes the Spring development easy using auto-configuration and starters. Also, Spring Boot provides post-production monitoring and application grade with the Actuator.

We used the Spring Initializr to create a Spring Boot application through the web interface and STS IDE. We also created a very simple Hello World REST application using the web-based Spring Initializr and Spring Tool Suite IDE, and we run this application where we used the embedded Tomcat container.

In the next *Chapter 2: Customizing Auto-Configuration*, we will discuss how to externalize the Spring Boot auto-configuration.

Questions

1. What is Spring Boot?
2. What does Spring Boot provide?
3. What are key components of Spring Boot?
4. What is starter?
5. What is auto-configuration in Spring Boot?
6. What is the Spring Boot CLI?
7. What is Spring Boot Actuator?
8. What is Spring Boot DevTools?

CHAPTER 2

Customizing Auto-configuration

In the previous chapter, we discussed Spring Boot's four essential key components and auto-configuration is one of them. The auto-configuration component makes Spring Boot a smart framework. The auto-configuration is a great feature and it simplifies the Spring application development. In this chapter, you will be given an overview of the Spring Boot Auto-configuration, including customization of auto-configuration. You'll also get an overview of the profiling.

Spring Boot provides several ways to set configuration properties such as JVM system properties, command line arguments, and environment variables. In this chapter, we will employ configuration properties to fine tune auto-configuration provided by Spring Boot by default.

In this chapter, we will cover the following topics:

- Understanding auto-configuration
  - o Enabling auto-configuration
  - o Disabling auto-configuration
- How the Spring Boot auto-configuration works?
  - o Auto-configuration classes
- Externalizing auto-configuration
  - o Order of evaluation for overridden properties
  - o Customizing name of the application.properties file

o Application configuration using a properties file

o Application configuration using a YAML file

o Multi-profile YAML documents

- Creating your own configuration properties

o Defining your own configuration properties in the application

o Declaring the configuration property and metadata

- Profiling

o Conditionally creating beans with profiles

o Activating profiles

o Profile-specific application configuration properties files

Understanding auto-configuration

In the Spring framework, if you need to configure **Spring Data JPA** in your Spring application, then you need to configure several beans in your application such as DataSource, JpaVendorAdapter, LocalContainerEntityManagerFactoryBean, and more. It takes lot of time to make it workable in your Spring application. Let's see the following configurations for Spring Data JPA:

```
@Configuration
public class InfrastructureConfig {
  //Configuring beans like DataSource, LocalContainerEntityManagerFactoryBean, etc.
  @Bean
  public DataSource dataSource(){
    EmbeddedDatabaseBuilder builder = new EmbeddedDatabaseBuilder().
setType(EmbeddedDatabaseType.H2);//in-memory
    builder.addScript("schema.sql");
    builder.addScript("data.sql");
    return builder.build();
  }

  @Bean
  public JpaVendorAdapter jpaVendorAdapter() {
    HibernateJpaVendorAdapter bean = new HibernateJpaVendorAdapter();
    bean.setDatabase(org.springframework.orm.jpa.vendor.Database.H2);
    bean.setGenerateDdl(true);
    return bean;
```

```
}

@Bean
public LocalContainerEntityManagerFactoryBean entityManagerFactory(
    DataSource dataSource, JpaVendorAdapter jpaVendorAdapter) {
  LocalContainerEntityManagerFactoryBean bean = new
LocalContainerEntityManagerFactoryBean();
  bean.setDataSource(dataSource);
  bean.setJpaVendorAdapter(jpaVendorAdapter);
  bean.setPackagesToScan("com.doj.springapp.model");
  return bean;
  }
}
```

The preceding code snippet is for the Spring Data JPA module. This configuration is only for one Spring Data JPA module. But any enterprise application might have many modules such as Spring MVC, Spring Security, HSQLDB, and so on. In this case, the configuration of these modules is hectic to manage in your Spring application. Spring Boot comes with the auto-configuration feature to reduce the complexity of the configuration in your Spring application, and it also reduces a lot of boilerplate codes.

The auto-configuration is a very important feature of Spring Boot; without it Spring Boot is nothing. The auto-configuration configures your Spring application automatically based on the starters JAR dependencies available on your application's classpath. For example, if Spring Data JPA is on your Spring application's classpath, then you do not need to configure it manually on your Spring application. Spring Boot auto-configures Spring Data JPA with its related beans such as DataSource, JpaVendorAdapter and LocalContainerEntityManagerFactoryBean, and so on. This means you do not need to write the above configuration code for Spring Data JPA. Let's see how the Spring Boot auto-configuration works and how does it enable and disable.

Enabling Spring Boot auto-configuration

There is no special requirement to enable the Spring Boot auto-configuration in your Spring application. You can get the auto-configuration by adding the @EnableAutoConfiguration or @SpringBootApplication annotation to one of your @Configuration classes. A single @SpringBootApplication annotation has auto-configuration, component scan and extra configuration in their application class. This means that the @SpringBootApplication annotation is equivalent to three annotations such as @Configuration, @EnableAutoConfiguration, and @ComponentScan with their default attributes. Let's see the following figure:

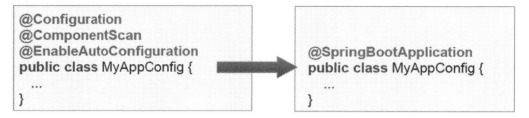

Figure 2.1: Enabling auto-configuration

Spring Boot does not force you to use the auto-configuration in your application. It is totally non-invasive. You can define your own configuration for any module, and you can replace the auto-configuration with your custom configuration. Suppose if you want to use your own DataSource configuration, you can define the configuration for it. The default configuration of the embedded database support backs away automatically. Let's see how to disable some part of the auto-configuration in the Spring Boot application.

Disabling the Spring Boot auto-configuration

Sometimes you find that the specific auto-configuration is not either fit for your application or you do not want to apply auto-configuration classes. Spring Boot allows you to exclude such auto-configuration classes from your Spring application using the exclude attribute of @SpringBootApplication and @EnableAutoConfiguration as shown in the following example:

```
package com.dineshonjava.prodos;

import org.springframework.boot.SpringApplication;
import org.springframework.boot.autoconfigure.SpringBootApplication;
import org.springframework.boot.autoconfigure.data.jpa.JpaRepositoriesAutoConfiguration;
import org.springframework.boot.autoconfigure.orm.jpa.HibernateJpaAutoConfiguration;

@SpringBootApplication(exclude = {JpaRepositoriesAutoConfiguration.class,
HibernateJpaAutoConfiguration.class})
public class ProdosApplication {

  public static void main(String[] args) {
    SpringApplication.run(ProdosApplication.class, args);
  }

}
```

You can also exclude the auto-configuration classes using the excludeName attribute of @SpringBootApplication and @EnableAutoConfiguration if the configuration classes are not on the classpath.

Let's discuss and understand the magic behind the Spring Boot auto-configuration.

How the Spring Boot auto-configuration works?

The Spring Boot auto-configuration is a magical and smart feature. It reduces a lot of boilerplate code from your Spring application. But you may be confused sometimes with what is going on behind the scenes. In this section, we will discuss and understand the magic behind the Spring Boot auto-configuration.

Spring Boot has several pre-written @Configuration classes for each module of the Spring framework. These pre-written auto-configuration classes will be available in your Spring application based on the contents of the classpath of your Spring application and whatever properties you have set in the Spring application. Spring Boot uses Spring's @Conditional annotation feature to create the Spring Boot auto-configuration magic.

The @Profile annotation is a specific case of the @Conditional annotation in the Spring framework. Spring Boot uses the same idea to the next level and provides the auto-configuration feature. This means that the @Conditional annotation configuration is extensively used in the auto-configuration, thus enabling Spring Boot. In this section, let's discuss how the Spring Boot auto-configuration works.

Auto-configuration classes

The auto-configuration classes are similar to any regular Spring @Configuration class. But the auto-configuration class is enriched with the @Conditional annotations. This conditional annotation decides whether auto-configuration will activate or not as a bean under certain circumstances.

As we know, Spring Boot supports Java-based configuration. Although Spring Boot also supports use of the SpringApplication class with XML sources , I would recommend that you use Java-based configuration for strong type safety and also recommend that the primary source must be a single @Configuration class. In case of multiple configuration classes, you can import additional configuration classes using the @Import annotation. I do not recommend using XML configuration files for additional configuration, but if you still want to use XML-based configuration, you can then use a @ImportResource annotation to load XML configuration files:

```
package com.dineshonjava.prodos.config;

import org.springframework.context.annotation.Configuration;
import org.springframework.context.annotation.Import;
import org.springframework.context.annotation.ImportResource;

/**
 * @author Dinesh.Rajput
 *
 */
@Configuration
@Import({InfrastructureConfig.class, SecurityConfig.class})
@ImportResource({"spring.xml"})
public class AppConfig {
 //...
}
```

We saw how to create the configuration classes. Let's see now how these configuration classes work in the Spring Boot application. For example, we have the auto-configuration JdbcTemplateAutoConfiguration class provided by the Spring framework itself as shown in the following code:

```
@Configuration
@ConditionalOnClass({ DataSource.class, JdbcTemplate.class })
@ConditionalOnSingleCandidate(DataSource.class)
@AutoConfigureAfter(DataSourceAutoConfiguration.class)
public class JdbcTemplateAutoConfiguration {

  private final DataSource dataSource;

  public JdbcTemplateAutoConfiguration(DataSource dataSource) {
   this.dataSource = dataSource;
  }

  @Bean
  @Primary
  @ConditionalOnMissingBean(JdbcOperations.class)
  public JdbcTemplate jdbcTemplate() {
```

```
    return new JdbcTemplate(this.dataSource);
}


@Bean
@Primary
@ConditionalOnMissingBean(NamedParameterJdbcOperations.class)
public NamedParameterJdbcTemplate namedParameterJdbcTemplate() {
    return new NamedParameterJdbcTemplate(this.dataSource);
}
//More beans definitions
}
```

Here, JdbcTemplateAutoConfiguration is annotated with @ConditionalOnClass({ DataSource.class,JdbcTemplate.class }), which means that auto-configuration of beans within JdbcTemplateAutoConfiguration will be considered only if the DataSource.class and JdbcTemplate.class classes are available on the classpath.

As you can see that the @Conditional annotations can also be used at the beans definition level. The @ConditionalOnMissingBean annotation can be used to register the new component in the absence of the required bean type or name. The @ ConditionalOnProperty annotation can be leveraged to create a bean based on the presence of some property definition. Out-of-the-box Spring Boot provides the following conditional annotations:

- @ConditionalOnClass
- @ConditionalOnMissingBean
- @ConditionalOnBean
- @ConditionalOnJava
- @ConditionalOnJndi
- @ConditionalOnMissingClass
- @ConditionalOnExpression
- @ConditionalOnNotWebApplication
- @ConditionalOnWebApplication
- @ConditionalOnProperty
- @ConditionalOnResource
- @ConditionalOnSingleCandidate

Most of the preceding conditional annotations are self-explanatory. You can find more details about these annotations from the Spring Boot documentation. If these annotations are not enough for your Spring application, you can create the custom conditions using the SpringBootCondition class and use this custom conditional class with the @Conditional annotation in your Spring application.

Spring Boot allows overriding the auto-configuration. In the next section, we will discuss how to externalize the Spring Boot auto-configuration in your Spring application.

Externalizing auto-configuration

Spring Boot has a lot of properties for fine tuning the auto-configuration according to your application requirements. For more detailed information about these properties, go to https://docs.spring.io/spring-boot/docs/2.2.0.BUILD-SNAPSHOT/reference/htmlsingle/#common-application-properties. You can use these properties to set up your Spring application via several property sources such as:

- JVM system properties
- Operating system environment variables
- Command-line arguments
- Application properties files
- Application YAML files

You are free to choose any property source to define your property values. Spring aggregates all properties from all property sources and provides a single source that is the Spring environment abstraction. The defined property values can be injected directly into your application beans using the @Value annotation. These properties can be accessed through the Spring Environment abstraction. Let's see the following figure to understand this in detail:

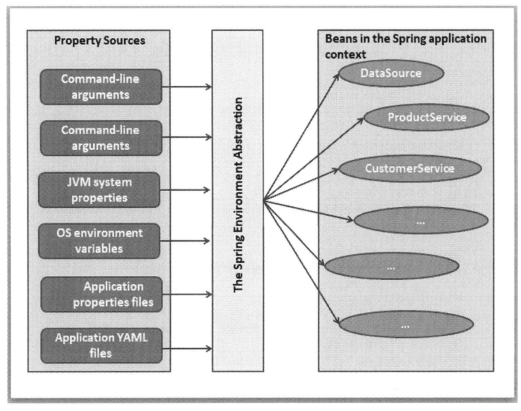

*Figure 2.2: The Spring environment abstraction pulls properties
from several sources and makes them available to beans in the application context.*

As you know we have several property sources to externalize your application properties. But these sources have a particular order of a sensible overriding of values of these properties in the Spring Boot application if you define the same properties on all property sources. Let's see the order of evaluation of these properties.

Order of evaluation for overridden properties

Spring Boot evaluates the order for the overridden properties as follows:

- The properties for the DevTools global settings are on your home directory (~/.spring-boot-devtools.properties) but DevTools must be active.

- The properties for the testing environment using the @TestPropertySource annotation on your tests.

- The defined properties as the command line arguments.

- Properties from SPRING_APPLICATION_JSON.

- In a web environment, the properties for init parameters of the ServletConfig object.

- In a web environment, the properties for init parameters of the ServletContext object.

- JNDI attributes from java:comp/env.

- Java system properties (System.getProperties()).

- The operating system environment variables.

- The properties with random.* using RandomValuePropertySource.

- The configuration properties files either with the application.properties or application.yml. The application property configuration files have their own order of precedence as follows:

  o Profile-specific application properties outside your packaged JAR, that is, in the /config subdirectory of the directory from which the application is run (application-{profile}.properties and YAML variants).

  o Profile-specific configuration files such as application-{profile}.properties and its YAML variants outside your packaged JAR but in a directory from which the application is run.

  o Profile-specific configuration files such as application-{profile}.properties and its YAML variants inside the packaged JAR file but in a package named config.

  o Profile-specific configuration files such as application-{profile}.properties and its YAML variants but at the root of the classpath.

  o Application configuration files such as application.properties and its YAML variants outside your packaged JAR but in the /config subdirectory of the directory from which the application is run.

  o Application configuration files such as application.properties and its YAML variants outside your packaged JAR but in a directory from which the application is run.

  o Application configuration files such as application.properties and its YAML variants inside your packaged JAR but in a package named config.

  o Application configuration files such as application.properties and its YAML variants inside your packaged JAR but at the root of the classpath.

  o The @PropertySource annotations on your @Configuration classes.

o   Default properties (specified using SpringApplication.setDefaultProp-
erties).

The preceding list of the property sources is according to the order of precedence. If
you define any property from a property source higher in the preceding list, Spring
Boot will override the same property defined in the property source lower in the
above list. Similarly, any property defined in a profile-specific application-{profile}.
properties will override the defined property value of the same properties in an
application.properties file at the same location as the application-{profile}.properties file.

Any properties you define in the application.properties file will be overridden by
the value of the defined same properties in the application.properties in the /config
subdirectory. We have seen the order of precedence of the several property sources
in the Spring Boot application. In Spring Boot, we can define properties either in
the .properties file or in the .yml file. By default, Spring Boot creates the application.
properties file in the src/main/resource directory of the Spring application.

Customizing the name of the application. properties file

Spring Boot does not force you to use the same property file created by default
(application.properties). You can change its name as per your choice but you to give
this name to the Spring Boot application by setting the spring.config.name property to
the new name of the file. Let's see the following code snippet:

```
package com.dineshonjava.prodos;

import org.springframework.boot.SpringApplication;
import org.springframework.boot.autoconfigure.SpringBootApplication;

@SpringBootApplication
public class ProdosApplication {
  public static void main(String[] args) {
    System.setProperty("spring.config.name", "prodos-application");
    SpringApplication.run(ProdosApplication.class, args);
  }
}
```

As you can see in the preceding code snippet, we are using the prodos-application.
properties file instead of the default application.properties file.

Note: But the value of the spring.config.name property must be defined as prodos-application and not prodos-application.properties; if you use prodos-application.properties, the file would get named as prodos-application.properties.properties.

Let's move on to the next section to see how to define properties in our configuration files either using the .properties file or its YAML variant.

Application configuration using a properties file

In the previous sections, we discussed about the application configuration using a properties file. The SpringApplication class loads properties from the application.properties file in the following locations and adds them to the Spring environment:

- A /config subdirectory of the current directory
- The current directory
- A classpath /config package
- The classpath root

You can also define the profile specific properties files in the same locations mentioned above. The properties defined in the profile-specific application properties file have a higher priority to override the same properties defined in the normal application properties file. Let's see how we can define some properties in the application property file:

```
//define embedded server configurations
server.port=8080
server.address=192.168.11.21
server.session-timeout=1800
server.context-path=/prodos
server.servlet-path=/admin
```

In the application.properties configuration file, we defined the embedded server in the Spring application. Spring Boot also provides another variant to configure a Spring application using a YAML file. Let's see in the next section.

Application configuration using a YAML file

The YAML file is an alternative to the .properties file and Spring Boot supports YAML files using the SpringApplication class. YAML is not a markup language; it is a configuration file used to define properties in the hierarchical configuration format. Spring Boot uses the SnakeYAML library to parse the YAML file. This library is automatically added to your application classpath by spring-boot-starters.

> **Note: If both the application.properties and application.yml files are present side by side at the same level of precedence, properties in application.yml will override the properties in application.properties.**

Spring Boot supports YAML for properties with hierarchical configuration data. YAML organizes the properties in groups. Let's see the following example for configuring the embedded server.

Configuring an embedded server

You can configure an embedded server in your Spring application as shown in the following the YAML configuration file:

```
//define embedded server configurations in YAML
server:
  port: 8080
  address: 192.168.11.21
  session-timeout: 1800
  context-path: /prodos
  servlet-path: /admin
```

In the preceding configuration, you can see both the application.properties and application.yml files. Spring Boot supports both the configuration files. You can choose any one of them to configure the properties in the Spring application.

Configuring a data source

Let's see some other configuration related to a data source. You can configure a data source in your Spring application as shown in the following YAML configuration file:

```
//define data source configurations
spring:
  datasource:
    url: jdbc:mysql://localhost/prodos
    username: prododb
```

password: prodopassword

driver-class-name: com.mysql.jdbc.Driver

The preceding configuration is for a data source in the YAML file. We will discuss more about it in the coming chapters.

Configuring Logging

By default, Spring Boot uses **Logback** (http://logback.qos.ch) for logging. And also, Spring Boot writes the logs to the console at an INFO level. You can take full control over the logging configuration by creating a logback.xml file at the root of the classpath. Let's see the following logback.xml file:

```xml
<configuration>
 <appender name="STDOUT" class="ch.qos.logback.core.ConsoleAppender">
  <encoder>
   <pattern>
   %d{HH:mm:ss.SSS} [%thread] %-5level %logger{36} - %msg%n
   </pattern>
  </encoder>
 </appender>

 <logger name="root" level="INFO"/>
 <root level="INFO">
  <appender-ref ref="STDOUT" />
 </root>
</configuration>
```

The logback.xml configuration file provides full control over the default configuration file. If you do not add this file to the classpath of the application (src/main/resources), then the default logging configuration file is more or less equivalent to the above configuration file. You can make in logging configuration file by changing the logging levels, specifying logs of the output file and pattern of logs.

But you can also make most of the changes without adding an external logging configuration file (logback.xml) along with the Spring Boot configuration either with the application.properties or application.yml file. Let's set the logging levels as shown in the following YAML configuration file:

```yaml
//define logging configurations
logging:
 level:
  root: WARN
```

```
org:
  springframework:
   security: DEBUG
```

In the preceding application.yml file, we set the root logging level to WARN but the we set the Spring security logs level to the DEBUG level. Now let's configure the logging output.

By default, Spring Boot writes logs to the console, but you can also write these logs to the rotating file (prodos.log). You can set a file or path in the application.yml file as shown in the following configuration:

```
//define logging configurations
logging:
 path: /var/logs/prodos/
 file: prodos.log
 level:
  root: WARN
  org:
   springframework:
    security: DEBUG
```

By default, Spring Boot includes the following:

- **SLF4J**: Logging facade

- **Logback**: SLF4J implementation

Spring Boot also supports other several logging frameworks such as Java Util Logging, Log4J, and Log4J2. But, it is recommended that you stick with the default logging framework in the Spring Boot application and also use the SLF4J abstraction in your application code. You can exclude the default logging framework and use another logging framework Log4J by just adding a dependency, as follows:

```
<dependency>
 <groupId>org.springframework.boot</groupId>
 <artifactId>spring-boot-starter-websocket</artifactId>
 <exclusions>
  <exclusion>
   <groupId>ch.qos.logback</groupId>
   <artifactId>logback-classic</artifactId>
  </exclusion>
 </exclusions>
```

```
</dependency>

<dependency>
 <groupId>org.slf4j</groupId>
 <artifactId>slf4j-log4j12</artifactId>
</dependency>
```

You can see that we added the log4j12 dependency in Maven and excluded the default logging framework, that is, logback.

Further, let's move on to see how a single YAML file works for multiple profiles configuration in the Spring application. Let's see, in the following section, how to define multiple profiles in a single YAML file.

Multi-profile YAML documents

As we have seen how to define profile-specific application properties files, so in case of the .properties file, you need to define number of files for the number of profiles you want to create, but in the YAML configuration file, you can define multiple profiles related properties in a single YAML file, which is an advantage of YAML over the properties configuration file.

Spring Boot provides a spring.profiles key to indicate when the document needs to be applied. Let's see the following example of how to define multiple profile-specific configurations in a single YAML file:

```
//define configurations profile specifically in a single YAML file
#Used for all profiles
logging:
 level:
  org.springframework: INFO


#'dev' profile only
---
spring:
 profiles: dev

database:
 host: localhost
 user: dev


#'prod' profile only
```

```
---
spring:
  profiles: prod

database:
  host: 192.168.200.109
  user: admin
```

In the preceding configuration application.yml file, we defined configurations related to the database according to the available profiles such as dev and prod in the Spring application. We can use a spring.profiles property to set the profile name. In the file, '---' implies a separation between profiles.

Let's now see how to define your own configuration properties in your Spring application.

Creating your own configuration properties

We have seen the configuration properties of the Spring's own component till now. Configuring these configuration properties is very simple, thus making it easy to inject the values into the components' properties. We can also fine tune this auto-configuration. The configuration properties are not for your own component beans created by Spring. These properties are only for some of the exclusive components of Spring. But Spring Boot allows us to create the configuration properties for your own beans in the Spring application. Let's see how to take advantage of the configuration properties in your own beans.

Defining your own configuration properties in the application

Spring Boot provides the @ConfigurationProperties annotation to help register your own beans as properties in your Spring application. You can use these properties by using either the application.properties or application.yml file. Creating your own configuration properties allows you to strongly type safe beans and validate the configuration in your Spring application. Let's see the following example.

Let's see how @ConfigurationProperties works. Suppose in your PRODOS application, you have a requirement to connect the third-party remote service such as feedback service of the product. To connect this remote service, we require some attributes such as service host, service port, timeout, and more. So we can set these attributes by providing hardcoded values. Rather than hardcode the host, port, and timeout, we can set these attributes with custom configuration properties. First, we need to add a separate class to the application to hold all configuration properties such as host, port, timeout, and so on. Let's see the following properties holder class:

```
package com.dineshonjava.prodos.client;

import org.springframework.boot.context.properties.ConfigurationProperties;
import org.springframework.stereotype.Component;

/**
 * @author Dinesh.Rajput
 *
 */
@Component
@ConfigurationProperties(prefix="feedback.client")
public class ConnectionSettings {

  private String host;
  private int port;
  private int timeout;
  public String getHost() {
   return host;
s }
  public void setHost(String host) {
   this.host = host;
  }
  public int getPort() {
   return port;
  }
  public void setPort(int port) {
   this.port = port;
  }
  public int getTimeout() {
   return timeout;
  }
  public void setTimeout(int timeout) {
   this.timeout = timeout;
  }
}
```

As you can see the preceding ConnectionSettings class is annotated with @ ConfigurationProperties to have a prefix of feedback.client. This class is also annotated with the @Component annotation so that Spring can scan it as a component automatically and create it as a bean in the Spring application context.

So, the configuration property holders are Spring beans that hold their properties injected from the Spring environment. You can use these configuration property holders in any other bean that needs those properties. For example, the FeedbackClientConfiguration class has a bean definition FeedbackClient and it needs those properties to set up all the required configuration before creating its bean in the Spring application context. Let's see the following example:

```
package com.dineshonjava.prodos.client;

import org.springframework.beans.factory.annotation.Autowired;
import org.springframework.boot.context.properties.EnableConfigurationProperties;
import org.springframework.context.annotation.Bean;
import org.springframework.context.annotation.Configuration;

/**
 * @author Dinesh.Rajput
 *
 */

@Configuration
@EnableConfigurationProperties(ConnectionSettings.class)
public class FeedbackClientConfiguration {

  // Spring initialized this automatically
  @Autowired
  ConnectionSettings connectionSettings;

  @Bean
  public FeedbackClient feedbackClient() {
    return new FeedbackClient(
      connectionSettings.getHost(),
      connectionSettings.getPort()
      );
  }
}
```

In the preceding configuration class, ConnectionSettings is injected with the FeedbackClientConfiguration class. And the FeedbackClient bean uses this property holder class. Now, we can reuse the ConnectionSettings class in any other bean that may need it. You can modify the ConnectSettings class without impacting the FeedbackClientConfiguration class. You can also apply the validation of the properties inside the property holder class.

The FeedbackClientConfiguration class is annotated with the @ EnableConfigurationProperties annotation. This annotation specifies and auto-injects the container bean.

Declaring the configuration property and metadata

Let's define the configuration properties in the application.yml (or application. properties) file. At the time of defining the configuration property in your Spring application, you may have noticed some warning message saying '**Unknown Property 'feedback'**. This warning message sometimes depends on the IDE, but I am using the Spring Tool Suite IDE for this application. Let's see the following figure:

Figure 2.3: The warning message for an unknown property

Currently, this warning message is seen because the Spring auto-configuration has not recognized the property. The feedback.client.port property is not related to the Spring default configuration, but it is declared for own application bean. You can fix it by creating metadata for your custom configuration properties. It is not mandatory to create it; your application can still work without the metadata. But to remove the warning message, you need to create the metadata for your custom configuration properties under src/main/resources/META-INF named as additional-spring-configuration-metadata.json.

If you are using the Spring Tool Suite, then you can create it by moving the cursor on the line with the missing metadata warning. Then, the cursor displays the quick-fix pop up as shown in the following screenshot:

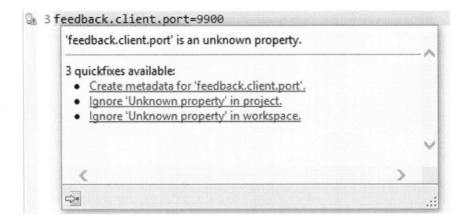

Figure 2.4: The quick-fix pop-up

Let's click on the **Create metadata for feedback.client.port** link. Then, the metadata for your own custom configuration property will be created in the src/main/resources/ META-INF directory of your Spring application. Let's see the following screenshot:

Figure 2.5: additional-spring-configuration-metadata.json metadata added to your application

You can see that the additional-spring.configuration-metadata.json file is added to the src/main/resources/META-INF directory of your Spring application. Let's add some more custom configuration properties to the configuration file as shown in the following code:

feedback.client.port=9900

feedback.client.host=192.168.10.21

feedback.client.timeout=4000

Similarly, let's create the metadata for the preceding custom configuration properties. And finally, let's open the additional-spring.configuration-metadata.json file as shown in the following code:

{"properties": [
  {

```
  "name": "feedback.client.port",
  "type": "java.lang.String",
  "description": "Set the port for the remote feedback service"
  },
  {
  "name": "feedback.client.timeout",
  "type": "java.lang.String",
  "description": "Set maximum timeout for the feedback service in milliseconds"
  },
  {
  "name": "feedback.client.host",
  "type": "java.lang.String",
  "description": "Set the hostname for the remote feedback service"
  }
]}
```

The preceding metadata for the feedback.client.port, feedback.client.host, and feedback.client.timeout properties are created and you can set up this metadata with the custom descriptions. These descriptions are displayed when you move the cursor over the property written in the application configuration file as shown in the following screenshot:

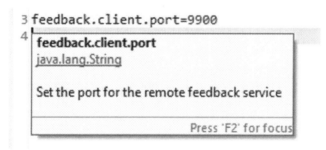

Figure 2.6: Metadata description message about the defined property

After creating the metadata for your own configuration properties, you can add these properties either to the application.properties or application.yml file. The suggestion will be kept open as we have typed feedback in the configuration files as shown in the following screenshot:

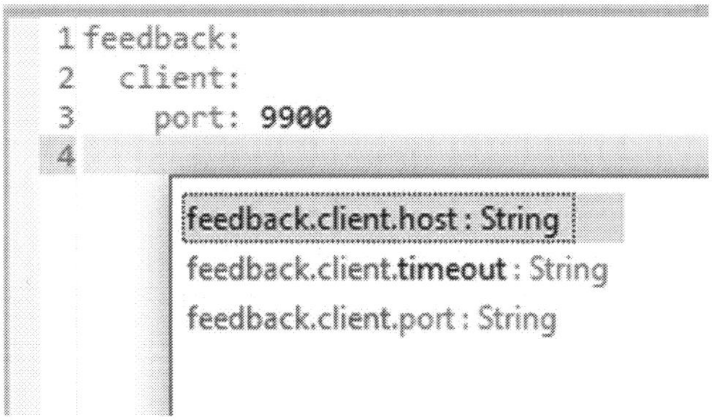

```
1 feedback:
2   client:
3     port: 9900
4
```

feedback.client.host : String
feedback.client.timeout : String
feedback.client.port : String

Figure 2.7: Suggestion quick-box popup for custom configuration properties

You can see in the preceding YAML configuration file that as we typed the feedback, all the suggested available configuration properties get displayed.

You can set your custom configuration properties as environment variables, or you can specify these properties as command-line arguments, or you can add these in any other places where the configuration properties can be set.

Let's move on to the next section and discuss the Spring profiles and how to use the Spring profiles in your application.

Profiling

The profiling is a process used to segregate the application configurations based on certain environments such as development, staging, and production. Spring provides support to create the application configurations based on the profiles. Spring has the @Profile annotation to limit parts of your application configurations to be loaded. You can use the @Profile annotation with any stereotype annotations such as @Component, @Configuration, and also with the @Bean annotation. Let's see the following example:

```
@Configuration
@Profile("production")
public class ProductionConfiguration {
  // ...
}
```

As you can see in the preceding configuration file, we used the @Profile annotation with the value production attribute. This means that the application configurations under the ProductionConfiguration class will be available only for the production profile. Actually, profiles are a type of conditional annotation configuration. The profile is a specific implementation of the @Conditional annotation where different configuration classes, beans, application properties are either applied or ignored based on the active profile at the runtime in your Spring application.

Conditionally creating beans with profiles

In the Spring application, normally, all declared beans in the configuration are created for all profiles, regardless of which profiles are active. But sometimes, the set of beans are required for certain profiles. In this case, Spring allows us to use @ Profile annotation to create profile specific beans. Let's see the following example:

```
@Bean
@Profile("dev")
public DataSource dataSource(){
  EmbeddedDatabaseBuilder builder = new EmbeddedDatabaseBuilder().
setType(EmbeddedDatabaseType.HSQL);//in-memory
  builder.addScript("schema.sql");
  builder.addScript("data.sql");
  return builder.build();
}
```

The preceding DataSource bean, with the embedded HSQL database, is available only for the dev profile in the Spring application. That's great for development, but it would be unnecessary in a production application. If you want the same DataSource bean with either the dev or qa profile, you can define the same DataSource bean as shown in the following code:

```
@Bean
@Profile({"dev", "qa"})
public DataSource dataSource(){
  EmbeddedDatabaseBuilder builder = new EmbeddedDatabaseBuilder().
setType(EmbeddedDatabaseType.HSQL);//in-memory
  builder.addScript("schema.sql");
  builder.addScript("data.sql");
  return builder.build();
}
```

Now, the DataSource bean will only be loaded if the dev or qa profiles are active. Let's discuss how to activate the Spring profiles in the Spring application.

Activating profiles

The profile-specific application configurations and settings are only applicable to the Spring application when you activate those profiles in your Spring application, otherwise creating profile-specific configurations are useless. Let's make the profiles active in the Spring application using the spring.profiles.active property as shown in the following example:

In application.yml like this:

```
spring:
  profiles:
    active:
      -production
```

In application.properties, use the following code:

```
spring.profiles.active=production
```

You can also set the spring.profiles.active property using the Environment property to specify which profiles are active. You can activate multiple profiles at one time using the spring.profiles.active property. Let's see the following example:

```
spring.profiles.active=production,mariadb
```

Spring allows us to create profile-specific application configuration properties files. Let's see how.

Profile-specific application configuration properties files

As discussed in the earlier section of this chapter, the application.properties file is one of the ways used to externalize the application auto-configuration. But you can externalize the auto-configuration based on the active profiles in the Spring application. Profile-specific configuration properties can be created as application-{profile}.properties (For example: application-dev.properties, application-qa.properties, and so on). By default, Spring has default profiles, which means there are no active profiles in the Spring application. If no profiles are used in the application, then the application loads the properties from the application-default.properties file.

The profile-specific application configuration files are always win with non-profile specific files at the same place of precedence.

Conclusion

In this chapter, we discussed the Spring Boot auto-configuration and a lot of things related to auto-configuration. Spring Boot is a very opinionated framework and never forces to use the default auto-configuration. Spring Boot allows you to enable or disable the default auto-configuration based on your requirement.

We saw how the Spring Boot auto-configuration works. Spring Boot sensibly uses the @Conditional annotation out-of-the-box. Configuration properties can be set in command-line arguments, environment variables, JVM system properties, properties files, or YAML files, among other options.

We saw Spring auto-configurations can be externalized using the application.properties or application.yml configuration files. We also saw how to create your own custom configuration properties in your Spring application. We discuused how Spring profiles provide a mechanism to control the configurations settings and bean creations based on the active profiles in the Spring application.

In the next *Chapter 3: Configuring Spring Data JPA and CRUD* operations, we will discuss how to configure Spring Data and ORM tools for the CRUD operations using Spring Boot.

Questions

1. What is auto-configuration in Spring Boot?
2. How to enable auto-configuration in Spring Boot?
3. How to disable auto-configuration in Spring Boot?
4. How to externalize auto-configuration?
5. What is the order of evaluation for overridden properties?
6. What is YAML?
7. How to define multi-profiles YAML documents?
8. What is profiling in Spring Boot?
9. How to activate profiles?

CHAPTER 3
Configuring Data and CRUD operations

The Spring framework provides comprehensive support for working with backend data using SQL relational or non-relational databases. Spring provides full support to use backend technologies from the JDBC access using JdbcTemplate to the object-relational mapping (ORM) solution technologies such as Hibernate. Additionally, Spring has a wonderful functionality for the backend data with magical Spring Data. It creates Repository implementations from interfaces and generates queries from the method names. We will discuss everything one by one in this chapter.

In the previous chapter, we discussed Spring Boot with its essential key components. We also discussed the auto-configuration component in detail, how to customize and externalize the existing default configurations provided Spring Boot. In this chapter, you will get a better understanding of Spring Data JPA and learn how to configure SQL DB H2. You will be given an overview of Spring Data JPA and how to configure SQL DB in the Spring Boot application.

Till now, we created a PRODOS Spring application using Spring Boot. Let's now learn how to configure data backend into our application. As we know, most of the applications offer data information in front of the users. So, you need to configure a database in the Spring PRODOS application to store the information about the products.

We will use the database in the PRODOS Spring application using the Spring support for **Java Database Connectivity (JDBC)**. After that, we will rework with the ORM (Hibernate) and then Spring Data **Java Persistence API (JPA)**, which eliminates even more boilerplate code. Let's start with the Spring support for JDBC. We will cover the following topics in this chapter:

- Using JDBC with the Spring application
    - o Adding a domain class
    - o Working with JdbcTemplate
    - o Creating a table schema and loading data
- Configuring a DataSource
    - o Embedded database support
    - o Production database support
    - o A JNDI DataSource support
- Working with Spring Data JPA
    - o A quick introduction to ORM with JPA
    - o Entity classes
    - o Creating and dropping JPA databases
    - o Introduction to Spring Data
    - o Configuring Spring Data JPA
    - o Creating Spring Data JPA repositories
    - o Customizing Spring Data JPA repositories
- Configuring the H2 database
- Configuring the MariaDB database

Using JDBC with the Spring application

Spring provides support to use JDBC with abstractions for working with relational data. As a Java developer, you can choose any one of the options such as JDBC, the JPA, and ORM supported by the Spring framework. But in this section, we will discuss the Spring JDBC support with an example.

Normally, if you use JDBC in the simple core Java application without the Spring framework, then you need to typically write a lot of boilerplate code such as loading driver, creating a database connection, preparing a SQL statement, etc. But the most irritating is handling SQL exception at the data access layer of the application; it is not good practice to handle exceptions at the data access layer. Let's see the following code snippet for JDBC without using Spring:

```
//Querying a database without JdbcTemplate
@Override
public Product findOne(String id) {
 Connection connection = null;
 PreparedStatement statement = null;
 ResultSet resultSet = null;
 try {
  connection = dataSource.getConnection();
  statement = connection.prepareStatement(
  "select id, name, type from Product");
  statement.setString(1, id);
  resultSet = statement.executeQuery();
  Product product = null;
  if(resultSet.next()) {
   product = new Product(
   resultSet.getString("id"),
   resultSet.getString("name"),
   resultSet.getString("type"));
  }
  return product;
 } catch (SQLException e) {
  // ??? What should be done here ???
 } finally {
  if (resultSet != null) {
   try {
    resultSet.close();
   } catch (SQLException e) {}
  }
  if (statement != null) {
   try {
    statement.close();
   } catch (SQLException e) {}
  }
  if (connection != null) {
   try {
    connection.close();
```

```
    } catch (SQLException e) {}
  }
 }
 return null;
}
```

The preceding code snippet has a big part of boilerplate code and developers are forced to handle checked the exception SQLException using various try-catch block. Even the earlier code does not have proper readability. The Spring framework provides the JdbcTemplate class to handle all the necessary things and boilerplate is typically required when working with JDBC. JdbcTemplate allows developers to perform SQL operations only against the relational database. Let's see the following code snippet with the JdbcTemplate class:

```
JdbcTemplate jdbcTemplate;

public Product findOne(String id){
  String sql = "select id, name, type from Product where id = "+id;
  return jdbcTemplate.queryForObject(sql, new RowMapper<Product>(){
    @Override
    public Product mapRow(ResultSet rs, int arg1) throws SQLException {
      product = new Product(
        resultSet.getString("id"),
        resultSet.getString("name"),
        resultSet.getString("type"));
      return product;
    }
  });
}
```

As you can see in the preceding code snippet, we performed the same SQL query, but here, there is no need to handle a lot of things such as SQLException, prepare a statement, the clean-up of those objects, and connection. And also, the preceding code is much simpler than the previous raw JDBC example. We just called the queryForObject() method of the JdbcTemplate class and mapped the results to a Product object.

Adding a domain class

In the application PRODOS, we have a database to store the product information, and we can also access the product information from the database. So, it is a good idea to create a domain class for the product information, and we could map the column names with the fields of the object. Let's create a domain class Product as shown in the following code:

```
package com.dineshonjava.prodos.domain;

import java.io.Serializable;

public class Product implements Serializable{

  private static final long serialVersionUID = 1L;

  private String id;
  private String name;
  private String type;

  public Product(String id, String name, String type) {
    super();
    this.id = id;
    this.name = name;
    this.type = type;
  }

  public String getId() {
    return id;
  }

  public void setId(String id) {
    this.id = id;
  }

  public String getName() {
    return name;
  }
```

```
public void setName(String name) {
  this.name = name;
}

public String getType() {
  return type;
}

public void setType(String type) {
  this.type = type;
}
}
```

Now, our domain class is ready for persistence. Let's see how to use JdbcTemplate to read and write them to a database.

Working with JdbcTemplate

Let's start to use JdbcTemplate in our Spring REST application PRODOS. Before we start using JdbcTemplate, we need to add the Maven dependency to the project classpath. We need to add the following Spring Boot's JDBC starter dependency to the pom.xml file:

```
<dependency>
  <groupId>org.springframework.boot</groupId>
  <artifactId>spring-boot-starter-jdbc</artifactId>
</dependency>
```

Now, the preceding dependency will add all the required libraries to your application's classpath for JdbcTemplate. But before using it, you need to add a database where your data will be stored. For development purposes, we can use an embedded database such as H2, HSQL and Derby. But in this example, I prefer using the H2 embedded database. Let's see the following Maven dependency that will be added to the pom.xml file:

```
<dependency>
  <groupId>com.h2database</groupId>
  <artifactId>h2</artifactId>
  <scope>runtime</scope>
</dependency>
```

After adding an in-memory database to your application, let's move on to write a repository class to fetch and save the product data from the in-memory database. Let's see the following ProductRepository interface that defines operation methods:

```
package com.dineshonjava.prodos.repository;

import com.dineshonjava.prodos.domain.Product;

public interface ProductRepository {

  Iterable<Product> findAll();
  Product findOne(String id);
  Product save(Product product);
}
```

Your product repository performs the following operations:

- Query for all products into a collection of Product objects
- Query for a single Product by its id
- Save a Product object

Now, we will implement the preceding repository interface. The JdbcTemplate class of Spring is auto-configured with your Spring application, and you can @Autowire it directly into your repository implementation, as shown in the following example:

```
package com.dineshonjava.prodos.repository;

import org.springframework.jdbc.core.JdbcTemplate;
import org.springframework.stereotype.Repository;

import com.dineshonjava.prodos.domain.Product;

@Repository
public class JdbcProductRepository implements ProductRepository {

  private JdbcTemplate jdbcTemplate;

  public JdbcProductRepository(JdbcTemplate jdbcTemplate) {
    super();
    this.jdbcTemplate = jdbcTemplate;
```

```
    }


    //...
}
```

As you can see, JdbcProductRepository is annotated with the @Repository annotation. This @Repository annotation is one of the stereotype annotations. The Spring application's context will automatically scan this annotated JdbcProductRepository and instantiate it as a bean in the Spring application context.

At the time of bean creation of the JdbcProductRepository bean, the Spring container injects JdbcTemplate into this repository bean via the construction. We can use a JdbcTemplate instance to query and insert it into the database.

In the preceding code, we have not explicitly used the @Autowired annotated construction to inject JdbcTemplate because in Spring 4.3.5 version, the single constructor is treated as the @Autowired annotated constructor by default, so no need to add the @Autowired annotation explicitly. If you have more than one constructor, then you need to use the @Autowired annotation.

You can also customize some properties of the JDBC template using the spring.jdbc.template.* properties, as shown in the following example:

```
spring.jdbc.template.max-rows=500
```

Let's take a look at the implementations of findAll() and findOne() of the JdbcProductRepository class:

```
@Override
public Iterable<Product> findAll() {
  return jdbcTemplate.query("select id, name, type from Product",
  this::mapRowToProduct);
}


@Override
public Product findOne(String id) {
  return jdbcTemplate.queryForObject("select id, name, type from Product where id=?",
  this::mapRowToProduct, id);
}


private Product mapRowToProduct(ResultSet rs, int rowNum) throws SQLException {
  return new Product(
    rs.getString("id"),
```

```
    rs.getString("name"),
    rs.getString("type"));
}
```

The preceding two methods are only reading data from the database, but inserting and updating are the other parts where we are playing with data. So, the update() method of the JdbcTemplate class can be used for any query that writes or updates data in the database. And, as shown in the following listing, it can be used to insert data into the database:

```
@Override
public Product save(Product product) {
  jdbcTemplate.update(
     "insert into Product (id, name, type) values (?, ?, ?)",
     product.getId(),
     product.getName(),
     product.getType());
  return product;
}
```

We defined all the three methods of ProductRepository. Now, once JdbcProductRepository class is complete, you can use it with the other beans such as services and controllers in your Spring application. Let's see the complete JdbcProductRepository class as shown in the following code:

```
package com.dineshonjava.prodos.repository;

import java.sql.ResultSet;
import java.sql.SQLException;

import org.springframework.jdbc.core.JdbcTemplate;
import org.springframework.stereotype.Repository;

import com.dineshonjava.prodos.domain.Product;

/**
 * @author Dinesh.Rajput
 *
 */
@Repository
public class JdbcProductRepository implements ProductRepository {
```

```java
private JdbcTemplate jdbcTemplate;

public JdbcProductRepository(JdbcTemplate jdbcTemplate) {
  super();
  this.jdbcTemplate = jdbcTemplate;
}

@Override
public Iterable<Product> findAll() {
  return jdbcTemplate.query("select id, name, type from Product", this::mapRowToProduct);
}

@Override
public Product findOne(String id) {
  return jdbcTemplate.queryForObject("select id, name, type from Product where id=?",
this::mapRowToProduct, id);
}

@Override
public Product save(Product product) {
  jdbcTemplate.update(
    "insert into Product (id, name, type) values (?, ?, ?)",
    product.getId(),
    product.getName(),
    product.getType());
  return product;
}

private Product mapRowToProduct(ResultSet rs, int rowNum) throws SQLException {
  return new Product(
    rs.getString("id"),
    rs.getString("name"),
    rs.getString("type"));
}
}
```

In the previous chapter, we created a REST web application with a controller class which returned hardcoded values Hello World!!! as a response. But after the JdbcProductRepository class is complete, you can now inject it into the controller class. Let's create the ProductController controller class and use it to provide a list of Product objects. Let's see the following controller class:

```java
package com.dineshonjava.prodos.controller;

import java.util.ArrayList;
import java.util.List;

import org.springframework.web.bind.annotation.GetMapping;
import org.springframework.web.bind.annotation.RestController;

import com.dineshonjava.prodos.domain.Product;
import com.dineshonjava.prodos.repository.ProductRepository;

/**
 * @author Dinesh.Rajput
 *
 */

@RestController
public class ProductController {

  private ProductRepository productRepository;

  public ProductController(ProductRepository productRepository) {
    super();
    this.productRepository = productRepository;
  }

  @GetMapping("/products")
  public List<Product> findAll(){
    List<Product> products = new ArrayList<>();
    productRepository.findAll().forEach(i -> products.add(i));
    return products;
  }
}
```

}

As you can see, ProductRepository is injected into the controller class and the controller class is using the injected findAll() method of the ProductRepository object. This method fetches all the products from the database.

Creating table schema and loading data

Let's create a table in the H2 database using the following query:

```
CREATE TABLE PRODUCT (
  name VARCHAR(50),
  type VARCHAR(50),
  id VARCHAR(10)
 );
```

In the preceding schema query, we need to run the H2 database, but how to run this query to the H2 database, and where do we need to put this query. So, Spring Boot will support you to run this query for your application. We need to create a file named schema.sql in the src/main/resources folder of the Spring application PRODOS.

After creating the table schema, let's preload the database with some product data. Spring Boot also supports the data loading by executing a file named data.sql from the root of the classpath when the application starts. That means, we need to place data.sql file in the src/main/resources folder of your Spring application PRODOS with the following data insertion queries:

```
INSERT INTO PRODUCT (id, name, type) values ('MOB01', 'Samsung A6 plus', 'Mobile');
```

```
INSERT INTO PRODUCT (id, name, type) values ('MOB02', 'iPhone X plus', 'Mobile');
```

```
INSERT INTO PRODUCT (id, name, type) values ('TLV01', 'Sony Bravia KLV-50W662F 50 Inch Full HD', 'Television');
```

```
INSERT INTO PRODUCT (id, name, type) values ('CAM01', 'Canon EOS 1500D Digital SLR Camera', 'DSLR Camera');
```

```
INSERT INTO PRODUCT (id, name, type) values ('SPK01', 'JBL Cinema 510 5.1 with Powered Subwoofer', 'Home Theater Speaker');
```

Let's see the following PRODOS application structure:

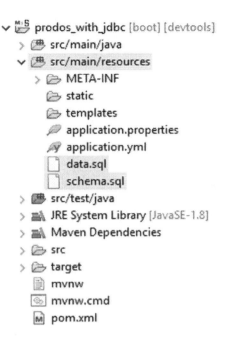

Figure 3.1: A Prodos application structure

Now, you can see that we created a table schema and loaded some data to the table. After the loading data into the table, it will look like as shown in the following screenshot:

SELECT * FROM PRODUCT;

NAME	TYPE	ID
Samsung A6 plus	Mobile	MOB01
iPhone X plus	Mobile	MOB02
Sony Bravia KLV-50W662F 50 Inch Full HD	Television ·	TLV01
Canon EOS 1500D Digital SLR Camera	DSLR Camera	CAM01
JBL Cinema 510 5.1 with Powered Subwoofer	Home Theater Speaker	SPK01

(5 rows, 3 ms)

Figure 3.2: A Prodos application table structure and data

We added the H2 Database and loaded the product data to the database. Spring Boot provides auto-configuration which is related to the H2 database. So here, we did not configure the DataSource explicit. An H2 database is a good option for the development environment, but it is not suitable for the production environment. So, Spring Boot allows you to customize it accordingly based on the development and production environments.

Configuring a DataSource

A DataSource class is all about configuring the URL along with some credentials to establish a database connection. So, the javax.sql.DataSource interface is available in Java and it provides a standard mechanism to establish a database connection. Let's see how to configure a DataSource for the in-memory embedded database such as H2, HSQL, Derby, and more.

In-memory embedded database support

As mentioned earlier, the in-memory embedded database is a good option for the development environment. But the in-memory embedded database does not provide the persistent storage. As your application starts, the in-memory embedded database is prepared and as your application ends, it throws away data.

Spring Boot provides support to the auto-configure in-memory embedded database such as H2, HSQL, and Derby databases. You can just add the Maven dependency to an embedded database that you want to use. There is no need to provide any connection URLs.

```
<dependency>
  <groupId>com.h2database</groupId>
  <artifactId>h2</artifactId>
  <scope>runtime</scope>
</dependency>
```

But still you can customize using the following configuration:

```
@Bean
public DataSource dataSource(){
  EmbeddedDatabaseBuilder builder =
    new EmbeddedDatabaseBuilder().setType(EmbeddedDatabaseType.H2);//in-memory
  builder.addScript("schema.sql");
  builder.addScript("data.sql");
  return builder.build();
}
```

Production database support

Spring Boot also auto-configures the production database connection using a pooling DataSource. In the production environment, pooling DataSource is a more suitable for database. Spring Boot uses some specific default implementation of the connection pooling as follows:

- By default, as of Spring Boot 2.0 uses HikariCP. The HikariCP data source provides high performance and concurrency. The HikariCP gets automatically added to your Spring application when you configure the spring-boot-starter-jdbc or spring-boot-starter-data-jpa starter to the Maven pom.xml file.

- We can also use the Tomcat pooling DataSource.

- Another option is the Commons DBCP2 data source.

We have seen the connection pooling auto-configuration. Now, let's see how to externalize the configuration properties in spring.datasource.* as shown in the following code:

```
spring.datasource.url=jdbc:mariadb://localhost:3306/mydb
spring.datasource.username=mydbuser
spring.datasource.password=mydbpass
spring.datasource.driver-class-name=org.mariadb.jdbc.Driver
```

If you do not specify the spring.datasource.url property, then Spring Boot tries to auto-configure an embedded database.

In Spring Boot 2, the spring.datasource.driver-class-name **property is optional. If you do not specify it, then Spring Boot will resolve it for most databases from the URL.**

You can also fine tune the settings of the specific data source implementation using the following respective prefixes:

- spring.datasource.hikari.*

- spring.datasource.tomcat.*

- spring.datasource.dbcp2.*

For example, if you are using the Tomcat connection pool, then you can customize the additional settings as shown in the following code:

```
# Number of ms to wait before throwing an exception if no connection is available.
spring.datasource.tomcat.max-wait=10000

# Maximum number of active connections that can be allocated from this pool at the same time.
spring.datasource.tomcat.max-active=50

# Validate the connection before borrowing it from the pool.
spring.datasource.tomcat.test-on-borrow=true
```

A JNDI DataSource support

Spring Boot provides support to use a JNDI DataSource. It is useful when your application is deployed to the application server such as JBoss. You can configure your DataSource using the application server's built-in features and access the DataSource in your application using JNDI.

Spring Boot provides the spring.datasource.jndi-name property to access the DataSource from a specific JNDI location. Let's see the following example:

spring.datasource.jndi-name=java:jboss/datasources/prodos

Working with Spring Data JPA

In the previous section, we discussed how to work with data using Spring's JdbcTemplate. But sometimes, we need a more powerful tool to handle the backend. In the JDBC example, we had a domain object with the table. So, it might get more complicated when we handle a number of columns with several tables. Spring Boot also supports JPA and ORM technologies.

A quick introduction to ORM with JPA

Object-relational mapping (**ORM**) means mapping Java Persistence Objects to the relational databases. It is a technique used to fetch and manipulate the data using the object-oriented programming paradigm. So, as a developer, you do not need to rely on the database structure and vendor-specific SQL statements, you need to rely on object-oriented concepts and write ORM implementation specific queries. That means ORM allows you to write database independent queries to fetch and manipulates data.

ORM provides a separate data access layer without depending on the vendor-specific properties. It allows you to change the database infrastructure without any or minimal changes in the data access layer in the application. The ORM also makes development much faster and reduces the amount of source code.

The following is a list of popular ORM tools:

- Hibernate
- iBATIS
- Java Data Objects (JDO)
- Java Object Oriented Querying (jOOQ)
- DataNucleus

- Ebean

- EclipseLink

- MyBatis

- Object Relational Bridge (Apache OJB)

- ObjectDB

- OpenJPA

- ORMLite

- QuickDB ORM

- TopLink

The **Java Persistence API (JPA)** is a Java implementation for the object-relational mapping for Java developers. It provides a standard way that allows you to map objects to relational databases. The JPA uses the JPA entity classes; these classes present the structure of a database table and its fields present the columns of the database tables.

For Java development, Hibernate is the most popular JPA implementation. Spring Boot provides support to several JPA implementations but the Hibernate is used by default. Hibernate is used widely in large-scale applications and it is a mature product. For the Spring Boot application, you need to add the spring-boot-starter-data-jpa starter to the POM file to provide Hibernate as the JPA implementation:

```
<dependency>

 <groupId>org.springframework.boot</groupId>

 <artifactId>spring-boot-starter-data-jpa</artifactId>

</dependency>
```

The preceding Maven dependency provides the Spring Data JPA module to your application and it adds other dependencies to Hibernate, Spring Data JPA, and Spring support for the core ORM.

Let's discuss how to create a JPA entity class in the application.

Creating the entity class

Let's create an entity class in your Spring application for the Product table in the H2 database as the following:

```
package com.dineshonjava.prodos.domain;

import java.io.Serializable;

import javax.persistence.Column;
import javax.persistence.Entity;
import javax.persistence.GeneratedValue;
import javax.persistence.Id;
import javax.persistence.Table;

/**
 * @author Dinesh.Rajput
 *
 */
@Entity
@Table(name="PRODUCT")
public class Product implements Serializable{

    private static final long serialVersionUID = 1L;

    @Id
    @GeneratedValue
    private String id;

    @Column(nullable = false)
    private String name;

    @Column(nullable = false)
    private String type;

    @Column(name="desc", nullable=false, length=512)
    private String description;

    @Column(nullable = false)
```

```java
private String brand;

public Product() {
 super();
}
public Product(String id, String name, String type, String description,
   String brand) {
 super();
 this.id = id;
 this.name = name;
 this.type = type;
 this.description = description;
 this.brand = brand;
}
public String getId() {
 return id;
}
public void setId(String id) {
 this.id = id;
}
public String getName().{
 return name;
}
public void setName(String name) {
 this.name = name;
}
public String getType() {
 return type;
}
public void setType(String type) {
 this.type = type;
}
public String getDescription() {
 return description;
}
public void setDescription(String description) {
 this.description = description;
}
```

```
public String getBrand() {
  return brand;
 }
 public void setBrand(String brand) {
  this.brand = brand;
 }
}
```

As you can see, the preceding class is annotated with the JPA @Entity annotation. That means any simple POJO class is treated as an Entity class if that is annotated with the JPA @Entity annotation. The preceding class is also annotated with the @ Table annotation to provide the name of the table; if you do not use this @Table annotation, then JPA creates a database table called the name of the class at the time of application initialization.

In the entity class, some fields are mapped to the database table columns. The entity class must also contain a unique ID that is used as a primary key in the database. Its ID property is annotated with @Id. And also, its id field is annotated with the @GeneratedValue annotation and defines the ID automatically generated by the database.

The @Column annotation in the entity class defines the column's name, and you can also define other properties such as the column's length and check whether the column is nullable:

```
@Column(name="desc", nullable=false, length=512)
private String description;
```

The preceding code has the @Column annotation with the column's name in the database as desc and the length of the column is 512 and it is not nullable.

At the time of running this application, the table PRODUCT was created in the database. You can ensure it using the spring.jpa.show-sql property. Let's set this property as true in the application.properties file.

```
spring.jpa.show-sql=true
```

You can see the following logging of SQL statements to the console to verify the table PRODUCT has been created:

```
2019-02-12 22:57:02.988  INFO 6744 --- [  restartedMain] org.hibernate.tuple.PojoInstantiator    : HHH000182: No default (no-argument) constructor for class:
com.dineshonjava.prodos.domain.Product (class must be instantiated by Interceptor)
Hibernate: drop table product if exists
Hibernate: drop sequence if exists hibernate_sequence
Hibernate: create sequence hibernate_sequence start with 1 increment by 1
Hibernate: create table product (id varchar(255) not null, desc varchar(512) not null, name varchar(255) not null, type varchar(255) not null, primary key (id))
2019-02-12 22:57:03.276  INFO 6744 --- [  restartedMain] o.h.t.schema.internal.SchemaCreatorImpl   : HHH000476: Executing import script
'org.hibernate.tool.schema.internal.exec.ScriptSourceInputNonExistentImpl@17cdac71'
2019-02-12 22:57:03.277  INFO 6744 --- [  restartedMain] o.h.e.t.j.p.i.JtaPlatformInitiator        : HHH000490: Using JtaPlatform implementation:
[org.hibernate.engine.transaction.jta.platform.internal.NoJtaPlatform]
```

Figure 3.3: Table Creation of SQL statements to the console

Earlier, the JPA Entity class was specified with a persistence.xml file, but Spring Boot allows you to create an entity class without a persistence.xml file. Spring Boot provides Entity Scanning for the entity classes. By default, Spring Boot scans all packages under your main configuration class that is annotated with @SpringBootApplication.

Creating and dropping JPA databases

You can set the spring.jpa.hibernate.ddl-auto property for creating and dropping JPA databases as shown in the following code:

spring.jpa.hibernate.ddl-auto=create-drop

The preceding spring.jpa.hibernate.ddl-auto property is set to a create-drop value, which means JPA databases will be dropped and created at the start time of the application. But, in Spring Boot, by default, JPA databases are created automatically if you are using an embedded database such as H2, HSQL, or Derby. But Spring Boot allows you to customize the PA settings by using the spring.jpa.* properties.

We discussed the JPA entity class and its annotations. In Spring Boot, you can use this entity class with Spring Data. Let's now discuss Spring Data and its related projects.

Introduction to Spring Data

The pivotal team created a very magical project, that is, Spring Data. Spring Data has reduced a lot of configuration and boilerplate code from the data access layer in your Spring application. It provides a familiar and consistent programming model at the data access layer in your Spring application with any underlying data store.

Earlier, if you wanted to use any data access technologies such as relational database, non-relational database, and cloud-based data services then, you have required a lot of configuration related to any specific data access technologies. But Spring Data reduces this configuration and makes it easy to use these data access technologies in the Spring application.

Spring Data is an umbrella project which contains many other subprojects for the specific data access technologies. Here are some of the following subprojects of Spring Data:

- Spring Data Commons: Core Spring concepts underpinning every Spring Data module.

- Spring Data JPA: Subproject for the JPA persistence support against a relational database.

- Spring Data MongoDB: Subproject for the MongoDB support against a non-relational database.

- Spring Data Redis: Subprojects for a Redis key-value store.

- Spring Data for Apache Cassandra: Subprojects for a Cassandra database.

- Spring Data Neo4j: Subprojects for a Neo4j graph database.

- Spring Data for Apache Solr: Subprojects for Apache Solr for your search-oriented Spring applications.

There are many more subprojects available under the Spring Data umbrella project. Here are some other community modules under this Spring Data umbrella project:

- Spring Data Aerospike: Spring Data module for Aerospike.

- Spring Data ArangoDB: Spring Data module for ArangoDB.

- Spring Data Couchbase: Spring Data module for Couchbase.

- Spring Data Azure Cosmos DB: Spring Data module for Microsoft Azure Cosmos DB.

- Spring Data DynamoDB: Spring Data module for DynamoDB.

- Spring Data Elasticsearch: Spring Data module for Elasticsearch.

- Spring Data Hazelcast: Provides Spring Data repository support for Hazelcast.

- Spring Data Jest: The Spring Data module for Elasticsearch based on the Jest REST client.

- Spring Data Vault: Vault repositories built on top of Spring Data KeyValue.

Let's see the important features of the Spring Data project:

- The most interesting features of Spring Data is its ability to automatically create repositories, based on a repository specification interface.

- The query derivation from the repository method names.

- Support for the custom repository code.

- A consistent approach for all data access technologies.

- XML and JavaConfig-based Spring integration.

We discussed the Spring Data project, so now let's discuss one of subprojects *Spring Data JPA* of the Spring Data in the next section.

Configuring Spring Data JPA to the project

Spring Boot provides the JPA starter to add the Spring Data JPA to your Spring application. Let's see the following starter dependency that needsto be added to your Maven pom.xml file to get all the required dependencies, including transitive dependencies as well your Spring application:

```
<dependency>
 <groupId>org.springframework.boot</groupId>
 <artifactId>spring-boot-starter-data-jpa</artifactId>
</dependency>
```

The Maven JPA starter dependency includes Hibernate as the JPA implementation by default. But if you want to use another JPA implementation with your Spring application, then you need to exclude Hibernate as the default JPA implementation. Let's see the following Maven dependencies configuration:

```
<dependency>
 <groupId>org.springframework.boot</groupId>
 <artifactId>spring-boot-starter-data-jpa</artifactId>
 <exclusions>
  <exclusion>
   <artifactId>hibernate-entitymanager</artifactId>
   <groupId>org.hibernate</groupId>
  </exclusion>
 </exclusions>
</dependency>

<dependency>
  <groupId>com.oracle.toplink</groupId>
  <artifactId>toplink</artifactId>
  <version>10.1.3</version>
</dependency>
```

In the preceding configuration, we excluded the Hibernate JPA implementation with Spring Data JPA and added the top link as JPA implementation to your Spring application. We added Spring Data JPA in the Spring Application. Now, let's create Spring Data JPA repositories.

Creating Spring Data JPA repositories

Spring Data provides a Repository marker interface to make any interface similar to the Spring Data repository. Along with this interface, Spring Data also provides another CrudRepository interface for CRUD operations. This interface provides the CRUD functionalities in the Spring application to our entity class.

Spring Data JPA repositories interfaces are used to access data from the relational database. You do not need to write JPA queries as these are automatically created from your method names. Let's see the following example.

Creating ProductRepository using the Repository marker interface

First, we will create a ProductRepository interface using the Repository marker interface. But in this case, we wrote our own methods for the CRUD functionalities:

```
package com.dineshonjava.prodos.repository;

import org.springframework.data.repository.Repository;

import com.dineshonjava.prodos.domain.Product;

public interface ProductRepository extends Repository<Product, String>{

  Iterable<Product> findAll();

  Product findById(String id);

  Product save(Product product);
}
```

Creating ProductRepository using the CrudRepository interface

Let's create the same ProductRepository interface using the CrudRepository interface. Then, you do not need to write any CRUD methods as these methods are inherited from the CrudRepository interface, as shown in the following example:

```
package com.dineshonjava.prodos.repository;

import org.springframework.data.repository.CrudRepository;
import com.dineshonjava.prodos.domain.Product;

public interface ProductRepository extends CrudRepository<Product, String>{
  //No need to define generic CRUD methods
}
```

The preceding ProductRepository interface now extends the CrudRepository interface of the Spring Boot JPA. Another interesting thing, the <Product, String> type arguments define this repository created for the Product entity class with the type of ID as String. And also, CrudRepository provides multiple CRUD methods which are as follows:

Method	Description
long count()	This method returns the total number of entities.
Iterable<T> findAll()	This method returns all the available rows in the table of the given type.
Optional<T> findById(ID Id)	This method returns one row by id from the table.
void delete(T entity)	This method deletes an entity from the table.
void deleteAll()	This method deletes all entities of the repository from table.
<S extends T> save(S entity)	This method inserts an entity to the table.

You can see that one method has the Optional<T> return type, which means it returns only one item. Java 8 has introduced Optional<T> instead of T. So, Optional is used for a single value container with either one value or no value. It is also used to prevent null pointer exceptions in case of no value found.

To test the created ProductRepository, let's insert some data into the table, PRODUCT. So for development purpose, either we can insert data into a table using the CommandLineRunner interface or we can create a data.sql file with insert queries at the src/main/resource folder of your Spring application.

Using CommandLineRunner

This interface allows you to execute additional code before the application has fully started:

```
import org.springframework.boot.CommandLineRunner;
import org.springframework.boot.SpringApplication;
import org.springframework.boot.autoconfigure.SpringBootApplication;
import org.springframework.context.annotation.Bean;


@SpringBootApplication
public class ProdosApplication {
  public static void main(String[] args) {
    SpringApplication.run(ProdosApplication.class, args);
  }

  @Bean
  CommandLineRunner runner(){
    return args -> {
     // Place your code here
    };
  }
}
```

Using the data.sql file

Let's create a data.sql file and place this file in the src/main/resources folder of the Spring application. This file contains the following insert queries:

INSERT INTO PRODUCT (id, name, type, brand, desc) values ('MOB01', 'Samsung A6 plus', 'Mobile', 'Samsung', 'Samsung A6 plus is very nice phone with 24mp front camera');

INSERT INTO PRODUCT (id, name, type, brand, desc) values ('MOB02', 'iPhone X plus', 'Mobile', 'Apple', 'iPhone X plus is very nice phone with 24mp front camera');

INSERT INTO PRODUCT (id, name, type, brand, desc) values ('TLV01', 'Sony Bravia KLV-50W662F 50 Inch Full HD', 'Television', 'Sony', 'Sony Bravia is full HD tv');

INSERT INTO PRODUCT (id, name, type, brand, desc) values ('CAM01', 'Canon EOS 1500D Digital SLR Camera', 'DSLR Camera', 'Canon', 'Best DSLR camera in the market');

INSERT INTO PRODUCT (id, name, type, brand, desc) values ('SPK01', 'JBL Cinema 510 5.1 with Powered Subwoofer', 'Home Theater Speaker', 'JBL', 'This sound system is suitable for the Home Theater');

We inserted all the above when the application started and you can check it via the H2 database console. We will discuss how to use H2 database console later in this chapter.

Till now, we discussed the Spring Data JPA repository and we created a repository interface by extending the Spring Data JPA CrudRepository interface. It provides generic CRUD functionalities but we will see how to add the customize method to the repository.

Customizing Spring Data JPA repositories

You can add your own queries according to your business requirement in the Spring Data repositories. Suppose you want to access all products from the database by a specific type, you need to declare the following method:

```
//Fetch products by type
List<Product> findByType(String type);
```

As you can see the preceding method, the method name must start with a prefix that is findBy and after the prefix; you need to define that entity class field that is used in the query:

```
package com.dineshonjava.prodos.repository;

import java.util.List;
import org.springframework.data.repository.CrudRepository;
import com.dineshonjava.prodos.domain.Product;

public interface ProductRepository extends CrudRepository<Product, String>{

  // Fetch products by type
  List<Product> findByType(String type);

  // Fetch products by name
  List<Product> findByName(String name);

  // Fetch products by brand
  List<Product> findByBrand(String brand);
}
```

The preceding repository has three methods for finding products by type, name, and brand. There are other multiple fields after the By keyword such as And and Or keywords. We can concatenate the method name with the And and Or keywords as shown in the following code:

```
package com.dineshonjava.prodos.repository;

import java.util.List;
import org.springframework.data.repository.CrudRepository;
import com.dineshonjava.prodos.domain.Product;

public interface ProductRepository extends CrudRepository<Product, String>{

  //Fetch products by brand and type
  List<Product> findByBrandAndType(String brand, String type);

  //Fetch products by brand or type
  List<Product> findByBrandOrType(String brand, String type);
}
```

The preceding repository has used the And and Or keywords with a findBy keyword to fetch the products from the database. We can also use sorting with the query method in the ProductRepository interface. Queries can be sorted using the OrderBy keyword as shown in the following code:

```
package com.dineshonjava.prodos.repository;

import java.util.List;
import org.springframework.data.repository.CrudRepository;
import com.dineshonjava.prodos.domain.Product;

public interface ProductRepository extends CrudRepository<Product, String>{

  //Fetch products by type and sort by name ascending
  List<Product> findByTypeOrderByNameAsc(String type);
}
```

The preceding ProductRepository has a query method to fetch all products by type and sort by the product's name. There are many more keywords supported by Spring Data. The Spring Data query method signatures can also have the following keywords:

- IsAfter, After, IsGreaterThan, GreaterThan
- IsGreaterThanEqual, GreaterThanEqual
- IsBefore, Before, IsLessThan, LessThan
- IsLessThanEqual, LessThanEqual
- IsBetween, Between
- IsNull, Null
- IsNotNull, NotNull
- IsIn, In
- IsNotIn, NotIn
- IsStartingWith, StartingWith, StartsWith
- IsEndingWith, EndingWith, EndsWith
- IsContaining, Containing, Contains
- IsLike, Like
- IsNotLike, NotLike
- IsTrue, True
- IsFalse, False
- Is, Equals
- IsNot, Not
- IgnoringCase, IgnoresCase

You can use the above keywords with the Spring Data query method as shown in the following code:

```
List<Product> findByTypeAndBrandIgnoresCase(String type, String brand);
```

Using the @Query annotation

Sometimes, developers are not comfortable with writing a query method for a complex query. Spring Data allows you to create queries using the SQL statements via the @Query annotation. Let's see the following example:

```
package com.dineshonjava.prodos.repository;

import java.util.List;
import org.springframework.data.jpa.repository.Query;
import org.springframework.data.repository.CrudRepository;
```

```
import com.dineshonjava.prodos.domain.Product;

public interface ProductRepository extends CrudRepository<Product, String>{

  // Fetch products by brand
  @Query("select p from Product p where p.brand = ?1")
  List<Product> findByBrand(String brand);

  // Fetch products by name and type
  @Query("select p from Product p where p.name = ?1 and p.type = ?2")
  List<Product> findByNameAndType(String name, String type);
}
```

You can use like query with the @Query annotation, as shown in the following example:

```
import java.util.List;

import org.springframework.data.jpa.repository.Query;

import org.springframework.data.repository.CrudRepository;

import com.dineshonjava.prodos.domain.Product;

public interface ProductRepository extends CrudRepository <Product, String> {

  //Fetch products by type using SQL
  @Query("select p from Product p where p.type like %?1")
  List<Product> findByTypeEndsWith(String type);
}
```

Using pagination and sorting

Spring Data JPA also provides support to fetch the data from the database with pagination and sorting. Spring Data JPA provides the PagingAndSortingRepository interface to offer some methods for accessing data using pagination and sorting. The PagingAndSortingRepository interface extends the CrudRepository interface. We can use this PagingAndSortingRepository interface with a larger amount of data. Let's see the following example:

```
package com.dineshonjava.prodos.repository;

import java.util.List;
import org.springframework.data.domain.Page;
```

```
import org.springframework.data.domain.Pageable;
import org.springframework.data.domain.Sort;
import org.springframework.data.jpa.repository.Query;
import org.springframework.data.repository.PagingAndSortingRepository;
import com.dineshonjava.prodos.domain.Product;


public interface ProductRepository extends PagingAndSortingRepository<Product, String>{


    // Fetch products by brand with pagination and given sorting option
    @Query("select p from Product p where p.brand = ?1")
    Page<Product> findByBrand(String brand, Pageable pageable, Sort sort);
}
```

The preceding ProductRepository extends the PagingAndSortingRepository interface and has one query method to fetch the products with pagination and using a given sorting option. The PagingAndSortingRepository class adds two additional methods to the ProductRepository as shown in the following table:

Method	Description
Iterable<T> findAll(Sort sort)	This method returns data sorted by the given options.
Page<T> findAll(Pageable pageable)	This method returns data according to given paging options.

We discussed how to customize the Spring Data JPA repositories using the query methods and the @Query annotation. We can create the Spring Data JPA repository as per our requirement. We can write more complex queries using the @Query annotation.

The product data has been added to the H2 database and we have also written the Spring Data JPA repository to fetch the product data. Let's now learn how to configure the H2 database in the application and access the H2 database web console to ensure whether the product data is there or not.

Configuring the H2 Database

The H2 database is an in-memory database. Let's configure this H2 database in your Spring application by adding an H2 database dependency to the pom.xml file as shown in the following code:

```
<dependency>
  <groupId>com.h2database</groupId>
  <artifactId>h2</artifactId>
  <scope>runtime</scope>
</dependency>
```

After adding the preceding Maven dependency, the H2 database will be added to your application and you can use it.

You can check the H2 database using a browser-based console provided by the H2 database. Spring Boot auto-configures it for you as we add the H2 dependency to classpath. If you are using the Spring Boot developer tools, then you can access the H2's console, but if you are not using DevTool, then you need to set the spring.h2.console.enabled property with a value of true. But talk about this property in the production environment.

```
spring.h2.console.enabled = true
```

By default, the H2's console is available in the /h2-console path but you can change it accordingly by setting the following property in the application.properties file:

```
spring.h2.console.enabled=true
spring.h2.console.path=/h2-console
```

After running the Spring Boot application, you can access the H2 console of our application PRODOS by navigating to http://localhost:8181/prodos/h2-console/ on your favourite browser as shown in the following screenshot:

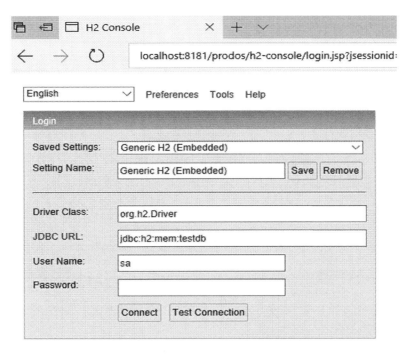

Figure 3.4: The H2 web console

You can set jdbc:h2:mem:testdb as the JDBC URL and leave the **Password** field empty in the login window. Click on the **Connect** button to log in to the console as shown in the following screenshot:

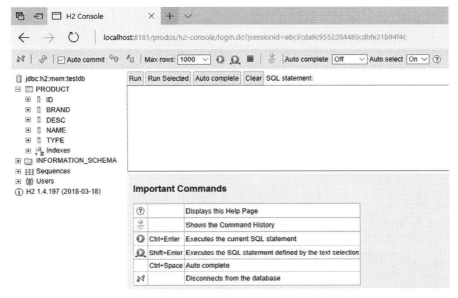

Figure 3.5: A product table in the H2 web console

In the preceding screenshot, you can see our Product table in the database. Now, you can ensure that data defined in the data.sql file has been inserted or not at the time of running the application. You can fetch the inserted data by querying as select * from the product on the H2 console and see the output on the H2 console, as shown in the following screenshot:

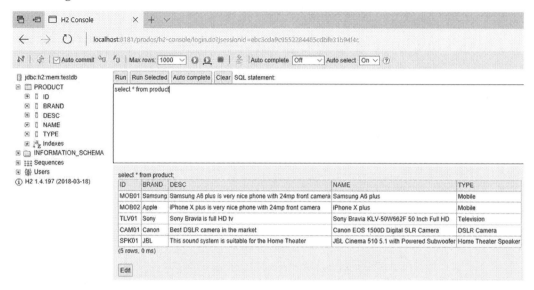

Figure 3.6: Select query result of the product table in the H2 web console

In the preceding screenshot, the Product table has five rows we inserted at the start of the application. We have seen how to use the H2 database in our Spring application. We know that the H2 database is not a better option for the production environment. In production, we need to configure rich featured database such as MariaDB, Oracle DB, IBM DB2, and more. Let's see how to configure the MariaDB relational database in the application.

Configuring the MariaDB database

Let's configure the MariaDB database in our PRODOS application instead of the H2 database. You need to replace the H2 database Maven dependency with the MariaDB dependency to the pom.xml file as shown in the following code:

```
<dependency>
 <groupId>org.mariadb.jdbc</groupId>
 <artifactId>mariadb-java-client</artifactId>
</dependency>
```

Now, we added the MariaDB database dependency to our application. We need to create a database for our application in MariaDB. Let's create a PRODODB database in MariaDB for our PRODOS application using HeidiSQL as shown in the following code:

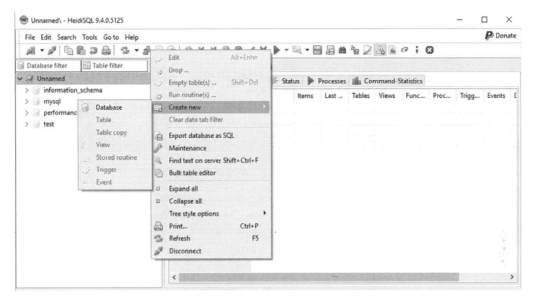

Figure 3.7: Creating PRODODB in MariaDB using HeidiSQL

Now, we created a database in MariaDB. But the database table is still created automatically by JPA.

Let's set some property configuration related to the MariaDB database in the application.properties file of the application. First, you need to define the database connection using the spring.datasource.* and spring.jpa.* properties as shown in the following code:

```
spring.datasource.url=jdbc:mariadb://localhost:3306/prododb
spring.datasource.username=root
spring.datasource.password=root
spring.datasource.driver-class-name=org.mariadb.jdbc.Driver
spring.jpa.generate-ddl=true
spring.jpa.hibernate.ddl-auto=create-drop
```

In the preceding application.properties file, we defined the database connection by setting the database's URL, username, password, and database driver class. Also, we set the spring.jpa.generate-ddl-auto property to create-drop value (Other values are none, validate, update, create, and create-drop). This property defines the behaviour of the database initialization. And the spring.jpa.generate-ddl property defines whether JPA should initialize the database or not (using true/false values).

Now, after running the application, you should see the tables in MariaDB. The following screenshot shows the HeidiSQL UI after the database has been created. Your application is now ready to be used with MariaDB:

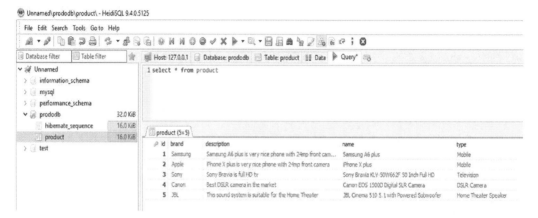

Figure 3.8: Application inside MariaDB

You can see that the Product table is created under prododb, which has entries already present in it.

We learned how to configure MariaDB in your application for the production environment.

Conclusion

In this chapter, we discussed how Spring Boot works for the data layer and learned a lot of things. We created an application using Spring's JdbcTemplate to fetch the database.

We covered how to configure a DataSource for embedded database and production database. We also discussed JNDI data source support and we created an application using Spring Data JPA. We also created the JPA entity class and Spring Data JPA repositories. We also saw how Spring Data JPA automatically created queries from the method's names. We also customized a JPA repository in the application.

We created an application using the H2 database with Spring Data JPA and also configured the H2 database web console to query the inserted data into the database. Finally, we configured MariaDB in the same application instead of the H2 database.

In the next *Chapter 4: Creating REST APIs with Spring Boot*, we will discuss how to create the REST services using the Spring Boot.

Question

1. What is JDBC?
2. How to create Entity classes?
3. What is JdbcTemplate in Spring?
4. How to configure a DataSource?
5. How to work with Spring Data JPA?
6. What is ORM?
7. What is any implementation of ORM?
8. What is JNDI?

CHAPTER 4

Creating REST APIs with Spring Boot 2.2

Today, the web application development approaches have changed due to the diversity of the application clients such as mobile devices, tablets, voice-based devices, smart watches, and many more. The present-day web application does not depend on the web browser. The web browsers are moving to legacy technologies!

There are several companies getting more than 50 or 60 percent traffic from the mobile devices, so the browser is no longer used as the primary means of accessing the internet. There are many browser-based applications based on the running JavaScript such as Angular, ReactJS, and so on.

In order to handle a vast variety of the client-side technologies, we need to design our web application in such a way that it adopts a common design where the client-side user interface is pushed close to the client and the same APIs are exposed by the server so that all clients can communicate to these APIs for the backend functionalities.

In this chapter, we will discuss the REST architectural style and how to define REST endpoints in Spring MVC, how to enable hyperlinked REST resources, and automatically generate repository-based REST endpoints with Spring Data REST. We will cover the following topics in this chapter:

- An introduction to the REST architectural style
    - o REST architectural constraints
    - o Uniform interface principles
- Create a RESTful web service with Spring Boot
    - o Using the @RestController annotation
    - o Retrieving data from the server
    - o Sending data to the server
    - o Updating data on the server
    - o Deleting data from the server
- Adding Hypermedia to the RESTful APIs
    - o Using Spring HATEOAS
        - Using the Resource and Resources classes
        - Implementing the Resource Assemblers
        - Changing the embedded relationship name
- Create a RESTful web service using Spring Data REST
- Consuming REST endpoints
    - o Consuming REST endpoints with RestTemplate
        - Retrieving resources using the GET method
        - Updating resources using the PUT method
        - Deleting resources using DELETE method
        - Posting resource data using the POST method
    - o Consuming REST endpoints with Traverson
    - o Consuming REST endpoints with WebClient

An introduction to the REST architectural style

The term **REST** stands for **REpresentational State Transfer**. It was first defined by Roy Fielding in 2000. REST is not a framework or tool; it is an application architectural style and design for web services. The web services work over the internet using the HTTP protocol. There are many web service architectural styles used to create web services. REST is one of the REST architectural styles based on the HTTP protocol design.

Roy Fielding defined a set of constraints. Any web application that follows these constraints is known as REST application. These constraints are applied to the architecture. REST applications use HTTP requests to GET, PUT, POST, and DELETE data. This REST application creates an **Application Program Interface** (**API**) to play with data. Data in the REST application represents resources. And the resources get manipulated and it is state-transferred between the client and server using typically JSON or XML. For example:

- **Resource**: Product (mobile)
- **Service**: Product information about mobile (GET)
- **Representation**: Name, type, brand, price as JSON or XML format

Let's discuss the following six constraints for the REST architecture.

REST architectural constraints

The REST architectural model has a set of constraints, so a REST application must follow the following constraints:

- Client-server
- Stateless
- Cacheable
- Uniform interface
- Layered system
- Code-on-demand

Let's take a look at these constraints in more detail.

Client-server

The REST architecture must provide a separation of concern between the client and server. The clients should not be responsible for any data storage; it must be part of the server so that the portability of the client code could be improved. The servers are not responsible for rendering the user interface or do not hold any user state. The server must be the same for any type of user interface and must be more scalable. The server and client must act independently.

Stateless

In the REST architecture-based application, the server must be stateless, which means that it does not hold any information about the client state. Any client can send several requests to the server and these requests must be treated independently. This means every request must contain all the necessary information so that the server can understand it and process it accordingly. The server must not hold any information related to the client but the client can hold the server information.

Cacheable

The REST application must be cacheable for some resources. Many clients ask for the same resources frequently; in this case, the server must cache the responses to improve the application's performance.

Layered system

In the REST architecture-based application, we can introduce the layered system architecture. A client is not aware of whether it is communicated directly to the end server or to an intermediary along the way. The intermediary system may be anything such as a load-balancer server. An intermediary can improve the system scalability by enabling load balancing and by providing shared caches. In the layered system, you can also enforce security policies.

Code-on-demand

This is an optional constraint. According to this constraint, you can run some code on demand to the client side such as an applet or scripts.

A uniform interface

The REST architecture allows both the client and server to evolve independently, so the requests from different clients look the same, but the client might differ such as a mobile application, a Java web application, and a browser. The uniform interface is an important constraint and this constraint defines the interface between the clients and servers. According to this constraint, every REST application should have the following elements.

The uniform interface principle

The four guiding principles of the uniform interface are described as follows.

Identifying the resources

For each client, the resource must be available with their unique identifiers and also have the cohesive URI to make this resource available. For example, here is the following URI structure:

HTTP/1.1 GET http://localhost:8181/prodos/products/MOB01

The preceding REST resource easily exposes the directory structure so that the client can access the resource easily.

Resource representation

In the preceding REST resource, we defined a REST URI to identify a resource, but this URI does not know how to return that resource to the client. So, the resource representation is also very important for the REST architectural application. This representation can be in HTML, XML, JSON, TXT, and so on. When the client calls the URI http://localhost:8181/prodos/products/MOB01, the server responds with a representation of the resource as shown in the following code:

```
    {
  id: "MOB01",
  name: "Samsung A6 plus",
  type: "Mobile",
  description: "Samsung A6 plus is a very nice phone with a 24mp front camera",
  brand: "Samsung"
    }
```

Self-descriptive messages

The request messages should have enough information so that the server is able to understand how to process this request and generate a response accordingly. Suppose if the client wants to access a REST API with the JSON content type. Let's see the following request message describing the details:

GET /#!/prodos/products/MOB01 HTTP/1.1
User-Agent: Chrome/37.0.2062.94
Accept: application/json
Host: localhost

As you can see the preceding meta information is needed in the request and response.

Hypermedia as the Engine of Application State (HATEOAS)

Clients deliver state via body contents, query-string parameters, request headers and the requested URI (the resource name). Services deliver the state to clients via body content, response code, and response headers. This part is often overlooked when talking about REST. It returns all the necessary information in response to the client on how to navigate and have access to all application resources. For example:

```
//Request
HTTP/1.1 GET http://localhost:8080/prodos/products
//Response
    {
_embedded: {
products: [
{
 name: "Samsung A6 plus",
 type: "Mobile",
 description: "Samsung A6 plus is very nice phone with 24mp front camera",
 brand: "Samsung",
 _links: {
  self: {
   href: "http://localhost:8080/prodos/products/MOB01"
  },
  product: {
   href: "http://localhost:8080/prodos/products/MOB01"
  }
 }
    },
    {
name: "Sony Bravia KLV-50W662F 50 Inch Full HD",
type: "Television",
description: "Sony Bravia is full HD tv",
brand: "Sony",
_links: {
 self: {
  href: "http://localhost:8080/prodos/products/TLV01"
 },
```

```
   product: {
     href: "http://localhost:8080/prodos/products/TLV01"
   }
 }
     },
     {
name: "Canon EOS 1500D Digital SLR Camera",
type: "DSLR Camera",
description: "Best DSLR camera in the market",
brand: "Canon",
_links: {
 self: {
   href: "http://localhost:8080/prodos/products/CAM01"
 },
 product: {
   href: "http://localhost:8080/prodos/products/CAM01"
 }
}
   }
 ]
},
_links: {
 self: {
   href: "http://localhost:8080/prodos/products"
 },
 profile: {
   href: "http://localhost:8080/prodos/profile/products"
 },
 search: {
   href: "http://localhost:8080/prodos/products/search"
 }
}
   }
```

We discussed the REST Architecture model and its six constraints. If a service violates any constraint except the Code-On-Demand constraint, it strictly cannot be referred to as a RESTful application. In the next section, we will create a RESTful application using Spring Boot 2.2.

Create a RESTful web service with Spring Boot

In Spring Boot, let's create a RESTful web service. We created a PRODOS application, and now we will create a controller class. The controller classes handle all HTTP requests. Let's right click on the com.dineshonjava.prodos.controller package and select **New** | **Class** from the menu. Let's give a name to our class ProductController:

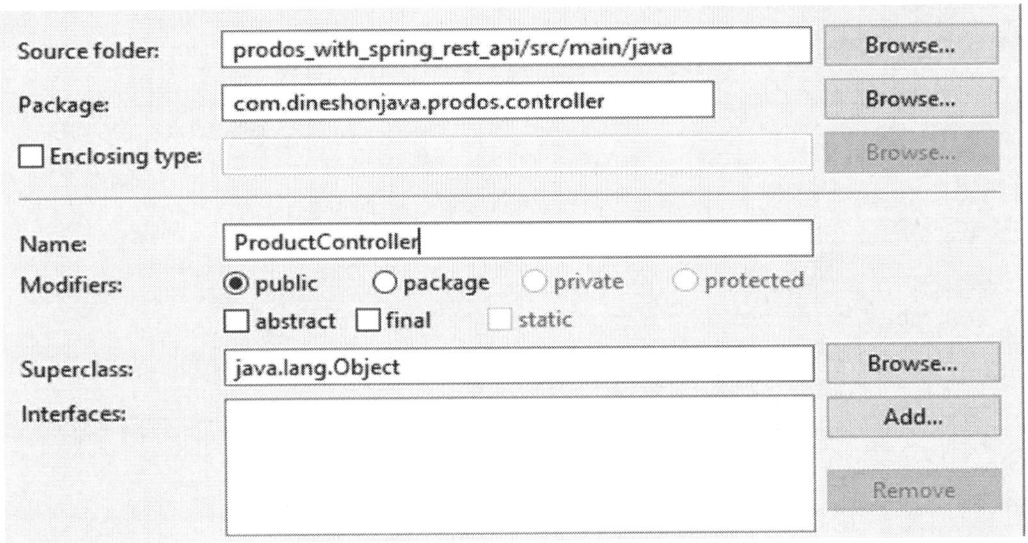

Source folder:	prodos_with_spring_rest_api/src/main/java	Browse...
Package:	com.dineshonjava.prodos.controller	Browse...
☐ Enclosing type:		Browse...
Name:	ProductController	
Modifiers:	◉ public ◯ package ◯ private ◯ protected	
	☐ abstract ☐ final ☐ static	
Superclass:	java.lang.Object	Browse...
Interfaces:		Add...
		Remove

Figure 4.1:Creating a ProductController class

After creating a ProductController class, let's see the project structure. It should look like the following screenshot:

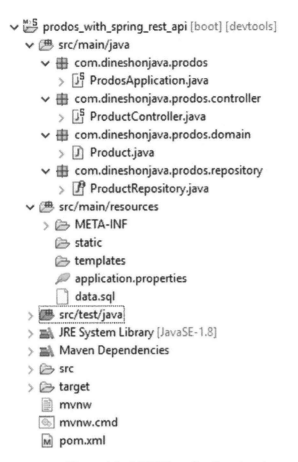

Figure 4.2: A REST application structure

Using the @RestController annotation

Open your ProductController controller class in the STS IDE and annotate this controller class with the @RestController annotation. Let's see the following source code of the ProductController class:

```
package com.dineshonjava.prodos.controller;


import org.springframework.web.bind.annotation.RestController;


@RestController
public class ProductController {


}
```

In the preceding controller class, the @RestController annotation indicates that this controller class will be the REST controller for the RESTful web service. Now you can add the application functionalities to this REST controller class.

Retrieving data from the server

In our PRODOS application, we created a new ProductController as a REST controller annotated by the @RestController annotation. So, as we know that the @RestController annotation is one of the stereotype meta-annotations just like @Controller, @Service, and so on. The classes annotated with the @RestController annotation are also eligible for the component scanning, and the important thing is that all request handler methods under this controller file return the value directly to the body of the response rather than using the view resolver to render the model data to the view.

Let's add a request handler method to the created REST controller to retrieve data from the server, as shown in the following code:

```
package com.dineshonjava.prodos.controller;

import java.util.ArrayList;
import java.util.List;
import org.springframework.web.bind.annotation.GetMapping;
import org.springframework.web.bind.annotation.RestController;
import com.dineshonjava.prodos.domain.Product;
import com.dineshonjava.prodos.repository.ProductRepository;

@RestController
public class ProductController {

  private ProductRepository productRepository;

  public ProductController(ProductRepository productRepository) {
    super();
    this.productRepository = productRepository;
  }
  @GetMapping("/products")
  public List<Product> findAll(){
    List<Product> products = new ArrayList<>();
```

```
    productRepository.findAll().forEach(i -> products.add(i));
    return products;
  }
}
```

In the preceding REST controller class, we defined a request handler method, the findAll() method. This method is annotated with the @GetMapping annotation to indicate that the findAll() method is responsible for handling the GET request for URI /prodos/products. The @GetMapping annotation is a short cut for the @RequestMapping annotation with the GET method.

@GetMapping("/products") is equivalent to the @RequestMapping("/products", method=GET)

As of version 4.3.5, Spring has introduced these short request mapping annotations for specific HTTP methods, which are as follows:

- @GetMapping
- @PostMapping
- @PutMapping
- @DeleteMapping
- @PatchMapping

The findAll() request handler method will retrieve all products from the server using the ProductRepository object, which we created in the previous chapter. The ProductRepository object is @Autowired with the ProductController class.

Let's run the application and navigate to http://localhost:8181/prodos/products, as shown in the following screenshot:

```
[
  - {
        id: "MOB01",
        name: "Samsung A6 plus",
        type: "Mobile",
        description: "Samsung A6 plus is very nice phone with 24mp front camera",
        brand: "Samsung"
    },
  - {
        id: "MOB02",
        name: "iPhone X plus",
        type: "Mobile",
        description: "iPhone X plus is very nice phone with 24mp front camera",
        brand: "Apple"
    },
  - {
        id: "TLV01",
        name: "Sony Bravia KLV-50W662F 50 Inch Full HD",
        type: "Television",
        description: "Sony Bravia is full HD tv",
        brand: "Sony"
    },
  - {
        id: "CAM01",
        name: "Canon EOS 1500D Digital SLR Camera",
        type: "DSLR Camera",
        description: "Best DSLR camera in the market",
        brand: "Canon"
    },
  - {
        id: "SPK01",
        name: "JBL Cinema 510 5.1 with Powered Subwoofer",
        type: "Home Theater Speaker",
        description: "This sound system is suitable for the Home Theater",
        brand: "JBL"
    }
]
```

Figure 4.3: All Products data in the JSON format

Now, let's say that we want to create another endpoint that fetches a single Product by product ID. We can use the placeholder variable with the request handler path for the handler method. The handler method accepts this placeholder using the @PathVariable annotation. Let's add the following request handler method to the ProductController class:

```
@GetMapping("/products/{id}")
public Product findProductById(@PathVariable String id){
  return productRepository.findById(id).isPresent() ? productRepository.findById(id).get() : null;
}
```

The preceding code snippet will return the single product information by the product ID by navigating to the http://localhost:8181/prodos/products/MOB01 URI, as shown in the following screenshot:

```
{
    id: "MOB01",
    name: "Samsung A6 plus",
    type: "Mobile",
    description: "Samsung A6 plus is very nice phone with 24mp front camera",
    brand: "Samsung"
}
```

Figure 4.4: Single Product data in the JSON format

In the preceding request handler findProductById() method, the id parameter is passed to the findById() method of the ProductRepository object to fetch the Product. It also returns an Optional<Product> object. The returned Optional<Product> object indicates that a product with the given ID may not exist in the Product database. That is why we checked whether the product was present or not before returning a value. If the product is present with the given product ID, you call the get() method on the Optional<Product> object to return the actual Product.

If there is no product for the given ID, you will return null. In this case, the client will receive the empty body with the HTTP status code of 200 (OK). This is not an ideal way to handle the requests because the status code 200 means everything is fine at the server end. We can provide a better approach to handle such empty result cases by returning a response with an HTTP 404 (NOT FOUND) status.

Let's make some small changes in the above written request handler findProductById() method as follows:

```
@GetMapping("/products/{id}")
public ResponseEntity<Product> findProductById(@PathVariable String id){
  return productRepository.findById(id).isPresent() ?
  new ResponseEntity<>(productRepository.findById(id).get(), HttpStatus.OK) :
  new ResponseEntity<>(null, HttpStatus.NOT_FOUND);

}
```

The preceding request handler findProductById() method returns a ResponseEntity<Product> object instead of a Product object. If the product of the given product ID is found, the found Product object is wrapped in a ResponseEntity object with an HTTP status code 200(OK). But if the product of the given product ID is not found, then the null value is wrapped in a ResponseEntity object along with an HTTP status code 404 (NOT FOUND) to indicate that the client is trying to fetch a product that does not exist in the database.

Sending data to the server

Now, we will create a request handler method in the ProductController REST class to send data to the server. This means we will create an API for sending data to the server instead of fetching data from the server. Let's write a postProduct() method in ProductController to handle that request and save the product data to the database using the save() method of the ProductRepository object:

```
@PostMapping(value= "/products", consumes="application/json")
@ResponseStatus(HttpStatus.CREATED)
public Product postProduct(@RequestBody Product product) {
  return productRepository.save(product);
}
```

The preceding request handle method is annotated with the @PostMapping annotation due to which it handle an HTTP POST request. We specify a path /products. We also specify the other consumes attribute. The consumes attribute defines the request input content type. Here, we set the application/json value to the consumes attribute. It is a content type that matches application/json.

We pass the Product parameter to the request handler method and this parameter is annotated with a @RequestBody annotation to indicate that the body of the request should be converted to a Product object and bound to the parameter. After conversion, it passes to the save() method on the ProductRepository interface.

The postProduct() request handler method is also annotated with the @ ResponseStatus(HttpStatus.CREATED) annotation. It indicates that the client request was successfully completed with a resource creation at the given endpoint. However, we can also use the HTTP status code 200 but it will not be descriptive enough in this case. So, the @ResponseStatus(HttpStatus.CREATED) annotation is a good idea to use in cases where you want to send data to the server from the client.

Let's run the application and create a new product to the server from the client. Here, I am using the Postman REST client to test the created API as shown in the following screenshot:

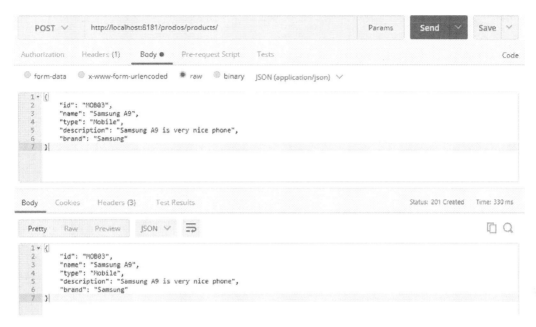

Figure 4.5: Sending Product data to the server

As you can see in the preceding screenshot, we created a resource at the server using the Postman REST client. The REST client shows the response status code as 201. Although, we can create a resource on the server using the @PostMapping annotation for POST requests, we can also use PUT and PATCH request methods for resources update. Let's discuss about the @PutMapping and @PatchMapping annotations in the next section.

Updating data on the server

Spring provides two request mapping annotations to update data on the server, @ PutMapping and @PatchMapping. So, before using any one of them, we need to know why are there two different ways to update data on the server using the HTTP PUT and PATCH methods.

The PUT HTTP method is often used to update the resource data on the server. The PUT requests are used to send the resource data from the client to the server for a given resource ID. The PUT method performs the wholesale replacement operation for a resource rather than an update operation. But the PATCH request method performs a partial update on the resource data on the server.

Let's see the following PUT HTTP request handler method that we added to the ProductController class. For example, suppose you want to change the description of a product:

@PutMapping("/products/{id}")

```
public Product putProduct(@RequestBody Product product) {
  return productRepository.save(product);
}
```

After adding the PUT request handler method to the ProductController class, let's run the application and test the PUT requests using the Postman REST client, as shown in the following screenshot:

Figure 4.6: Updating Product data on the server using the PUT method

If you are using the define method mentioned above to update the date on the server, then the client will need to submit the complete product information in the PUT request. So, in the above defined method, put the product data at the given URI, / products/{id}. So, this method replaces all data on the server related to the given URI irrespective of whether data is there or not. If you forget to set some property of the product, then the property's value would be overwritten with null.

So, let's see how to handle requests to do a partial update using the HTTP PATCH requests. Spring's @PatchMapping annotation is used to achieve the partial resource update on the server. Here is the following request handler method that needs to be added to the ProductController class:

```java
@PatchMapping(path="/products/{id}", consumes="application/json")
public Product patchProduct(@PathVariable String id, @RequestBody Product patch) {
  Product product = productRepository.findById(id).get();
  if (patch.getBrand() != null) {
    product.setBrand(patch.getBrand());
  }
  if (patch.getDescription() != null) {
    product.setDescription(patch.getDescription());
  }
  if (patch.getName() != null) {
    product.setName(patch.getName());
  }
  if (patch.getType() != null) {
    product.setType(patch.getType());
  }
  return productRepository.save(product);
}
```

The preceding patchProduct() request handler method is annotated with the @PatchMapping annotation instead of @PutMapping to indicate that this method will handle HTTP PATCH requests instead of PUT requests.

So, Spring MVC's mapping annotations for update request include @PatchMapping and @PutMapping which do not provide any specific way to handle the requests. These annotations only indicate that the PATCH request handler method is for the partial update and the PUT request handler method is for a complete update on the server. So these different methods to update data on the server provide an approach that allows the client to only send the properties that should be changed and enables the server to retain the existing data for any properties not specified by the client.

After adding the PATCH request handler method to the ProductController class, let's run the application and test the PATCH requests using the Postman REST client as shown in the following screenshot:

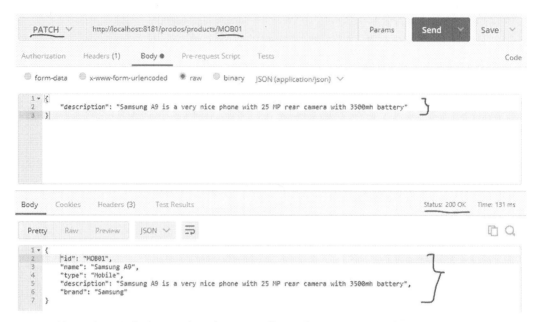

Figure 4.7: Updating Product data partially on the server using the PATCH method

In the preceding screenshot, we are updating a product with the given ID (http://localhost:8181/prodos/products/MOB01), and we want to update only the description about the product that is why we are only passing the product description in the request body. Finally, the description of the product has been changed and the remaining data is as is.

We discussed how to fetch and post resources using @GetMapping and @PostMapping. We also discussed the two different ways of updating a resource with @PutMapping and @PatchMapping. Further, we will discuss how to handle the delete request to delete data from the server.

Deleting data from the server

You can also create an API to delete data from the server. Sometimes, the old product information is not needed anymore; in this case, a client should be able to delete those products from the server. We can create one more request handler method in the ProductController class to serve the requests to remove the resources from the server using the HTTP DELETE request method.

Spring MVC provides a mapping annotation for the DELETE HTTP method that is the @DeleteMapping annotation. For example, let's say you want your API to allow you to delete a product resource. The following controller method should do the trick:

```
@ResponseStatus(code=HttpStatus.NO_CONTENT)
@DeleteMapping("products/{id}")
public void deleteProduct(@PathVariable String id) {
  try {
   productRepository.deleteById(id);
  } catch (EmptyResultDataAccessException e) {}
}
```

The preceding deleteProduct() request handler method is responsible for handling the DELETE HTTP requests for the path (products/{id}) deleteProduct() and delete the product for a given product ID from the server. The deleteProduct() method is annotated with the @DeleteMapping annotation and this is used to map the HTTP DELETE request to the handler method using the products/{id} request path.

In the deleteProduct() method, delete the product of a given product ID using the deleteById() method of the ProductRepository object. And the product ID is provided as a path variable in the URI. Now, if the product exists for the given the deleteProduct() method, it will delete it else this method will throw an EmptyResultDataAccessException exception. You will notice that the deleteProduct() request handler method is also annotated with @ResponseStatus(code=HttpStatus.NO_CONTENT), which means the deleteProduct() method ensures that the response's HTTP status is 204 (NO CONTENT) and there is no need to revert any data to the client for a deleted product.

Let's run the application after adding the request DELETE handler method and test it using the Postman REST client as shown in the following screenshot:

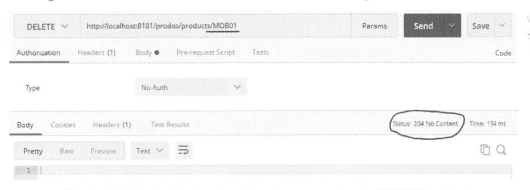

Figure 4.8: Deleting Product data from the server using the DELETE method

As you can see in the preceding screenshot, we deleted a product with a given product ID (DELETE http://localhost:8181/prodos/products/MOB01) using the Postman REST client. And you can see the response returned with the status code 204 (NO CONTENT).

Now, your RESTful application PRODOS has APIs. The client of your application can consume these APIs easily. The client can retrieve all products, create a new product, delete a product, and update product details using these APIs. But the client has to remember these APIs. We can make these API, even more, easier for the client so that the client does not need to remember these APIs. Let's add Hypermedia to the RESTful APIs in the next section.

Adding Hypermedia to the RESTful APIs

In the previous section, we created RESTful APIs for the CRUD functionalities. These APIs are very fair for the client but the client must be aware of the API URL. The client may have the API URL hardcoded locally at the client-side. For example, if a client wants to retrieve all products from the server using the /prodos/products GET request path. This request path may be hardcoded at the client side to retrieve all products, but how to access a particular product resource by the given product ID. The client may have more URLs to be hardcoded.

The hardcoded URL structure at the client side may be risky for a moment if the API URL scheme changes. So, hardcoded API URLs at the client code may be obsolete and broken. In this case, the client code needs to be updated if there are any changes made in the API URL patterns. This problem can be solved using the uniform interface's HATEOAS property. So, the HATEOAS approach comes into picture to solve the problem of the client with the RESTful API. Now, the client needs to only remember an initial URI. Once the client loads the initial URI's response, all the links of application state transitions will be available to the client and the client is able to select the links provided by the server.

HATEOAS is one of the principles of the Uniform interface of the REST constraints. It means we are creating self-describing REST APIs. The client can discover the next or previous links available at runtime from the server. These APIs will return the resources to contain links to related resources. This enables the clients to use an API without having prior information about the API URL patterns or with minimal understanding of the API's URLs. The Spring framework provides a module for HATEOAS.

Using Spring HATEOAS

The Spring framework provides support to add the hypermedia to the RESTful APIs by adding the Spring HATEOAS module to your application. The Spring HATEOAS project provides hyperlink support for the RESTful APIs. This module offers a set of classes and resource assemblers to add the hyperlinks to resources.

Let's add the hypermedia support to your previous REST application PRODOS where we created REST APIs. You can enable hypermedia in your PRODOS application by adding the Spring HATEOAS starter dependency as shown in the following code:

```
<dependency>
  <groupId>org.springframework.boot</groupId>
  <artifactId>spring-boot-starter-hateoas</artifactId>
</dependency>
```

The preceding starter dependency adds the Spring HATEOAS module to your application along with the auto-configuration to enable Spring HATEOAS. No configuration related change is required in your PRODOS application; the only change required is to change the return resource types instead of domain types. Let's add the hyperlink to the one of the previously created APIs, which returns all products using a GET request to the /prodos/products, as shown in the following screenshot:

```
[
  - {
        id: "MOB01",
        name: "Samsung A6 plus",
        type: "Mobile",
        description: "Samsung A6 plus is very nice phone with 24mp front camera",
        brand: "Samsung"
    },
  - {
        id: "MOB02",
        name: "iPhone X plus",
        type: "Mobile",
        description: "iPhone X plus is very nice phone with 24mp front camera",
        brand: "Apple"
    },
  - {
        id: "TLV01",
        name: "Sony Bravia KLV-50W662F 50 Inch Full HD",
        type: "Television",
        description: "Sony Bravia is full HD tv",
        brand: "Sony"
    },
  -
```

Figure 4.9: Product resources without hyperlinks

Using the Resource and Resources classes

Spring HATEOAS has two classes, Resource and Resources, to represent hyperlinked resources. The Resource class is used for a single resource but the Resources class is used for a list of resources. Let's make the changes to the findAll() method of the ProductController class to add hyperlinks to the list of products:

```
package com.dineshonjava.prodos.controller;

import java.util.ArrayList;
import java.util.List;
import org.springframework.hateoas.Resource;
import org.springframework.hateoas.Resources;
import org.springframework.hateoas.mvc.ControllerLinkBuilder;
import org.springframework.web.bind.annotation.GetMapping;
import org.springframework.web.bind.annotation.RestController;
import com.dineshonjava.prodos.domain.Product;
import com.dineshonjava.prodos.repository.ProductRepository;

@RestController
public class ProductController {

  private ProductRepository productRepository;

  public ProductController(ProductRepository productRepository) {
   super();
   this.productRepository = productRepository;
  }

  @GetMapping(value = "/products", produces="application/json")
  public Resources<Resource<Product>> findAll(){
   List<Product> products = new ArrayList<>();
   productRepository.findAll().forEach(i -> products.add(i));
   Resources<Resource<Product>> productResources = Resources.wrap(products);
   productResources.add(ControllerLinkBuilder.linkTo(ProductController.class).
slash("products").withRel("products"));
   return productResources;
  }
  //...
}
```

The preceding findAll() method of the ProductController class has been changed with the Resources<Resource<Product>> return type instead of the list of products directly. The wrap() method of the Resources class is used to wrap the list of products as an instance of Resources<Resource<Product>>. This instance is returned by the findAll()

method for getting the request http://localhost:8181/prodos/products/ request, as shown in the following screenshot:

```
{
  - _embedded: {
    - productList: [
      - {
          id: "MOB01",
          name: "Samsung A6 plus",
          type: "Mobile",
          description: "Samsung A6 plus is very nice phone with 24mp front camera",
          brand: "Samsung"
        },
      - {
          id: "MOB02",
          name: "iPhone X plus",
          type: "Mobile",
          description: "iPhone X plus is very nice phone with 24mp front camera",
          brand: "Apple"
        },
      - {
          id: "TLV01",
          name: "Sony Bravia KLV-50W662F 50 Inch Full HD",
          type: "Television",
          description: "Sony Bravia is full HD tv",
          brand: "Sony"
        },
      - {
          id: "CAM01",
          name: "Canon EOS 1500D Digital SLR Camera",
          type: "DSLR Camera",
          description: "Best DSLR camera in the market",
          brand: "Canon"
        },
      - {
          id: "SPK01",
          name: "JBL Cinema 510 5.1 with Powered Subwoofer",
          type: "Home Theater Speaker",
          description: "This sound system is suitable for the Home Theater",
          brand: "JBL"
        }
    ]
  },
  - _links: {
    - products: {
        href: "http://localhost:8181/prodos/products"
      }
  }
}
```

Figure 4.10: Product resources with the hyperlink

In the preceding screenshot, the API request from http://localhost:8181/prodos/ products/ returns the resource with the following code snippet of JSON:

```
_links: {
 products: {
  href: "http://localhost:8181/prodos/products"
 }
}
```

Spring HATEOAS provides a link builder class that is ControllerLinkBuilder. This is a very useful class of Spring HATEOAS used to build the links. This class is smart enough to take the hostname without specifying and it also provides several methods to help you build the links.

We are not only giving the hostname to the link builder but we are also not specifying the /prodos/products path. Instead, we are passing the ProductController class as a parameter to the linkTo() method of the ControllerLinkBuilder class of Spring HATEOAS. The ControllerLinkBuilder class uses the base path of the ProductController class as the foundation of the Link object you're creating.

Next, we used the slash() method of the ControllerLinkBuilder class. This method defines the URI (/products) after the base URL (/prodos) of the controller and gives value to the URL. Finally, it generates the URL's /prodos/products path as the result. And after that, we specified a relation name for the hyperlink and in our example, the relation is name ID products.

We used the ControllerLinkBuilder class and its methods such as linkTo() and slash() to eliminate the hardcoding with the link, but we can modify the link builder code even better. We can directly use the controller's method name instead of the controller class to generate the complete URL without using the slash() method of the ControllerLinkBuilder class as shown in the following code:

```
@GetMapping(value = "/products", produces="application/json")
public Resources<Resource<Product>> findAll(){
   List<Product> products = new ArrayList<>();
 productRepository.findAll().forEach(i -> products.add(i));

 Resources<Resource<Product>> productResources = Resources.wrap(products);
 productResources.add(linkTo(methodOn(ProductController.class).findAll()).withRel("products"));
 return productResources;
}
```

We are using the linkTo() and methodOn() methods of the ControllerLinkBuilder class. In the preceding code, the ControllerLinkBuilder class is used to generate the link using the base URL of the request handler method instead of the base URL of the controller. Here, we need to pass the controller class to the methodOn() method and then it allows you to make a call to the findAll() method, which is intercepted by the ControllerLinkBuilder class to drive the entire URL that is path mapped to the findAll() method.

Till now, we added a single link to the resource returned by the API http://localhost:8181/prodos/products/ but this API returns a list of the products. Now, we need to add the link to each product within the list. Spring HATEOAS provides support to generate the link to each resource within the return list by the API without looping through each of the Resource<Product> elements. Let's implement the resource assembler to generate the link to each product within the product list.

Implementing the resource assemblers

We have to create a utility class that will be responsible for generating the link for each product resource. But it is not possible using the Resources.wrap() method because this method creates a Resource object for each product in the list. Now, the utility class will convert the Product object to the new ProductResource object. Here, the ProductResource object is very similar to the Product object, but the ProductResource object is able to carry the links. Let's see the ProductResource class as shown in the following code:

```
package com.dineshonjava.prodos.domain;

import org.springframework.hateoas.ResourceSupport;

public class ProductResource extends ResourceSupport{

  private String name;
  private String type;
  private String description;
  private String brand;

  public ProductResource(Product product) {
    this.name = product.getName();
    this.type = product.getType();
    this.description = product.getDescription();
    this.brand = product.getBrand();
  }
```

```java
public String getName() {
  return name;
}

public void setName(String name) {
  this.name = name;
}

public String getType() {
  return type;
}

public void setType(String type) {
  this.type = type;
}

public String getDescription() {
  return description;
}

public void setDescription(String description) {
  this.description = description;
}

public String getBrand() {
  return brand;
}

public void setBrand(String brand) {
  this.brand = brand;
  }
}
```

The preceding ProductResource class extends the ResourceSupport class and it inherits methods to manage the list of links and also inherits a list of Link objects. In the preceding code, I created a single constructor for the ProductResource class and this constructor accepts a Product object and copies the values of the properties from the Product object to its own properties.

Now, we need to create an assemble class that will help in converting the Product objects to the ProductResource objects. Let's see the following code:

```
package com.dineshonjava.prodos.domain;

import org.springframework.hateoas.mvc.ResourceAssemblerSupport;
import com.dineshonjava.prodos.controller.ProductController;

public class ProductResourceAssembler extends ResourceAssemblerSupport<Product,
ProductResource> {

  public ProductResourceAssembler() {
   super(ProductController.class, ProductResource.class);
  }

  @Override
  protected ProductResource instantiateResource(Product product) {
   return new ProductResource(product);
  }

  @Override
  public ProductResource toResource(Product product) {
   return createResourceWithId("products/"+product.getId(), product);
  }
}
```

The preceding ProductResourceAssembler class extends the ResourceAssemblerSupport class by taking <Product, ProductResource> as a type argument. This class has a default constructor that calls the superclass constructor by taking the ProductController and ProductResource classes as the arguments. The first argument ProductController class is used to determine the base path for any URLs in links and the second argument ProductResource class is used to inform the superclass to create a ProductResource class. The ProductResourceAssembler class also overrides the two methods, instantiateResource() and toResource(), of the ResourceAssemblerSupport class for the following purposes:

- The instantiateResource() method is used to instantiate a ProductResource object given a Product object.

- The toResource() method is used to create a ProductResource object from a Product and this method automatically provides a self-link with the URL being derived from the id property of the Product object.

As you can see in the preceding code, both the methods return the ProductResource object, but there the only difference is that the instantiateResource() method instantiates a Resource object (ProductResource) only but the toResource() method does not only instantiate the Resource object, but also populates it with links. The createResourceWithId() method internally calls the instantiateResource() method to create the Resource object.

Let's change the findAll() method code of the ProductController class, as shown in the following code, to use the ProductResourceAssembler class to generate the links for each product within the list:

```
@GetMapping(value = "/products", produces = "application/json")
public Resources<ProductResource> findAll() {
 List<Product> products = new ArrayList<>();
 productRepository.findAll().forEach(i -> products.add(i));
 List<ProductResource> productResourceList = new ProductResourceAssembler().
toResources(products);
 Resources<ProductResource> productResources = new Resources<ProductResource>(productRe
sourceList);
 productResources.add(linkTo(methodOn(ProductController.class).findAll()).withRel("products"));
 return productResources;
}
```

Here are the following changes in the preceding method code as from the previous implementation:

- The return type of the findAll() method is Resources<ProductResource> instead of Resources<Resource<Product>>.

- The product list is passed to the toResources() method in a ProductResourceAssembler class.

Another part is very similar to the preceding code. After making these changes in the ProductController class, restart the application and navigate to the REST API at http://localhost:8181/prodos/products/ and see the output as shown in the following screenshot:

```
{
    _embedded: {
        productResourceList: [
            {
                name: "Samsung A6 plus",
                type: "Mobile",
                description: "Samsung A6 plus is very nice phone with 24mp front camera",
                brand: "Samsung",
                _links: {
                    self: {
                        href: "http://localhost:8181/prodos/products/MOB01"
                    }
                }
            },
            {
                name: "iPhone X plus",
                type: "Mobile",
                description: "iPhone X plus is very nice phone with 24mp front camera",
                brand: "Apple",
                _links: {
                    self: {
                        href: "http://localhost:8181/prodos/products/MOB02"
                    }
                }
            },
            {
                name: "Sony Bravia KLV-50W662F 50 Inch Full HD",
                type: "Television",
                description: "Sony Bravia is full HD tv",
                brand: "Sony",
                _links: {
                    self: {
                        href: "http://localhost:8181/prodos/products/TLV01"
                    }
                }
            },
            {
                name: "Canon EOS 1500D Digital SLR Camera",
                type: "DSLR Camera",
                description: "Best DSLR camera in the market",
                brand: "Canon",
                _links: {
                    self: {
                        href: "http://localhost:8181/prodos/products/CAM01"
                    }
                }
            },
            {
                name: "JBL Cinema 510 5.1 with Powered Subwoofer",
                type: "Home Theater Speaker",
                description: "This sound system is suitable for the Home Theater",
                brand: "JBL",
                _links: {
                    self: {
                        href: "http://localhost:8181/prodos/products/SPK01"
                    }
                }
            }
        ]
    },
    _links: {
        products: {
            href: "http://localhost:8181/prodos/products"
        }
    }
}
```

embedded

Figure 4.11: Product resources with the links for each product

Changing the embedded relationship name

Spring HATEOAS also allows you to change the name to the embedded relationship using the @Relation annotation. In the following code snippet, the current relationship names are shown:

```
{
  "_embedded": {
   "productResourceList": [

     ...

   ]
  }
}
```

Let's make the following change in the code of the ProdcutResource class:

```
@Relation(value="product", collectionRelation="products")
public class ProductResource extends ResourceSupport{
//...
}
```

After making the change in the ProductResource class, restart the application again and navigate to the same REST API. The embedded relationship name has been changed as shown in the following code:

```
{
  "_embedded": {
   "products": [

     ...

   ]
  }
}
```

We created a REST application using the Spring HATEOAS to add links to your REST API rather than creating something that is straightforward and simple. Let's see the following application structure:

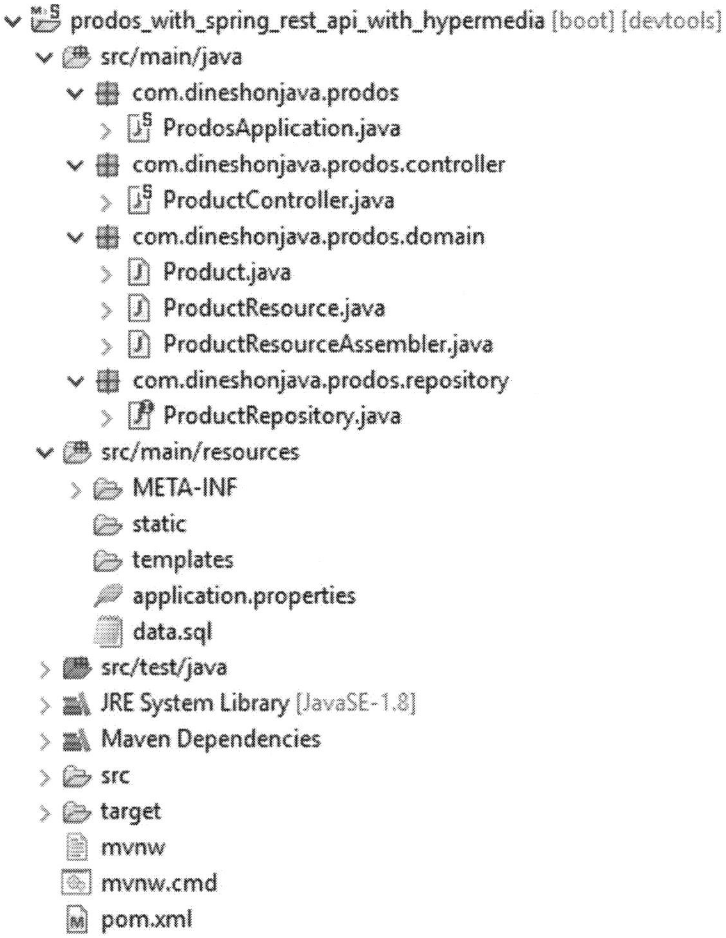

∨ 🗲 prodos_with_spring_rest_api_with_hypermedia [boot] [devtools]
   ∨ 🗁 src/main/java
      ∨ ⊞ com.dineshonjava.prodos
         > 🗎 ProdosApplication.java
      ∨ ⊞ com.dineshonjava.prodos.controller
         > 🗎 ProductController.java
      ∨ ⊞ com.dineshonjava.prodos.domain
         > 🗎 Product.java
         > 🗎 ProductResource.java
         > 🗎 ProductResourceAssembler.java
      ∨ ⊞ com.dineshonjava.prodos.repository
         > 🗎 ProductRepository.java
   ∨ 🗁 src/main/resources
      > 🗁 META-INF
      🗁 static
      🗁 templates
      🖉 application.properties
      ▦ data.sql
   > 🗁 src/test/java
   > 🗟 JRE System Library [JavaSE-1.8]
   > 🗟 Maven Dependencies
   > 🗁 src
   > 🗁 target
      🗎 mvnw
      🗎 mvnw.cmd
      🗎 pom.xml

Figure 4.12: A REST application with Spring HATEOAS
for including hypermedia in the REST APIs.

Here, we used Spring MVC to create the REST services, but Spring Data provides another way to create the RESTful web services using the Spring Data REST project. Now, let's discuss how to create the REST web services using Spring Data REST in the next section.

Create a RESTful web service using Spring Data REST

Spring Data REST is another subproject of the Spring Data umbrella family. It automatically creates REST APIs for you without any rest controller in your application using the created repositories by Spring Data. You can add the following Maven starter dependency to your build:

```
<dependency>
  <groupId>org.springframework.boot</groupId>
  <artifactId>spring-boot-starter-data-rest</artifactId>
</dependency>
```

We added the preceding Maven dependency to the pom.xml file of the Spring application to implement RESTful web services with Spring. Spring Data REST, by default, finds all public repositories of your application to create the RESTful web services for your entities. The above starter provides auto-configuration that enables automatic RESTful web services created for the Spring Data repositories, including Spring Data JPA, Spring Data Cassandra, Spring Data MongoDB, and so on.

You can also set the endpoint path for the RESTful web services for your application in the application.properties file as shown in the following code:

```
spring.data.rest.basePath=/api
```

After setting the preceding base path for your RESTful web services, all services will be available at http://localhost:8080/api/ endpoint. The data is returned by Spring Data REST in the JSON format, including hypermedia or links. Let's create a Spring Boot application with the following structure:

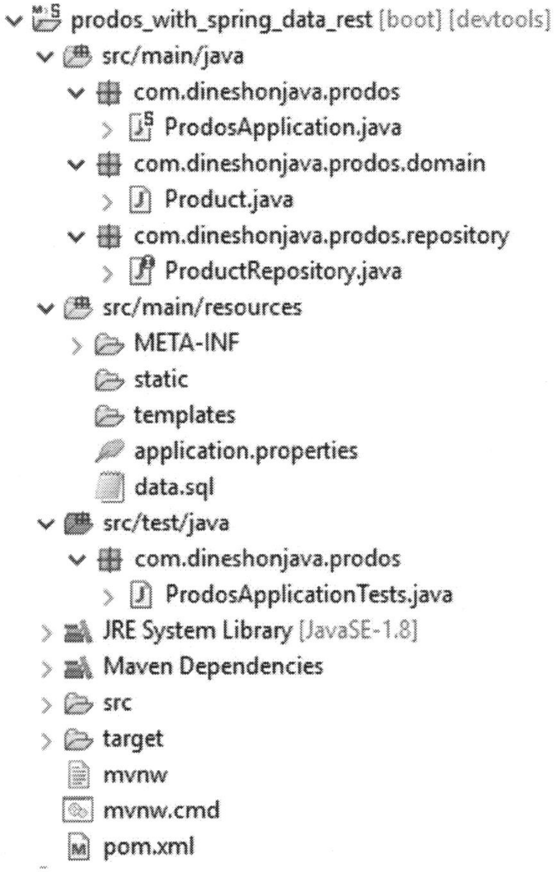

```
∨ ᵐ˙ᔆ prodos_with_spring_data_rest [boot] [devtools]
  ∨ ⊕ src/main/java
    ∨ ⊞ com.dineshonjava.prodos
      > ⌐ˢ ProdosApplication.java
    ∨ ⊞ com.dineshonjava.prodos.domain
      > Ⓙ Product.java
    ∨ ⊞ com.dineshonjava.prodos.repository
      > ⌐ ProductRepository.java
  ∨ ⊕ src/main/resources
    > ⌐ META-INF
    ⌐ static
    ⌐ templates
    ⌐ application.properties
    ⌐ data.sql
  ∨ ⊕ src/test/java
    ∨ ⊞ com.dineshonjava.prodos
      > Ⓙ ProdosApplicationTests.java
  > ⩗ JRE System Library [JavaSE-1.8]
  > ⩗ Maven Dependencies
  > ⌐ src
  > ⌐ target
  ⌐ mvnw
  ⌐ mvnw.cmd
  ⌐ pom.xml
```

Figure 4.13: The Spring Data REST application structure

In the preceding screenshot, we added the only starter of Spring Data REST in the classpath, nothing else. All code is same as in the previous such as repositories and entities. Let's run this application as a Spring Boot application and navigate to the http://localhost:8080/api/ endpoint, as shown in the following screenshot:

```
{
 - _links: {
    - products: {
        href: "http://localhost:8080/api/products"
      },
    - profile: {
        href: "http://localhost:8080/api/profile"
      }
   }
}
```

Figure 4.14: Response of the base URL of the Spring Data REST application

In the preceding screenshot, there are links to the products list and profile. Let's click on the product's link http://localhost:8080/api/products. Spring Data Rest renders all products available in the database in the JSON format, including a link to each product resource. Let's take a look at the following screenshot:

```
{
    - _embedded: {
        - products: [
            - {
                name: "Samsung A6 plus",
                type: "Mobile",
                description: "Samsung A6 plus is very nice phone with 24mp front camera"
                brand: "Samsung",
                - _links: {
                    - self: {
                        href: "http://localhost:8080/api/products/MOB01"
                    },
                    - product: {
                        href: "http://localhost:8080/api/products/MOB01"
                    }
                }
            },
            - {
                name: "iPhone X plus",
                type: "Mobile",
                description: "iPhone X plus is very nice phone with 24mp front camera",
                brand: "Apple",
                - _links: {
                    - self: {
                        href: "http://localhost:8080/api/products/MOB02"
                    },
                    - product: {
                        href: "http://localhost:8080/api/products/MOB02"
                    }
                }
            },
            - {
                name: "Sony Bravia KLV-50W662F 50 Inch Full HD",
                type: "Television",
                description: "Sony Bravia is full HD tv",
                brand: "Sony",
                - _links: {
                    - self: {
                        href: "http://localhost:8080/api/products/TLV01"
                    },
                    - product: {
                        href: "http://localhost:8080/api/products/TLV01"
                    }
                }
            }
        ]
    },
    - _links: {
        - self: {
            href: "http://localhost:8080/api/products"
        },
        - profile: {
            href: "http://localhost:8080/api/profile/products"
        },
        - search: {
            href: "http://localhost:8080/api/products/search"
        }
    }
}
```

Figure 4.15: Response for the product list API

The preceding screenshot displays the product list as the resources and having a self-link for each product. You can also access the self-link for the product by using the path name, which is derived from the entity name as the following:

```
{
    name: "Samsung A6 plus",
    type: "Mobile",
    description: "Samsung A6 plus is very nice phone with 24mp front camera",
    brand: "Samsung",
  - _links: {
     - self: {
          href: "http://localhost:8080/api/products/MOB01"
        },
     - product: {
          href: "http://localhost:8080/api/products/MOB01"
        }
    }
}
```

Figure 4.16: Response for the single product API

Spring Data REST does not only provide fetch functionalities but it also provides all CRUD operations. You can use the following HTTP methods for the CRUD operations:

- GET   => Read

- POST   =>Create

- PUT/PATCH   =>Update

- DELETE   =>Delete

Spring Data REST provides the @RestResource annotation that allows you to set the relation name and path you want to give the entity. Let's see the following code:

```
@Entity
@Table(name="PRODUCT")
@RestResource(rel="products", path="products")
public class Product implements Serializable{

...

}
```

In this case, you're setting them both to products. Now, when you request the home resource, you see the products link with the correct pluralization:

```
{
_links: {
 products: {
  href: "http://localhost:8080/api/products"
 },
```

```
  profile: {
    href: "http://localhost:8080/api/profile"
  }
 }
}
```

Now, when you make a GET request to the http://localhost:8080/api/products path, you will see a new endpoint called /search. When you call the http://localhost:8080/api/products/search path, it returns the following response:

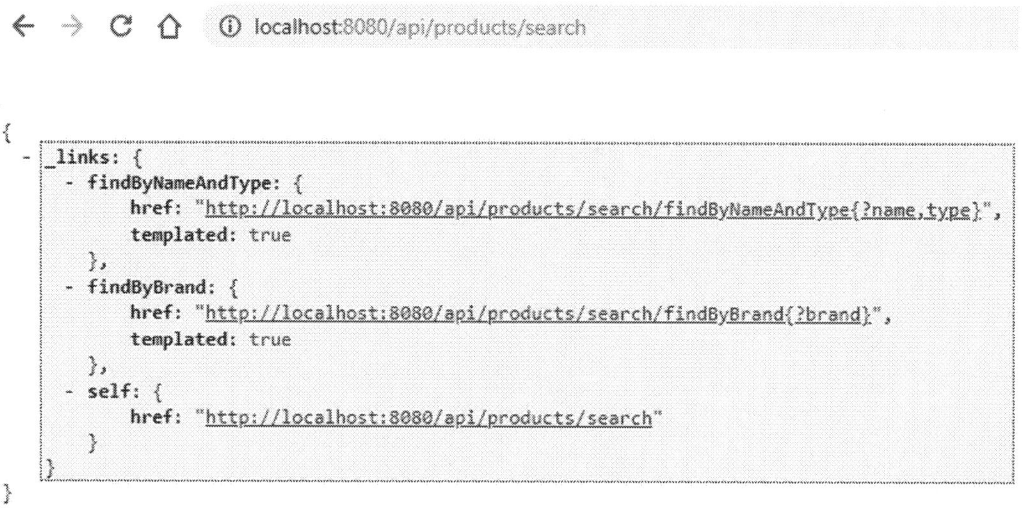

```
{
 - _links: {
    - findByNameAndType: {
        href: "http://localhost:8080/api/products/search/findByNameAndType{?name,type}",
        templated: true
      },
    - findByBrand: {
        href: "http://localhost:8080/api/products/search/findByBrand{?brand}",
        templated: true
      },
    - self: {
        href: "http://localhost:8080/api/products/search"
      }
  }
}
```

Figure 4.17: Response for the product search API

In the preceding response, you can see that both the queries are now available in our service. The following URL demonstrates how to fetch products by brand: http://localhost:8080/api/products/search/findByBrand?brand=Samsung

← → C ⌂ ⓘ localhost:8080/api/products/search/findByBrand?brand=Samsung

```
{
  - _embedded: {
    - products: [
      - {
          name: "Samsung A6 plus",
          type: "Mobile",
          description: "Samsung A6 plus is very nice phone with 24mp front camera",
          brand: "Samsung",
        - _links: {
          - self: {
              href: "http://localhost:8080/api/products/MOB01"
            },
          - product: {
              href: "http://localhost:8080/api/products/MOB01"
            }
          }
        }
      ]
    },
  - _links: {
    - self: {
        href: "http://localhost:8080/api/products/search/findByBrand?brand=Samsung"
      }
    }
}
```

Figure 4.18: Response for the product search API with the brand name

In the previous section, we discussed and created the REST endpoints that can be consumed by a client external to your application. Let's see how to consume REST endpoints in the next section.

Consuming REST endpoints

There are a lot of external clients that can consume REST endpoints. The Postman is one of the tools used for consuming and testing the REST endpoints. Similarly, RestClient is another tool. External applications such as Android, IOS, other programmatically clients consume REST endpoints to access or send data to the server.

The JS-based framework such as Angular and ReactJS also use the REST endpoints for accessing data from the server to be rendered in the UI components. A **Single-Page Application (SPA)** is one of the examples of using the REST endpoints. In this section, we will create a Spring application to consume REST endpoints. The following REST clients can be used to consume the REST endpoints in an external application:

- RestTemplate: The Spring framework provides RestTemplate as a synchronous REST client to consume the REST endpoints.

- Traverson: The Spring HATEOAS module provides Traverson as a synchronous REST client and this client is also hyperlink-aware.

- WebClient: This REST client is introduced in Spring 5 and it is a reactive, asynchronous REST client.

In this section, we will discuss each client from the preceding list. Let's discuss how to consume the REST endpoints using the RestTemplate object.

Consuming REST endpoints with RestTemplate

RestTemplate is a high-level implementation of the HttpClient object. Internally, it is working with low-level HTTP libraries. The RestTemplate object eliminates mostly tedious and boilerplate code that is required to call any remote API using the HTTP protocol.

The Spring framework provides RestTemplate like JdbcTemplate to avoid boilerplate code. The RestTemplate object provides several high-level method implementations to consume REST endpoints. Let's see the following table:

Method	Description
delete(…)	This method performs an HTTP DELETE request on a resource from the server.
exchange(…)	This method executes the HTTP method you specify against a URL and returns it as ResponseEntity containing an object.
execute(…)	This method executes the HTTP method you specify against a URL and returns the object in the response body.
getForEntity(…)	This method sends data to the server using an HTTP GET request and returns a ResponseEntity containing an object.
getForObject(…)	This method sends data to the server using an HTTP GET request and returns an object mapped from a response body.
headForHeaders(…)	This method sends an HTTP HEAD request to the server and returns the HTTP headers.
optionsForAllow(…)	This method sends an HTTP OPTIONS request to the server and returns the Allow header.

patchForObject(...)	This method sends an HTTP PATCH request to the server and returns the resource using the response body.
postForEntity(...)	This method posts data on the server and returns with a ResponseEntity object that contains a created object.
postForLocation(...)	This method posts data on the server to a URL and returns the URL of the newly created resource.
postForObject(...)	This method posts data on the server for a given URL and returns an object mapped from the response body.
put(...)	This method updates the resource using the PUT HTTP request method to the specified URL.

The previous listed methods of the RestTemplate object provide high-level functionality for the HTTP protocol. So, using RestTemplate, we do not need to worry about how to handle the exception, how to close HTTP connection, etc. RestTemplate manages this boilerplate internally.

In your Spring application, you can use RestTemplate by creating its bean or create an instance of RestTemplate:

```
@Bean
public RestTemplate restTemplate() {
  return new RestTemplate();
}
```

As of 5.0, the non-blocking, reactive org.springframework.web.reactive.client. WebClient offers a modern alternative to RestTemplate with sufficient support for both, sync and async, and as well for streaming scenarios. The RestTemplate object will be deprecated in a future version and will not have major new features added going forward.

Let's create a REST API's client application using Spring Boot and Spring MVC. As of now, we will use Thymeleaf for the UI layer. This client application will consume the REST endpoint created by the REST application in the previous section. Let's see the application structure of the client application. Let's see the GET request using RestTemplate:

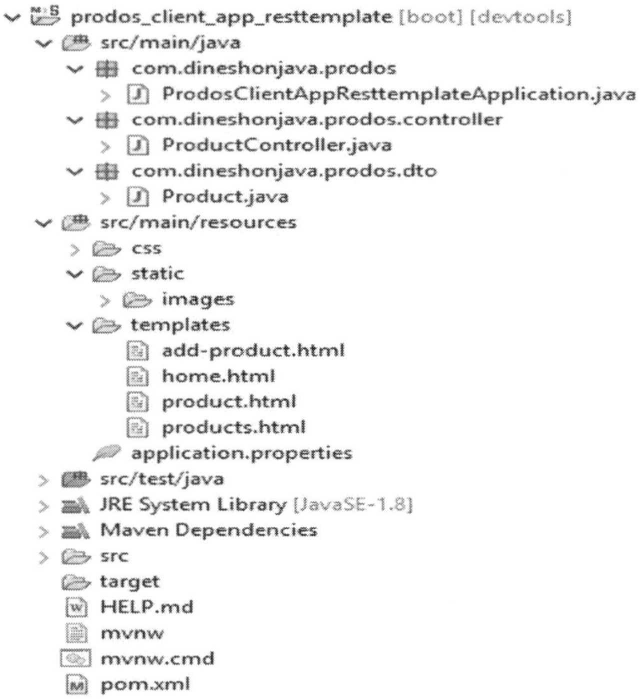

Figure 4.19: A REST client application structure

The preceding screenshot shows a web application that will consume REST endpoints to retrieve and post the data to the server. In the preceding screenshot, we created a ProductController class, which is very different from the REST application controller class. This is a simple and traditional controller class annotated with the @Controller annotation as shown in the following code:

```
@Controller
public class ProductController {
    //...
}
```

Let's define methods in this controller class and create the GET request by using RestTemplate.

Retrieving resources using the GET method

For example, if your client application wants to access the list of the products or single product details from the PRODOS REST API application. We will use the PRODOS REST application without hypermedia in this case because the RestTemplate does not support the hyperlinks in the resources.

We can use the getForObject() method to fetch the list of the products from the PRODOS REST API application. Let's see the following code that uses RestTemplate to fetch data from the API endpoints:

```
@Controller
public class ProductController {

  private final String BASE_URL = "http://localhost:8181/prodos";

  @Autowired
  RestTemplate restTemplate;

  @GetMapping("/products")
  public String findAllProducts(ModelMap model) {
    List<Product>  products = restTemplate.getForObject(BASE_URL+"/products", List.class);
    model.put("products", products);
    return "products";
  }

  @GetMapping("/products/{id}")
  public String findProductById(ModelMap model, @PathVariable String id) {
    Product  product = restTemplate.getForObject(BASE_URL+"/products/{id}", Product.class, id);
    model.put("product", product);
    return "product";
  }
  //...
}
```

In the preceding code, we are using the getForObject() method to fetch data from the REST endpoints. The getForObject() method of the RestTemplate class accepts a String URL and class type for the return value. The first method of the findAllProducts() controller class fetches the product list from the given REST endpoint. The second method fetches a single product for a specific product ID from the specified REST endpoint.

Let's see another overloaded version of the getForObject() method as shown in the following code:

```
@GetMapping("/products/{id}")
public String findProductById(ModelMap model, @PathVariable String id) {
  Map<String,String> urlVariables = new HashMap<>();
```

```
urlVariables.put("id", id);
 Product product = restTemplate.getForObject(BASE_URL+"/products/{id}", Product.class,
urlVariables);
 model.put("product", product);
 return "product";
}
```

Here, we're using the getForObject() variant that accepts a String URL, class type, and the URL variables. The id parameter passed to getForObject() is used to fill in the {id} placeholder in the given URL.

If you want to inspect the response header data, then you can use the getForEntity() method to fetch data from the REST endpoints. The getForEntity() method returns the ResponseEntity object instead of Product object. Let's see the following code:

```
@GetMapping("/products/{id}")
public String findProductById(ModelMap model, @PathVariable String id) {
 Map<String,String> urlVariables = new HashMap<>();
 urlVariables.put("id", id);
 ResponseEntity<Product> product = restTemplate.getForEntity(BASE_URL+"/products/{id}",
Product.class, urlVariables);
 log.info("Fetched time: " +responseEntity.getHeaders().getDate());
 model.put("product", responseEntity.getBody());
 return "product";
}
```

We created two methods in the ProductController class to fetch data from the REST endpoints. Let's run the client application and navigate to the http://localhost:9000/prodosapp/ URL in the browser:

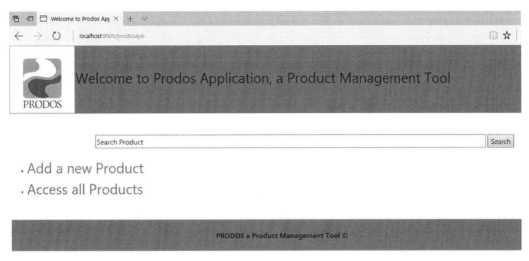

Figure 4.20: The home page of the PRODOS client application

Click on the **Access all Products** link, as shown in the preceding screenshot. It will render all available products:

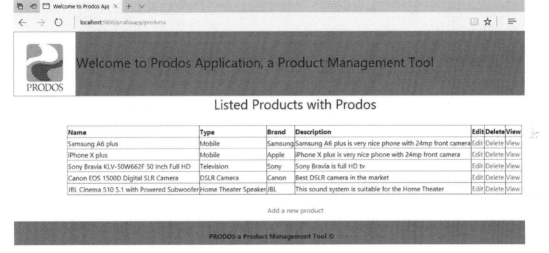

Figure 4.21: Product list page of the PRODOS application

The preceding screenshot displays the products retrieved by calling a REST endpoint (http://localhost:8181/prodos/products) using RestTemplate in the ProductController class. You can also access the specific product details by clicking on the view link as shown in the following screenshot:

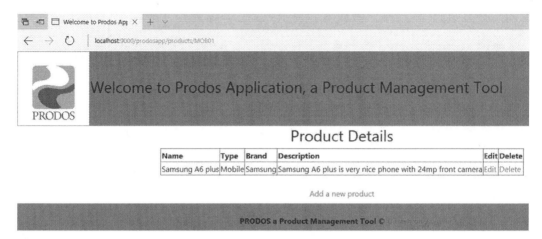

Figure 4.23: Product details page of the PRODOS client application

The preceding screenshot displays the product details (with product id : MOB01). This product details is fetched from the REST endpoint (http://localhost:8181/prodos/products/MOB01) using RestTemplate in the product controller class.

Let's create a new product in the specific REST endpoint.

Creating resource data using the POST method

Let's create a method for ProductController to create a product resource using the REST endpoint. Suppose if you want to create a new product in the PRODOS REST application's product list. You can use an HTTP POST request in the /products/ REST endpoint with the product data in the request body.

The RestTemplate object provides three methods to send a POST request such as postForObject(), postForLocation(), and postForEntity(). Each method has the same overloaded versions for specifying the URL.

If you want to receive the newly created resource after the POST request, then use the following implementation:

```
@PostMapping("/create-product")
public String createProduct(ModelMap model, Product product) {
   model.put("product", restTemplate.postForObject(BASE_URL+"/products/", product, Product.
class));
 return "product";
}
```

If you want to have the location of the newly created resource rather than having the newly created resource, then you can use the following implementation with the postForLocation() method:

```
public URI createProduct(Product product) {
  return restTemplate.postForLocation(BASE_URL+"/products/", product);
}
```

If you want to have both, the newly created resource and location of the newly created resource, then you can use the postForEntity() method of RestTemplate as shown in the following code:

```
public Product createProduct(Product product) {
  ResponseEntity<Product> responseEntity = restTemplate.postForEntity(BASE_URL+"/products/",
  Product.class);
  log.info("New resource created at " +responseEntity.getHeaders().getLocation());
  return responseEntity.getBody();
}
```

Let's see the following screenshot to create a new product using the createProduct() preceding request handler method. This request handler method uses the postForObject() method of the RestTemplate object with the REST endpoint (POST http://localhost:8181/prodos/products):

Figure 4.24: Create a new Product page

After entering data in the form, click on the **Create Product** button. A new product is created on the server using the REST endpoint. You can verify it by fetching all products again. Let's see the following screenshot:

Name	Type	Brand	Description	Edit	Delete	View
Samsung A6 plus	Mobile	Samsung	Samsung A6 plus is very nice phone with 24mp front camera	Edit	Delete	View
iPhone X plus	Mobile	Apple	iPhone X plus is very nice phone with 24mp front camera	Edit	Delete	View
Sony Bravia KLV-50W662F 50 Inch Full HD	Television	Sony	Sony Bravia is full HD tv	Edit	Delete	View
Canon EOS 1500D Digital SLR Camera	DSLR Camera	Canon	Best DSLR camera in the market	Edit	Delete	View
JBL Cinema 510 5.1 with Powered Subwoofer	Home Theater Speaker	JBL	This sound system is suitable for the Home Theater	Edit	Delete	View
Poco	Mobile	Xiomi	It is very nice mobile	Edit	Delete	View

Figure 4.25: Product list page after adding a new product

The product is added to the bottom of the product list. Let's discuss how to update a resource from the client application.

Updating resources using the PUT method

If you want to update a resource on the server by sending the HTTP PUT request, Spring's RestTemplate provides the put() method to do this. This method takes a URI as a String and updates the product object and class type as arguments. Let's suppose you want to update a product resource with the data from a new Product object. The following code should do the trick:

```
@PostMapping({"/edit/create-product"})
public String updateProduct(ModelMap model, Product product) {
  restTemplate.put(BASE_URL+"/products/", product, Product.class);
  return "redirect:/products";
}
```

Deleting resources using the DELETE method

Let's create a method in the ProductController class to delete a Product from the list of the products. To make this happen, you can call the delete() method from RestTemplate:

```
@GetMapping("/delete/{id}")
public String deleteProduct(@PathVariable String id) {
  restTemplate.delete(BASE_URL+"/products/{id}", id);
  return "redirect:/products";
}
```

In the preceding code, we called the delete() method of the RestTemplate object by taking two arguments. The first argument is the URL and the second argument is the URL variable value to be deleted.

We discussed how to use the RestTemplate object to consume the REST endpoints. As we know that RestTemplate has some limitations. It cannot be used when we work with the REST services with hypermedia. The RestTemplate object is not useful if you want to consume the REST endpoints, including hyperlinks in its response. Let's see an alternate of the RestTemplate to consume the REST endpoints.

Consuming REST endpoints with Traverson

Spring HATEOAS provides Traverson out-of-the-box to consume the REST endpoints with hypermedia. It is very similar to configure Traverson in your Spring application. Let's see the following code:

```
@Bean
public Traverson traverson() {
    return new Traverson(URI.create("http://localhost:8080/api"), MediaTypes.HAL_JSON);
}
```

or

```
Traverson traverson = new Traverson(URI.create("http://localhost:8080/api"), MediaTypes.HAL_JSON);
```

We instantiated the object Traverson class using the argument constructor. So, the first argument is URL. We assigned an initial base URL of the REST PRODOS application. And the second argument is the media type. We specified JSON responses with the HAL-style hyperlinks so that Traverson knows how to parse the incoming resource data.

Let's update the request handler method of the ProductController class. Now we will use the Traverson rest client to consume the REST endpoints. So, the following code is changed to find all products using the REST endpoint:

```
@Controller
public class ProductController {

    ...
    @Autowired
    Traverson traverson;
    @GetMapping("/")
    public String home() {
        return "home";
    }

    @GetMapping("/products")
    public String findAllProducts(ModelMap model) {
```

```
    ParameterizedTypeReference<Resources<Product>> productType = new ParameterizedTypeR
eference<Resources<Product>>() {};
    Resources<Product> productResources = traverson.follow("products").
toObject(productType);
  model.put("products", productResources.getContent());
  return "products";
 }
 ...
}
```

In the preceding code, we are using the Traverson object to fetch the product list from the REST API. The follow() method of the Traverson object allows you to navigate to resource the relation name of the link which is products. Now, your application call is navigated to the products and finally, we call the toObject() method to ingest the contents of that resource. But the toObject()method needs an argument for the type of data you want to read it as a Resources<Product> object.

So, Traverson allows you to consume the REST APIs. Those are HATEOAS-enabled APIs. Your client code can easily navigate to these HATEOAS-enabled APIs and consume its resources. But Traverson also has some limitations such as it cannot provide any method for writing to or deleting from those APIs unlike the RestTemplate provides method for writing to or deleting from the APIs.

You can still use Traverson for the POST, PUT, and DELETE requests using RestTemplate. For example, you can add a new Product to the PRODOS REST application. Then, you can see the following createProduct() method using Traverson and RestTemplate together to post a new Product to the API:

```
@PostMapping("/create-product")
public String createProduct(Product product) {
  Link productLink = traverson.follow("products").asLink();
  this.restTemplate.postForEntity(productLink.expand().getHref(), product, Product.class);
  return "redirect:/products";
}
```

In the earlier code, we created the link using the asLink() method of the Traverson object. And then, we used the postForEntity() method of the RestTemplate object to post a new product to the API.

Consuming REST endpoints with WebClient

As of Spring 5, WebClient has been introduced as a REST API client. The Spring WebFlux module provides WebClient to your Spring application. WebClient has more functionalities if you compare it with RestTemplate. WebClient is full reactive.

Let's add the following Spring WebFlux module Maven starter dependency to WebClient in your application:

```
<dependency>
 <groupId>org.springframework.boot</groupId>
 <artifactId>spring-boot-starter-webflux</artifactId>
</dependency>
```

This starter dependency will not only add the module libraries to your classpath, but it will also auto-configure the Spring WebFlux module in your application. So you can directly use WebClient in your Spring application, as shown in the following code:

```
@Controller
public class ProductController {

 @Autowired
  private WebClient webClient;

  public ProductController(WebClient.Builder webClientBuilder) {
    this.webClient = webClientBuilder.baseUrl("http://localhost:8181/prodos/").build();
  }

  @GetMapping("/products")
  public  String findAllProducts(ModelMap model) {
    Flux<Product> products = this.webClient.get().uri("/products").retrieve().bodyToFlux(List.
class);
   model.put("products", products);
   return "products";
  }

  ...

}
```

Similarly, we can create other request handler methods in the ProductController class using WebClient to consume the REST endpoints. In this chapter, we discussed how to create and how to consume the REST APIs.

Conclusion

In this chapter, we discussed the REST architectural model and its constraints and we created a REST application and a lot of REST endpoints for the CRUD functionalities. We learned the following topics in this chapter:

- The REST application architectural patterns with all its constraints, including Uniform Interface principles.

- We created a RESTful web service application using Spring Boot using the @RestController annotation. This application provides all services required for the CRUD functionalities.

- After that, we added the Spring HATEOAS modules to the REST application to enable hyperlinking of resources returned from Spring MVC controllers.

- We learned how to create HATEOAS-enabled REST APIs using the Spring Data REST repositories. It can automatically be exposed as REST APIs using the defined repositories in your Spring application.

- Finally, we discussed to consume the REST endpoints using the client's application. We created a client application PRODOS web application that used RestTemplate to make HTTP requests against REST APIs.

- And we also used the Traverson class to consume the REST API. It enables clients to navigate an API using hyperlinks embedded in the responses.

In the next *Chapter 5: Securing REST APIs with Spring Security*, we will discuss how to secure the REST services using Spring Security.

Questions

1. What is REST?
2. What are RESTful web services?
3. What are REST architectural constraints?
4. How to create a RESTful web service with Spring Boot?
5. What is difference between @RestController and @Controller?
6. What is HATEOAS?
7. How to consume REST API?

8.   What is RestTemplate?

9.   What is the difference between RESTful web services and SOAP web services?

10. What is resource in the REST framework?

11. Which HTTP methods are supported by RESTful web services?

CHAPTER 5
Securing REST APIs

In the previous chapter, we created REST APIs and learned about the various principles to create a RESTful application service. We also created a REST client application to consume the created RESTful endpoints. In our PRODOS application, we fetched the product list or product details and also created a REST endpoint to post a new product to the server. We can send a DELETE request to delete a product from the server. So anyone can access these REST endpoints and perform an operation on the server. In this case, we will need to secure these REST endpoints so that only authorized users can perform the CRUD operations using the REST endpoints.

Since the information provided by any REST application may be valuable, there are a lot of crooks or hackers who are eyeing to steal the application data. As software developers, we need to take precautions to protect the information that is provided by the REST APIs.

But how can we secure our REST APIs from the outside intruders? The Spring framework allows you to secure these REST endpoints. In this chapter, we will learn how to apply security to secure RESTful APIs using Spring Security, OAuth2 and JWT. We will also explore **JSON Web Token (JWT)** for the RESTful APIs.

In this chapter, we will discuss the following topics in detail:

- Spring Security
  - o   Adding the Spring Security module
- Implementing and configuring Spring Security
  - o   In-memory user store configuration

       o   JDBC user store configuration

       o   LDAP user store configuration

       o   Custom user details service configuration

- Password encoding with Spring Security
- Secure your RESTful APIs with Spring Security and the JWT
- Secure your RESTful APIs with Spring Security and OAuth2

Spring Security

The Spring framework added the security module in 2003 and it was known as 'The Acegi Security System for Spring' at that time. The Spring framework refined the security module and rebranded it as 'Spring Security' (https://spring.io/projects/spring-security). It provides security services for the Java web-based applications. Let us see how to add the Spring Security module to your REST application to secure the REST endpoints.

Adding the Spring Security module

Adding the Spring Security module to your Spring Boot REST application is very easy. You can include the Spring Security starter Maven dependency in your application. Let us add the following Maven dependency configuration to the project's pom.xml file:

```
<dependency>
  <groupId>org.springframework.boot</groupId>
  <artifactId>spring-boot-starter-security</artifactId>
</dependency>
```

The preceding starter dependency does not only provide the required libraries to your REST application but also provides the default configurations required by the Spring Security module. I believe it is enough to provide the basic authentication to your REST application. You can start your application, and try to visit any REST endpoint or homepage of your application. You will have to go through the authentication process with the HTTP basic authentication.

By default, Spring Security creates a single user with the user name, which is user, and the password is printed on the console output as shown in the following screenshot:

```
2019-02-28 17:04:27.235  WARN 2232 --- [  restartedMain] aWebConfiguration$JpaWebMvcConfiguration :
2019-02-28 17:04:27.505  INFO 2232 --- [  restartedMain] .s.s.UserDetailsServiceAutoConfiguration :

Using generated security password: b3339650-96e7-47bf-a1f7-182d09a8e6ab

2019-02-28 17:04:27.652  INFO 2232 --- [  restartedMain] o.s.s.web.DefaultSecurityFilterChain    :
2019-02-28 17:04:27.868  INFO 2232 --- [  restartedMain] o.s.b.w.embedded.tomcat.TomcatWebServer :
```

Figure 5.1: Printed password by Spring Security.

The preceding password is randomly generated and written in the logs. Let us see by default what Spring Security auto-configuration provides to your REST application:

- All REST endpoints or all HTTP request paths require authentication.

- Initially, Spring Security does not configure any specific role.

- Spring Security uses an AuthenticationManager and builds an in-memory single user with the username user.

- By default, it uses the HTTP basic authentication mechanism.

- It ignores paths such as /css, /images, and so on for static resources.

After you start your REST application, you need to make a GET request to the REST endpoint of your previous REST application by navigating to http://localhost:8181/prodos/products as shown in the following screenshot:

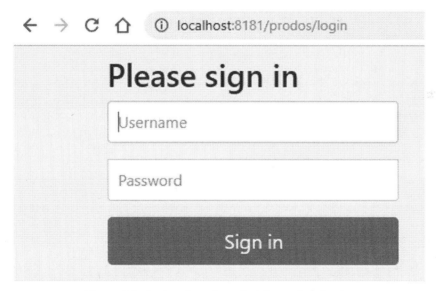

Figure 5.2: Spring Security asked for authentication

Spring Security redirects you to the login page before you can start accessing the API data. It displays a dialogue box prompting the user to input the username and password. The login page is designed by the Spring Security module. You can also create your own custom login page. As you know, the REST API is not only consumed by any browser, it can be accessed by any REST client either programmatically or using tools such as Postman. You can also use the REST client tool such as Postman to access the REST endpoint at http://localhost:8181/prodos/products, as shown in the following screenshot:

Figure 5.3: Postman provides an error Status 401 Unauthorized
when it accesses to secure REST API.

In the preceding screenshot, you can see that the Postman client returns an error Status code **401 Unauthorized** request because the REST API requires the basic authentication using the username and password.

To make a successful GET request, you need to provide credentials for the basic authentication. The default username is user and the password is the same that was printed on the console output screen. Let us provide the basic authentication details and access the same REST endpoint, as shown in the following screenshot with the Postman client:

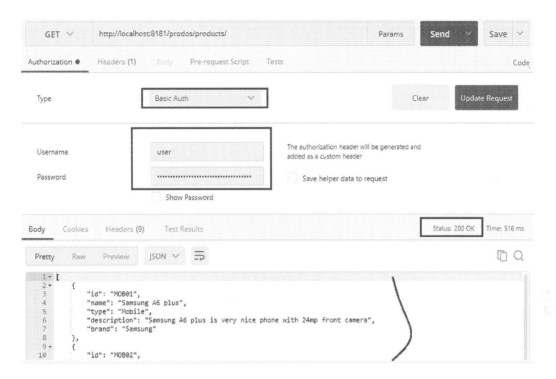

Figure 5.4: Postman provides a successful response Status 200
when it accesses the secure REST API

Now, after we provide the username and password, access the data from the REST endpoint (http://localhost:8181/prodos/products), perform the GET request successfully with Status 200 OK, the response is sent to the product list as the JSON resource.

We have seen how Spring Security works to secure the PRODOS REST application but currently, we have used the default configuration provided by the Spring Security starter in the Spring Boot application. The default configuration is not suitable for our REST application because we need to provide multiple users and passwords to access our REST endpoints.

To meet your own security expectations, you can customize the default configuration by providing your own Spring Security configuration. Let us discuss this in the next section.

Implementing and configuring Spring Security

In the current version (2.2.0) of Spring Boot, you can easily configure Spring Security to your PRODOS REST application by adding a new configuration class that extends the WebSecurityConfigurerAdapter class of the Spring Security module. Let's create a new configuration class SecurityConfig in your PRODOS REST application in the com.dineshonjava.prodos.security package as shown in the following code snippet:

```
package com.dineshonjava.prodos.security;


import org.springframework.context.annotation.Configuration;

import org.springframework.security.config.annotation.web.configuration.EnableWebSecurity;

import org.springframework.security.config.annotation.web.configuration.
WebSecurityConfigurerAdapter;


@Configuration
@EnableWebSecurity
public class SecurityConfig extends WebSecurityConfigurerAdapter {
}
```

The preceding configuration class is annotated with the @Configration and @ EnableWebSecurity annotations. These annotations switch off the default web security configuration in your application.

You can provide your own security configuration in this class. You can override the configure(HttpSecurity http) method as shown in the following code snippet:

```
@Override
protected void configure(HttpSecurity http) throws Exception {
 http
 .authorizeRequests()
  .anyRequest().authenticated()
  .and()
 .formLogin()
  .and()
 .httpBasic();
}
```

In this method, you can define the REST endpoints in your application that are secured and which are not. If you want to secure all REST endpoints to be secured then there is no need to override this method.

Suppose if you want to secure the REST endpoints such as /products and /product only, all other requests should be permitted for all users. Then, you need to configure the configure() method as shown in the following code snippet:

```
@Override
protected void configure(HttpSecurity http) throws Exception {
  http
  .authorizeRequests().antMatchers("/product", "/products").hasRole("ROLE_USER").
antMatchers("/", "/**").permitAll()
  .and()
  .formLogin()
   .and()
  .httpBasic();
}
```

In the preceding configuration of the configure() method, we configured the HTTP request interceptor by calling the authorizeRequests() method. We specified the URL paths and patterns using the antMatchers() method and also specified a granted authority of ROLE_USER. Now, the HTTP requests for /product and /products should be authenticated with a granted authority of ROLE_USER.

In the preceding configuration, we used two ant matchers because the Spring Security follows the order of the defined rules. Security rules declared first take precedence over those declared lower down.

The hasRole() and permitAll() methods are a couple of the methods used for declaring security requirements for request paths.

Method	Description
access(String)	This method allows access if the given SpEL expression evaluates to true.
anonymous()	This method allows access to anonymous users.
authenticated()	This method allows access to authenticated users.
denyAll()	This method denies access unconditionally.
fullyAuthenticated()	This method allows access if the user is fully authenticated.
hasAnyAuthority(String...)	This method allows access if the user has any of the given authorities.
hasAnyRole(String...)	This method allows access if the user has any of the given roles.

Method	Description
hasAuthority(String)	This method allows access if the user has the given authority.
hasIpAddress(String)	This method allows access if the request comes from the given IP address.
hasRole(String)	This method allows access if the user has the given role.
not()	This method negates the effect of any of the other access methods.
permitAll()	This method allows access without any authentication.
rememberMe()	This method allows access for users who are authenticated via remember-me.

We are configuring Spring Security in our PRODOS REST application, and that is why we are not going into much details about the other methods such as formLogin(), loginPage(), and so on. The loginPage() method is useful when you want to customize your login page. Let's now discuss how to configure a user store and how we can configure the user store with Spring Security.

There are several options available to store the users for Spring Security. We can choose any one as per the application requirement. Let's see the following user configurations:

- An in-memory user configuration
- A JDBC-based user configuration
- An LDAP-backed user configuration
- A custom user details configuration

You can configure the user store by overriding the configure() method of the WebSecurityConfigurerAdapter configuration base class. Let's see the following method to be added to the SecurityConfig class:

```
@Override
protected void configure(AuthenticationManagerBuilder auth) throws Exception {
  ...
}
```

Let's first see how to configure the in-memory user configuration.

An in-memory user configuration

An in-memory user configuration is very easy to use whenever you want to keep your user information in memory. It is better to use this configuration if you have only a small set of users and none of them is likely to change the information. Let's define the in-memory user store in theSpring security configuration as shown in the following code snippet:

```
public void configure(AuthenticationManagerBuilder auth) throws Exception {
  auth
    .inMemoryAuthentication()
      .withUser("dinesh").password("mypass").roles("USER").and()
      .withUser("arnav").password("yourpass").roles("ADMIN").and()
      .withUser("rushika").password("pass").roles("SUPPORT");
}
```

In the preceding configuration, we configured in-memory users using the AuthenticationManagerBuilder class. The inMemoryAuthentication() method is used to add user information directly to the security configuration file by calling the withUser() method. You can specify the password and granted permissions using the password() and roles() methods, respectively.

As an alternative, you can also add in-memory users to our application by adding the userDetailsService() method to our SecurityConfig class. Let's see the following code:

```
@Bean
@Override
public UserDetailsService userDetailsService() {
  UserDetails user = User.withDefaultPasswordEncoder()
    .username("arnav")
    .password("mypass")
    .roles("USER")
    .build();
  return new InMemoryUserDetailsManager(user);
}
```

The usage of in-memory users is good in the development phase, but the real application should save the users in the database.

A JDBC-based user configuration

If you want to put your user information in a relational database, then a JDBC-based user store seems appropriate for your application. Let's see how the following configuration configures Spring Security to authenticate the user and user information kept in the relational database:

```
@Configuration
@EnableWebSecurity
public class SecurityConfig extends WebSecurityConfigurerAdapter {

  ...

  @Autowired DataSource dataSource;

  public void configure(AuthenticationManagerBuilder auth) throws Exception {
   auth
    .jdbcAuthentication()
    .dataSource(dataSource);
  }
  ...
}
```

As you can see in the preceding configuration, the configure() method calls the jdbcAuthentication() method of AuthenticationManagerBuilder to fetch user information from the relational database with JDBC. For this requirement, you need to configure DataSource so that you know about the relational database. That is why we autowired and configured a DataSource class with the configure() method.

You can also override the default user queries for the preceding configuration. Let's change the preceding configuration to override the default user queries:

```
@Configuration
@EnableWebSecurity
public class SecurityConfig extends WebSecurityConfigurerAdapter {

  ...

  @Autowired DataSource dataSource;

  public void configure(AuthenticationManagerBuilder auth) throws Exception {
   auth
    .jdbcAuthentication()
    .usersByUsernameQuery("SELECT username, password, enabled FROM users WHERE
```

```
username = ?")
    .authoritiesByUsernameQuery("SELECT username, authority FROM authorities WHERE
username = ?")
    .dataSource(dataSource);
 }
  ...
}
```

In the preceding configuration, we have overridden the authentication and basic authorization queries using the usersByUsernameQuery() and authoritiesByUsernameQuery() methods.

An LDAP-backed user configuration

The Spring framework allows you to configure Spring Security with the LDAP-based authentication. The AuthenticationManagerBuilder class provides you with the ldapAuthentication() method. Let's see the following configuration for the LDAP authentication:

```
@Override
protected void configure(AuthenticationManagerBuilder auth) throws Exception {
 auth
  .ldapAuthentication()
  .userSearchFilter("(uid={0})")
  .groupSearchFilter("member={0}");
}
```

In the preceding configuration, we configured the configure() method with the LDAP-backed user configuration using the userSearchFilter() and groupSearchFilter() methods. These methods are used to provide filters for the base LDAP queries, which are used to search for users and groups.

In this chapter, we are not going define each user strategies in detail to avoid confusion for the beginners. We discussed Spring Security's built-in user stores with some common use cases. But for our REST application PRODOS, we will implement and configure custom user details service. Let's see this in the next section.

A custom user details configuration

In this configuration, we will build our own user detail service configuration. We have already used the Spring Data JPA in the last chapter to fetch the product list from the relational database. Here, also we will store the user information to the database and retrieve the user information using the Spring Data JPA.

Now, we have to create the Spring Data repository for the user information as well. But first, let's create the domain object and repository interface.

```
package com.dineshonjava.prodos.domain;

//imports
@Entity
@Table(name="USER")
public class ProdosUser {

  @Id
  @GeneratedValue(strategy = GenerationType.AUTO)
  @Column(nullable = false, updatable = false)
  private Long id;

  @Column(nullable = false, unique = true)
  private String username;

  @Column(nullable = false)
  private String password;

  @Column(nullable = false)
  private String role;

  public ProdosUser() {

  }

  public ProdosUser(String username, String password, String role) {
   super();
   this.username = username;
   this.password = password;
   this.role = role;
  }

  //setters and getters

}
```

We created a ProdosUser entity class to save the users to the database and this class is annotated with the @Entity annotation. This class has the id, username, password, and role as the fields. It may have more one field as per requirements. In the database, the passwords should not be saved to the database in plain text format. Passwords must be saved with hashing. You can any hashing algorithms provided by Spring Security such as BCrypt, PBKDF2, SHA-256, and many more. We will discuss the password encoder later in this chapter.

Let's create a new class called ProdosUserRepository in the com.dineshonjava.prodos. repository package as shown in the following code snippet:

```
package com.dineshonjava.prodos.repository;

import org.springframework.data.repository.CrudRepository;
import com.dineshonjava.prodos.domain.ProdosUser;

public interface ProdosUserRepository extends CrudRepository<ProdosUser, Long> {

  ProdosUser findByUsername(String username);
}
```

You can see that the preceding source code of the repository class is similar to what we did in the previous chapter for the product repository. There is one query method, findByUsername(), that we need in the next steps.

Now, let's create a class that implements the UserDetailsService interface of Spring Security. Spring Security uses this interface implementation for authentication and authorization. Let's see the following source code for the UserDetailServiceImpl class in the com.dineshonjava.prodos.service package:

```
package com.dineshonjava.prodos.service;

import org.springframework.beans.factory.annotation.Autowired;
import org.springframework.security.core.authority.AuthorityUtils;
import org.springframework.security.core.userdetails.User;
import org.springframework.security.core.userdetails.UserDetails;
import org.springframework.security.core.userdetails.UserDetailsService;
import org.springframework.security.core.userdetails.UsernameNotFoundException;
import org.springframework.stereotype.Service;
import com.dineshonjava.prodos.domain.ProdosUser;
import com.dineshonjava.prodos.repository.ProdosUserRepository;
```

```
/**
 * @author Dinesh.Rajput
 *
 */

@Service
public class UserDetailServiceImpl implements UserDetailsService {

    @Autowired
    private ProdosUserRepository userRepository;

    @Override

    public UserDetails loadUserByUsername(String username) throws UsernameNotFoundException
{

    ProdosUser prodosUser = userRepository.findByUsername(username);
        UserDetails user = new User(username, prodosUser.getPassword(), AuthorityUtils.
createAuthorityList(prodosUser.getRole()));
    return user;
  }


}
```

In the preceding UserDetailServiceImpl class, we autowired the ProdosUserRepository class with the UserDetailServiceImpl class to fetch the user information from the relational database at the time of Spring Security handles authentication. We implemented the loadUserByUsername() method of the UserDetailsService interface. This method returns the UserDetails object. This object is actually used by Spring Security for authentication and authorization.

Finally, we need to define our custom user detail service in the Spring Security configuration class instead of the in-memory user store. Let's change the SecurityConfig class as shown in the following code snippet:

```
package com.dineshonjava.prodos.security;

import org.springframework.beans.factory.annotation.Autowired;
import org.springframework.context.annotation.Configuration;
import org.springframework.security.config.annotation.authentication.builders.
```

```
AuthenticationManagerBuilder;
import org.springframework.security.config.annotation.web.builders.HttpSecurity;
import org.springframework.security.config.annotation.web.configuration.EnableWebSecurity;
import org.springframework.security.config.annotation.web.configuration.
WebSecurityConfigurerAdapter;
import org.springframework.security.crypto.bcrypt.BCryptPasswordEncoder;
import com.dineshonjava.prodos.service.UserDetailServiceImpl;


/**
 * @author Dinesh.Rajput
 *
 */

@Configuration
@EnableWebSecurity
public class SecurityConfig extends WebSecurityConfigurerAdapter {

  @Autowired
  private UserDetailServiceImpl userDetailsService;

  @Override
  protected void configure(HttpSecurity http) throws Exception {
    http
    .authorizeRequests()
     .anyRequest().authenticated()
    .and()
    .formLogin()
     .and()
    .httpBasic();
  }

  @Autowired
  public void configure(AuthenticationManagerBuilder auth) throws Exception {
    auth.userDetailsService(userDetailsService)
     .passwordEncoder(new BCryptPasswordEncoder());
  }
}
```

As discussed earlier, we should not save the password as plain text to the database. That is why we used the passwordEncoder() method to encode the password before a match with the database. In this case, we have used the Spring Security BCryptPasswordEncoder class to implement the password hashing.

Finally, we can add some test users to the database (currently using H2 database in our application). Let's see the following data.sql file; it has some initial test users that need to be inserted at the start of the application:

INSERT INTO USER (id, username, password, role) values (100, 'dinesh', '$2a$04$HCZQH4c0VIIz0K xO1Ux.c.REEM.sQZDyA8eZl8A48bBlYIczzSET6', 'USER');

INSERT INTO USER (id, username, password, role) values (101, 'anamika', '$2a$04$HCZQH4c0VIIz0 KxO1Ux.c.REEM.sQZDyA8eZl8A48bBlYIczzSET6', 'USER');

INSERT INTO USER (id, username, password, role) values (102, 'arnav', '$2a$04$Y5tgmB9IAsE4yPrA. oghQO9jfD6u4qSviHCbVXww3FXgOTnC4da0a', 'ADMIN');

INSERT INTO USER (id, username, password, role) values (103, 'rushika', '$2a$04$Y5tgmB9IAsE4yPrA. oghQO9jfD6u4qSviHCbVXww3FXgOTnC4da0a', 'ADMIN');

You can see in the preceding queries that we used the hashed passwords for each user to save in the database. You can use any BCrypt calculator found on the internet.

Now, you can run your application and see that there is a user table in the database and some user records are saved as shown in the following screenshot:

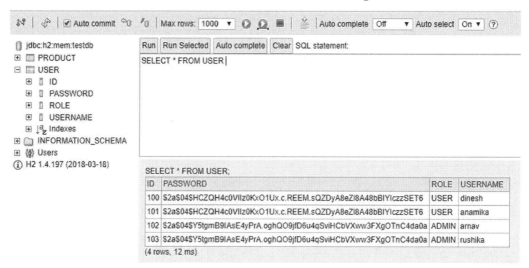

Figure 5.5: User-table in H2 web console

Let's make a call to the http://localhost:8181/prodos/products REST API. You will get a 401 unauthorized error without authentication. Now, make this call again by providing authentication and you will be able to make a call without any error. You will get a successful result with the products list. You will see a GET request to the /

products endpoint using the dinesh user as shown in the following screenshot:

Figure 5.6: Response of /products endpoint in Postman

Let's see the application structure:

Figure 5.7: The Prodos REST application structure

Let's discuss password encoding and see how it works.

Password encoding with Spring Security

You can see the following configuration code snippet that is used in the previous example of the HTTP basic authentication:

```
@Autowired
public void configure(AuthenticationManagerBuilder auth) throws Exception {
  auth.userDetailsService(userDetailsService)
    .passwordEncoder(new BCryptPasswordEncoder());
}
```

In the preceding code, we specified a password encoder by calling the passwordEncoder() method. To avoid password stealing, we need to use encoded passwords. The passwordEncoder() method takes the implementation of Spring Security's PasswordEncoder interface as follows:

- BCryptPasswordEncoder: This implementation class applies the bcrypt strong hashing encryption.

- NoOpPasswordEncoder: This implementation class applies no encoding.

- Pbkdf2PasswordEncoder: This implementation class applies the PBKDF2 encryption.

- SCryptPasswordEncoder: This implementation class applies the scrypt hashing encryption.

- StandardPasswordEncoder: This implementation class applies the SHA-256 hashing encryption.

We used the BCryptPasswordEncoder in our example. But you can choose any of the other implementations or even provide your own custom implementation if none of the out-of-the-box implementations meets your needs. The PasswordEncoder interface is simple. You need to check casing and maintain consistency.

```
public interface PasswordEncoder {
  String encode(CharSequence rawPassword);
  boolean matches(CharSequence rawPassword, String encodedPassword);
}
```

You can register your own custom password encoder in the same way as we have done in the previous example.

We have seen that Spring Security provides great solutions to the REST APIs for authentication and authorization for the Spring-based application. Previously, we discussed the simplest approach to utilize the HTTP basic authentication mechanism to secure your REST APIs. But sometimes, this mechanism is not suitable for the application which has separate frontend application in either ReactJS or in Angular. The HTTP basic authentication mechanism is good for development purpose and not fit for the production environment.

Securing your REST APIs using Spring Security and JWT

In this section, the custom **JSON Web Tokens (JWT)** will be used in our application instead of the HTTP basic authentication. JWT is used to implement authentication in the modern RESTful application. This token is small in size and it can be sent via a URL as well in the POST request parameter, and we can also send it inside the request header. This JWT contains all the required information about the user that contains the claims between the client and secured resource.

Now, we are going to use Spring Security and JWT in our RESTful application (PRODOS). Let's add the following Maven dependencies to the Maven configuration file of our application to implement the Spring Boot Security with the JWT token by accessing the database:

```
<dependency>
  <groupId>org.springframework.boot</groupId>
  <artifactId>spring-boot-starter-security</artifactId>
</dependency>


<dependency>
  <groupId>io.jsonwebtoken</groupId>
  <artifactId>jjwt</artifactId>
  <version>0.9.0</version>
</dependency>
```

The preceding Maven dependencies add Spring Security and JWT libraries to your RESTful web application. Now, Spring Security and JWT are available in the classpath of your application.

This application needs to follow the given steps to implement Spring Security with JWT:

1. First, we need to get the JWT-based token using the created endpoint (/auth/login).

2. The endpoint /auth/login will provide the response with the JWT token. You need to extract the token from the response.

3. Now, you can set this JWT token to the HTTP header authorization value as Bearer jwt_token.

4. Let's access the protected resources by sending an HTTP request to REST API.

5. If the accessed REST API is secured, then Spring Security will use the configured custom filter to validate the JWT token available in the request header.

6. If the JWT token is valid, then build an Authentication object and put this Authentication object to the Spring Security specific SecurityContextHolder object to complete the authentication progress.

7. After completing the authentication process, your client application can access the requested resource.

Let's see the following application structure after implementing Spring Security with JWT:

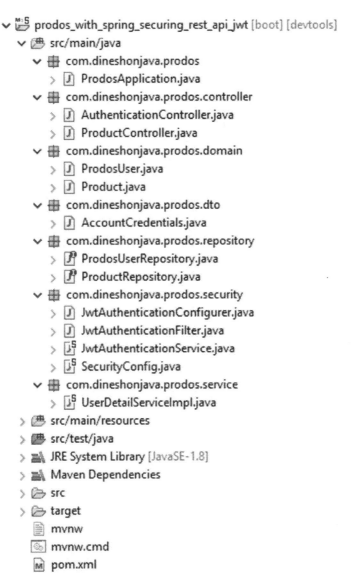

Figure 5.8: The Prodos REST application structure with Spring Security and JWT.

Now, we will discuss the newly created classes for enabling the JWT authentication in our REST APIs.

Let's create a new class called JwtAuthenticationService in the com.dineshonjava.prodos. security package as shown in the following code snippet:

```
package com.dineshonjava.prodos.security;


import java.util.Base64;
```

```java
import java.util.Date;
import java.util.List;

import javax.servlet.http.HttpServletRequest;

import org.springframework.beans.factory.annotation.Autowired;
import org.springframework.security.authentication.UsernamePasswordAuthenticationToken;
import org.springframework.security.core.Authentication;
import org.springframework.security.core.userdetails.UserDetails;
import org.springframework.stereotype.Component;

import com.dineshonjava.prodos.service.UserDetailServiceImpl;

import io.jsonwebtoken.Claims;
import io.jsonwebtoken.Jws;
import io.jsonwebtoken.JwtException;
import io.jsonwebtoken.Jwts;
import io.jsonwebtoken.SignatureAlgorithm;

/**
 * @author Dinesh.Rajput
 *
 */
@Component
public class JwtAuthenticationService {

  private static final String SECRETKEY = Base64.getEncoder().encodeToString("ProdosSecretZKey"
  .getBytes());;

  private static final String PREFIX = "Bearer";

  private static final String EMPTY = "";

  private static final long EXPIRATIONTIME = 86400000; //1 day in milliseconds

  private static final String AUTHORIZATION = "Authorization";

  @Autowired
```

```java
private UserDetailServiceImpl userDetailsService;

public String createToken(String username, List<String> roles) {

  Claims claims = Jwts.claims().setSubject(username);
  claims.put("roles", roles);

  Date now = new Date();
  Date validity = new Date(now.getTime() + EXPIRATIONTIME);

  return Jwts.builder()
    .setClaims(claims)
    .setIssuedAt(now)
    .setExpiration(validity)
    .signWith(SignatureAlgorithm.HS256, SECRETKEY)
    .compact();
}

public Authentication getAuthentication(HttpServletRequest request) {
  String token = resolveToken(request);
  if(token != null && validateToken(token)) {
  String username = getUsername(token);
  if(username != null) {
    UserDetails userDetails = this.userDetailsService.loadUserByUsername(username);
    return new UsernamePasswordAuthenticationToken(userDetails, null, userDetails.
getAuthorities());
  }
  }
  return null;
}

private String getUsername(String token) {
  return Jwts.parser()
    .setSigningKey(SECRETKEY)
    .parseClaimsJws(token)
    .getBody().getSubject();
}
```

```
private String resolveToken(HttpServletRequest req) {
 String bearerToken = req.getHeader(AUTHORIZATION);
 if (bearerToken != null && bearerToken.startsWith(PREFIX)) {
  return bearerToken.replace(PREFIX, EMPTY).trim();
 }
 return null;
}


private boolean validateToken(String token) {
 try {
  Jws<Claims> claims = Jwts.parser().setSigningKey(SECRETKEY).parseClaimsJws(token);

  if (claims.getBody().getExpiration().before(new Date())) {
   return false;
  }

  return true;
 } catch (JwtException | IllegalArgumentException e) {
  throw new IllegalArgumentException("Expired or invalid JWT token");
 }
}
}
```

In the preceding class, we defined a few constants such as EXPIRATIONTIME and SECRETKEY. The EXPIRATIONTIME defines the token validity time in milliseconds and SECRETKEY is used as a secret key to digitally sign the JWT token. Here, we created the SECRETKEY using a base64 encoded string. Another constant is PREFIX that defines the prefix of the token. Here, we defined PREFIX with the Bearer.

The createToken() method creates the JWT token and returns it to a caller. Also, the base64 encoded SECRETKEY is added to this token using the signWith() method and this signing key is again encoded with the SHA-512 algorithm. We also set the token creation and expiration time with the JWT token using the setIssuedAt() and setExpiration() methods, respectively. The setClaims() method is used to set the JWT payload using the Claims instance. This Claims instance has a username and the defined roles of the user.

The getAuthentication() method is used by the JwtAuthenticationFilter class to authenticate using the JWT token available in the header of the requests. We will discuss the JwtAuthenticationFilter class a little later.

The other methods are used to validate and resolve a token when a client makes a call the secured REST API.

Next, we need to create a simple POJO class for working as DTO to keep your credentials for the authentication process. Let's create a new class called AccountCredentials in the com.dineshonjava.prodos.dto package as shown in the following code:

```
package com.dineshonjava.prodos.dto;

import java.io.Serializable;

public class AccountCredentials implements Serializable{

  private static final long serialVersionUID = 1L;

  private String username;
  private String password;

  public String getUsername() {
    return username;
  }
  public void setUsername(String username) {
    this.username = username;
  }
  public String getPassword() {
    return password;
  }
  public void setPassword(String password) {
    this.password = password;
  }
}
```

The preceding AccountCredentials class has two fields, username and password. These fields are used to keep user credentials from the client. This AccountCredentials class is used by the following controller class:

```
package com.dineshonjava.prodos.controller;

import static org.springframework.http.ResponseEntity.ok;
import java.util.ArrayList;
import java.util.HashMap;
```

```
import java.util.List;
import java.util.Map;
import org.springframework.beans.factory.annotation.Autowired;
import org.springframework.http.ResponseEntity;
import org.springframework.security.authentication.AuthenticationManager;
import org.springframework.security.authentication.BadCredentialsException;
import org.springframework.security.authentication.UsernamePasswordAuthenticationToken;
import org.springframework.security.core.AuthenticationException;
import org.springframework.security.core.userdetails.UsernameNotFoundException;
import org.springframework.web.bind.annotation.PostMapping;
import org.springframework.web.bind.annotation.RequestBody;
import org.springframework.web.bind.annotation.RestController;

import com.dineshonjava.prodos.dto.AccountCredentials;
import com.dineshonjava.prodos.repository.ProdosUserRepository;
import com.dineshonjava.prodos.security.JwtAuthenticationService;

@RestController
public class AuthenticationController {

    @Autowired
    AuthenticationManager authenticationManager;

    @Autowired
    JwtAuthenticationService jwtAuthenticationService;

    @Autowired
    ProdosUserRepository prodosUserRepository;

    @PostMapping("/auth/login")
    public ResponseEntity<Map<Object, Object>> signin(@RequestBody AccountCredentials
    credentials) {

      try {
        authenticationManager.authenticate(
            new UsernamePasswordAuthenticationToken(credentials.getUsername(), credentials.
        getPassword()));
```

```
    List<String> list = new ArrayList<>();

    list.add(this.prodosUserRepository.findByUsername(credentials.getUsername())
      .orElseThrow(
        () -> new UsernameNotFoundException("Username " + credentials.getUsername() + "not
found"))
      .getRole());

    String token = jwtAuthenticationService.createToken(credentials.getUsername(), list);

    Map<Object, Object> model = new HashMap<>();
    model.put("username", credentials.getUsername());
    model.put("token", token);
    return ok(model);
  } catch (AuthenticationException e) {
    throw new BadCredentialsException("Invalid username/password supplied");

  }
 }

}
```

The preceding AuthenticationController class is a rest controller class. This class is used for login and authentication. This class handles the POST requests to the /auth/login endpoint. This controller class has a login() method which takes the AccountCredentials object as an argument. In this class, we have used AuthenticationManager to authenticate the user using the username and password.

After the successful authentication using the authenticate() method of the AuthenticationManager class, which takes an instance of the UsernamePasswordAuthenticationToken class as a constructor argument, this login() method creates a JWT token for the authenticated user using the createToken() method of the JwtAuthenticationService class. We have autowired the JwtAuthenticationService class with the controller class.

Finally, the login() method returns the username and generates the JWT token with ok() of the ResponseEntity object.

Further, let's create a new filter class called JwtAuthenticationFilter in the com. dineshonjava.prodos.security package as shown in the following code:

```
package com.dineshonjava.prodos.security;


import java.io.IOException;
```

```java
import javax.servlet.FilterChain;
import javax.servlet.ServletException;
import javax.servlet.ServletRequest;
import javax.servlet.ServletResponse;
import javax.servlet.http.HttpServletRequest;
import org.springframework.security.core.Authentication;
import org.springframework.security.core.context.SecurityContextHolder;
import org.springframework.web.filter.GenericFilterBean;

public class JwtAuthenticationFilter extends GenericFilterBean {

    private JwtAuthenticationService jwtAuthenticationService;

    public JwtAuthenticationFilter(JwtAuthenticationService jwtAuthenticationService) {
        this.jwtAuthenticationService = jwtAuthenticationService;
    }

    @Override
    public void doFilter(ServletRequest request, ServletResponse response, FilterChain filterChain)
        throws IOException, ServletException {

    Authentication authentication = jwtAuthenticationService.getAuthentication((HttpServletRequest) request);
    SecurityContextHolder.getContext().setAuthentication(authentication);
        filterChain.doFilter(request, response);
    }
}
```

The previously created JwtAuthenticationFilter class extends the GenericFilterBean class. The Spring web module provides the GenericFilterBean class as a generic superclass for any type of filter. The JwtAuthenticationFilter class will handle the authentication in all the other endpoints except the /auth/login endpoint. This class overrides the doFilter() method and this method fetches the Authentication object using the getAuthentication() method of the JwtAuthenticationService class. We need to pass the HttpServletRequest object as an argument to the getAuthentication() method. The returned authentication object will be added to the SecurityContext object.

Let's create the SecurityConfigurer implementation to apply our own custom configure class. The following is a configurer class for overriding any default SecurityConfigurer:

```
package com.dineshonjava.prodos.security;

import org.springframework.security.config.annotation.SecurityConfigurerAdapter;
import org.springframework.security.config.annotation.web.builders.HttpSecurity;
import org.springframework.security.web.DefaultSecurityFilterChain;
import org.springframework.security.web.authentication.UsernamePasswordAuthenticationFilter;

/**
 * @author Dinesh.Rajput
 *
 */
public class JwtAuthenticationConfigurer extends SecurityConfigurerAdapter<DefaultSecurityFilte
rChain, HttpSecurity> {

  private JwtAuthenticationService jwtAuthenticationService;

  public JwtAuthenticationConfigurer(JwtAuthenticationService jwtAuthenticationService) {
    this.jwtAuthenticationService = jwtAuthenticationService;
  }

  @Override
  public void configure(HttpSecurity http) throws Exception {
    JwtAuthenticationFilter jwtAuthenticationFilter = new JwtAuthenticationFilter(jwtAuthenticati
onService);
    http.addFilterBefore(jwtAuthenticationFilter, UsernamePasswordAuthenticationFilter.class);
  }
}
```

As you can see, we created a custom configurer class to apply your own custom filter that is JwtAuthenticationFilter. The JwtAuthenticationConfigurer class extends SecurityConfigurerAdapter which is a base class for SecurityConfigurer. It allows you to implement the methods you want to customize. You can apply this JwtAuthenticationConfigurer class to the SecurityBuilder object. The one configured in your security configuration class is SecurityConfig.

Let's see the changed SecurityConfig class from the previous example with the basic HTTP authentication as shown in the following code:

```
package com.dineshonjava.prodos.security;
```

```java
import org.springframework.beans.factory.annotation.Autowired;
import org.springframework.context.annotation.Bean;
import org.springframework.context.annotation.Configuration;
import org.springframework.http.HttpMethod;
import org.springframework.security.authentication.AuthenticationManager;
import org.springframework.security.config.annotation.authentication.builders.
AuthenticationManagerBuilder;
import org.springframework.security.config.annotation.web.builders.HttpSecurity;
import org.springframework.security.config.annotation.web.configuration.EnableWebSecurity;
import org.springframework.security.config.annotation.web.configuration.
WebSecurityConfigurerAdapter;
import org.springframework.security.config.http.SessionCreationPolicy;
import org.springframework.security.crypto.bcrypt.BCryptPasswordEncoder;

import com.dineshonjava.prodos.service.UserDetailServiceImpl;

/**
 * @author Dinesh.Rajput
 *
 */

@Configuration
@EnableWebSecurity
public class SecurityConfig extends WebSecurityConfigurerAdapter {

  @Autowired
  UserDetailServiceImpl userDetailsService;

  @Autowired
   JwtAuthenticationService jwtAuthenticationService;

  @Bean
   @Override
   public AuthenticationManager authenticationManagerBean() throws Exception {
     return super.authenticationManagerBean();
 }

  @Override
```

```
protected void configure(HttpSecurity http) throws Exception {
  http
  .authorizeRequests().antMatchers(HttpMethod.POST, "/auth/login").permitAll()
    .anyRequest().authenticated().and().apply(new JwtAuthenticationConfigurer(jwtAuthenticatio
nService))
    .and().csrf().disable().httpBasic().disable()
    .sessionManagement().sessionCreationPolicy(SessionCreationPolicy.STATELESS);
  }

  @Autowired
  public void configure(AuthenticationManagerBuilder auth) throws Exception {
    auth.userDetailsService(userDetailsService).passwordEncoder(new BCryptPasswordEncoder());
  }
}
```

In the preceding security configuration class, we made some changes to the configure(HttpSecurity http) method. We allowed the POST method request to the /auth/login endpoint without authentication. Other endpoints except /auth/login need authentication. And we also applied JwtAuthenticationConfigurer using the apply() method to configure our own custom filter that is JwtAuthenticationFilter. We disabled the HTTP basic authentication mechanism which we have used in the previous example. Also, we disabled the CSRF mechanism. We are not managing any session for our RESTful API application and that is why we set a STATELESS session creation policy.

Now, we configured Spring Security with JWT in our REST application. Let's run the application and call the /auth/login endpoint with the POST method using the Postman. You will get a JWT token in the response body as shown in the following screenshot:

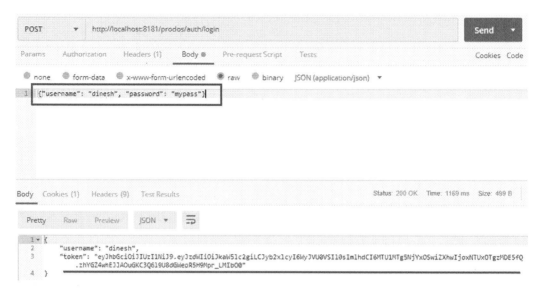

Figure 5.9: The JWT token created using the /auth/login endpoint.

As you can see in the preceding screenshot, the API /auth/login returned a JWT token for the username, dinesh. You can see the following example of a JWT token:

eyJhbGciOiJIUzI1NiJ9. eyJzdWIiOiJkaW5lc2giLCJyb2xlcyI6WyJVU0VSIl0sImlhdCI6-
MTU1MTg5NjYxOSwiZXhwIjoxNTUxOTgzMDE5fQ.zhYGZ4whEJJAOuGKC3Q6l9U8dGWeoR5H9-
Mpr_LMIbO0

The JWT token contains the following three different parts separated by dots:

- The first part is the header that defines the type of the token and the hashing algorithm.

- The second part is the payload that, typically, in the case of authentication, contains information about the user.

- The third part is the signature that is used to verify that the token hasn't been changed along the way.

After successfully getting the JWT token, you can use this JWT token to set the Bearer token in the authorization before calling the REST API http://localhost:8181/prodos/products. If you send this JWT token, then you can receive the product list as shown in the following screenshot:

Figure 5.10: The REST API call with the JWT token.

We have seen how the JWT token is passed to the request header to call a REST API. Let's see the following diagram which shows the functionality of the JWT authentication process:

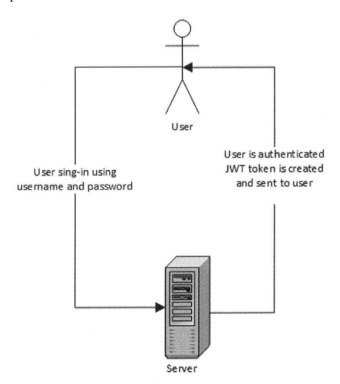

Figure 5.11: The JWT token authentication process in the REST API application.

As you can see in the preceding diagram, a user provides a username and password.

We implemented Spring Security in our PRODOS RESTful application to secure our REST APIs using the HTTP basic authentication mechanism, and we also used Spring Security with the JWT token mechanism for the authentication and authorization. However, these authentication mechanisms are also very popular but the OAuth2 support of the Spring Framework is very widely used in the industries. Let's see this in the next section.

Securing your REST APIs with Spring Security and OAuth2

The OAuth2 framework is a very popular authorization framework and widely used to secure REST APIs. The Spring framework provides good support for this authorization framework. In this section, we will implement a security mechanism using Spring Security and OAuth2 with JWT.

You can add Spring Security and OAuth2 with the JWT token store in your application classpath by adding the following Maven dependencies:

```
<dependency>
  <groupId>org.springframework.boot</groupId>
  <artifactId>spring-boot-starter-security</artifactId>
</dependency>
<dependency>
  <groupId>org.springframework.security.oauth</groupId>
  <artifactId>spring-security-oauth2</artifactId>
</dependency>
<dependency>
  <groupId>org.springframework.security</groupId>
  <artifactId>spring-security-jwt</artifactId>
</dependency>
```

Currently, Spring Boot doesn't provide any starter for the OAuth2 framework. You can take advantage of the Spring Boot auto-configuration feature by adding the following dependency to your application:

```
<dependency>
  <groupId>org.springframework.security.oauth.boot</groupId>
  <artifactId>spring-security-oauth2-autoconfigure</artifactId>
</dependency>
```

The preceding spring-security-oauth2-autoconfigure dependency allows you to externalize the OAuth2 configuration. Let's see some key components related to the OAuth2 architecture.

Key components for the OAuth2 architecture

Before implementing the OAuth2 architecture in our application, let's discuss some important key components of the OAuth2 architecture as shown in the following screenshot:

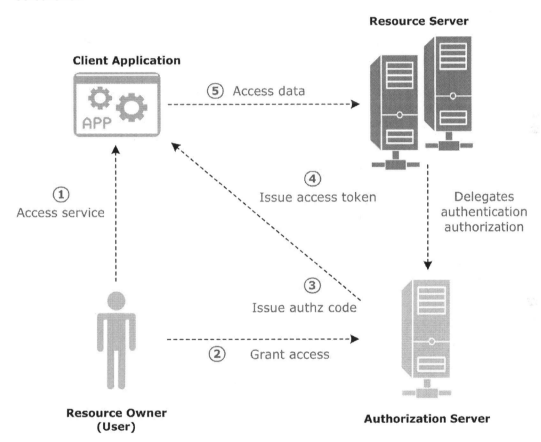

Figure 5.12: The diagram of an OAuth2 architecture.

An authorization server

An authorization server is the most important architectural component of the OAuth2 security mechanism for the API security implementation. This authorization server works to authorize the requests and it is a centralization authorization point for the authentication and authorization. This server provides the access token and other details to the client application based on the credentials provided by the client application. The client id and client secret key must be provided by the client before calling the authorization server.

Resource server

The Resource server is another key component of the OAuth2 authentication mechanism. This server allows the client application to access the resources using the access token. This means that you need a resource server to use the access token. The resource server can also be the same as the authorization server.

OAuth2

OAuth2 is an authorization framework. It can be used to enable web security to the application to access the resources from the client. The OAuth2 application server focuses on the grant type (authorization code), client ID, and client secret.

According to the OAuth2 documentation,

The OAuth 2.0 framework enables a third-party application to obtain limited access to an HTTP service, either on behalf of a resource owner by orchestrating an approval interaction between resource owner and HTTP service, or by allowing the third-party application to obtain access on its own behalf.

OAuth2 tokens

Tokens are implemented by the authorization server based on the provided credentials. There are two types of OAuth2 tokens, which are as follows:

- Access token: This token is used by each request and sent to the resource server. This token has validity for about an hour only but you can configure it according to your requirement.

- Refresh token: This token is used to get the new access token.

But in our application, we are using the **JWT token (JSON Web Token)**. It is used to represent the claims secured between two parties. A JWT token consists of three parts separated with a dot (.), that is, Header.payload.signature.

Resource owner: This is a user and an owner of the resource. Let's see the flow diagram of the OAuth2 framework.

The OAuth2 authorization flow diagram

Let's see the following flow diagram of the OAuth2 authorization framework:

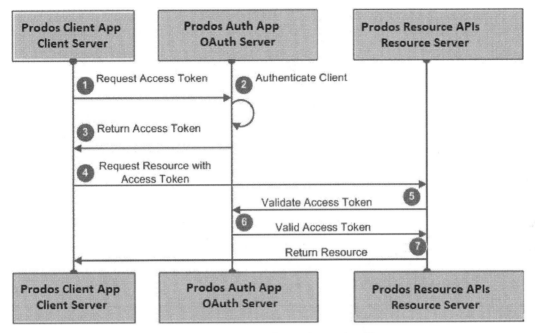

Figure 5.13: The OAuth2 authorization flow

As you can see in the preceding OAuth2 security flow diagram, there are three components **Client Server**, **OAuth Server**, and **Resource Server**. Let's see the flow:

1. **Prodos Client App** sends a request to the **Prodos OAuth App** server to access a token based on the credentials provided by the **Prodos Client App**.

2. The OAuth server authenticates the **Prodos Client App** as per the provided credentials.

3. **The Prodos OAuth Server** application returns an access token to the **Prodos Client App**.

4. Now, the **Prodos Client Application** sends a request with an access token for a protected resource to the **Prodos Resource Server** application.

5. The **Resource Server** validates the access token by sending the access token to the **OAuth Server** application.

6. The **OAuth Server** application validates the access token.

7. After validating the access token, the **Resource Server** application returns the protected resource.

Let's start the OAuth2 implementation with Spring Boot Security and the JWT token to secure our **Prodos Application** REST APIs.

Implementing the OAuth2 Server with Spring Boot Security

We are going to implement a **Prodos OAuth Server** application to provide the access token. Let's see the following project structure for the **OAuth Server** application:

```
∨ 🗂 prodos_with_spring_security_oauth2_server_app [boot] [devtools]
  ∨ 🗁 src/main/java
    ∨ ⊞ com.dineshonjava.prodos.security
      > ⬢ AuthServerApplication.java
    ∨ ⊞ com.dineshonjava.prodos.security.config
      > ⬢ AuthorizationServerConfig.java
      > ⬢ ResourceServerConfig.java
      > ⬢ SecurityConfig.java
    ∨ ⊞ com.dineshonjava.prodos.security.controller
      > ⬢ UserController.java
    ∨ ⊞ com.dineshonjava.prodos.security.domain
      > ⬢ ProdosUser.java
    ∨ ⊞ com.dineshonjava.prodos.security.repository
      > ⬢ ProdosUserRepository.java
    ∨ ⊞ com.dineshonjava.prodos.security.service
      > ⬢ UserDetailServiceImpl.java
  > 🗁 src/main/resources
  > 🗁 src/test/java
  > ▨ JRE System Library [JavaSE-1.8]
  > ▨ Maven Dependencies
  > 🗁 src
  > 🗁 target
    📄 mvnw
    📄 mvnw.cmd
    📄 pom.xml
```

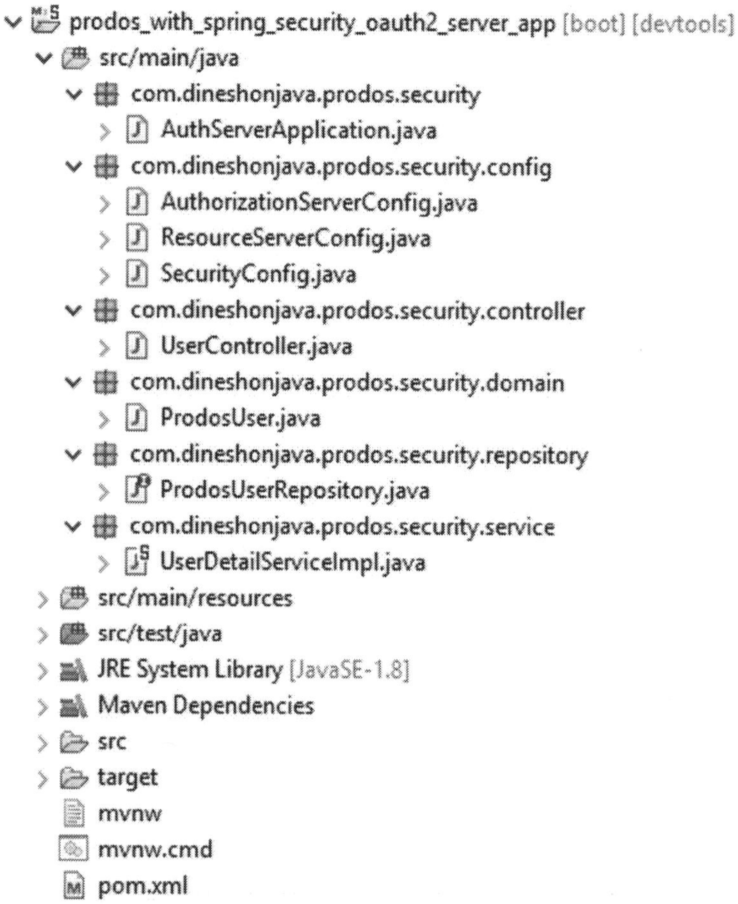

Figure 5.14: The OAuth2 server project structure

In the preceding application, we are using the JWT token store with the OAuth2 framework instead of the default token store. For the JWT token, you need to add the following Maven dependency:

```
<dependency>
 <groupId>org.springframework.security</groupId>
```

```
<artifactId>spring-security-jwt</artifactId>
</dependency>
```

Let's discuss the authorization server configuration files.

Authorization server configuration

The following class will provide the configuration to the authorization server application:

```
package com.dineshonjava.prodos.security.config;

import org.springframework.beans.factory.annotation.Autowired;
import org.springframework.context.annotation.Bean;
import org.springframework.context.annotation.Configuration;
import org.springframework.security.authentication.AuthenticationManager;
import org.springframework.security.crypto.bcrypt.BCryptPasswordEncoder;
import org.springframework.security.oauth2.config.annotation.configurers.
ClientDetailsServiceConfigurer;
import org.springframework.security.oauth2.config.annotation.web.configuration.
AuthorizationServerConfigurerAdapter;
import org.springframework.security.oauth2.config.annotation.web.configuration.
EnableAuthorizationServer;
import org.springframework.security.oauth2.config.annotation.web.configurers.
AuthorizationServerEndpointsConfigurer;
import org.springframework.security.oauth2.config.annotation.web.configurers.
AuthorizationServerSecurityConfigurer;
import org.springframework.security.oauth2.provider.token.store.JwtAccessTokenConverter;
import org.springframework.security.oauth2.provider.token.store.JwtTokenStore;

@Configuration
@EnableAuthorizationServer
public class AuthorizationServerConfig extends AuthorizationServerConfigurerAdapter{

  static final String CLIEN_ID = "dineshonjava";
  static final String CLIENT_SECRET = "$2a$04$TJmCr9KA4dRF1Gir.zQ1TO/
q9qELju1EzDpYhFBlbjxevCI7HZY5G";
  static final String GRANT_TYPE_PASSWORD = "password";
  static final String AUTHORIZATION_CODE = "authorization_code";
   static final String REFRESH_TOKEN = "refresh_token";
   static final String IMPLICIT = "implicit";
```

```java
static final String SCOPE_READ = "read";
static final String SCOPE_WRITE = "write";
  static final String TRUST = "trust";
static final int ACCESS_TOKEN_VALIDITY_SECONDS = 1*60*60;
  static final int FREFRESH_TOKEN_VALIDITY_SECONDS = 6*60*60;
private String privateKey = "111dinesh000";

@Autowired
private AuthenticationManager authenticationManager;

@Autowired
BCryptPasswordEncoder encoder;

@Bean
public JwtAccessTokenConverter tokenEnhancer() {
  JwtAccessTokenConverter converter = new JwtAccessTokenConverter();
  converter.setSigningKey(privateKey);
  return converter;
}

@Bean
public JwtTokenStore tokenStore() {
  return new JwtTokenStore(tokenEnhancer());
}

@Override
public void configure(AuthorizationServerEndpointsConfigurer endpoints) throws Exception {
  endpoints.authenticationManager(authenticationManager).tokenStore(tokenStore())
  .accessTokenConverter(tokenEnhancer());
}

@Override
public void configure(AuthorizationServerSecurityConfigurer security) throws Exception {
  security.tokenKeyAccess("permitAll()").checkTokenAccess("isAuthenticated()").
passwordEncoder(encoder);
  }

@Override
```

```
public void configure(ClientDetailsServiceConfigurer clients) throws Exception {
  clients.inMemory()
  .withClient(CLIEN_ID)
  .secret(CLIENT_SECRET)
  .authorizedGrantTypes(GRANT_TYPE_PASSWORD, AUTHORIZATION_CODE, REFRESH_TOKEN,
IMPLICIT )
  .scopes(SCOPE_READ, SCOPE_WRITE, TRUST)
  .accessTokenValiditySeconds(ACCESS_TOKEN_VALIDITY_SECONDS)
  .refreshTokenValiditySeconds(FREFRESH_TOKEN_VALIDITY_SECONDS);
 }
}
```

In the preceding authorization server configuration, we are using the JwtAccessTokenConverter and JwtTokenStore beans. These classes are helper classes used to provide JWT tokens based on the OAuth authentication information. We also added a private key to make the JWT token more robust. In this example, we are using the JwtTokenStore beans but Spring Security also provides you InMemoryTokenStore and JdbcTokenStore.

We override the configure(ClientDetailsServiceConfigurer clients) method. This method takes a ClientDetailsServiceConfigurer object as an argument. The ClientDetailsServiceConfigurer class is a configurer class that defines the client details service. In our example, we used the inMemory() method client details service implementation. Spring Security also provides the jdbc() method for the client details service implementation instead of the inMemory() client details implementation.

The AuthorizationServerSecurityConfigurer class is another configurer class that defines the security constraints on the token endpoint.

The authorization server configuration class also configured the AuthorizationServerEndpointsConfigurer class and that defines the authorization and token endpoints and the token services.

Here, we are not going to discuss each file of the authorization server application. All the other files are very similar to the ones we used in the previous examples. You can find the whole source code of the authorization server application from GitHub (https://github.com/dineshonjava/bpb-spring-boot-reactjs).

Let's create the resource server configuration files.

Implementing the resource server with Spring Boot Security

We will implement a **Prodos Resource Server** application to provide the protected resource EndPoints using the access token. Let's see the following project structure for the **Resource Server** application:

Figure 5.15: The resource server project structure

Let's discuss the resource server configuration files.

Resource server configuration

The following class will provide the configuration to the resource server application:

```
package com.dineshonjava.prodos.security.config;

import org.springframework.context.annotation.Configuration;
import org.springframework.security.config.annotation.web.builders.HttpSecurity;
import org.springframework.security.oauth2.config.annotation.web.configuration.
EnableResourceServer;
import org.springframework.security.oauth2.config.annotation.web.configuration.
ResourceServerConfigurerAdapter;
import org.springframework.security.oauth2.config.annotation.web.configurers.
ResourceServerSecurityConfigurer;
import org.springframework.security.oauth2.provider.error.OAuth2AccessDeniedHandler;

@Configuration
@EnableResourceServer
public class ResourceServerConfig extends ResourceServerConfigurerAdapter{

  private static final String RESOURCE_ID = "resource_id";

  @Override
  public void configure(ResourceServerSecurityConfigurer resources) {
    resources.resourceId(RESOURCE_ID).stateless(false);
  }

  @Override
  public void configure(HttpSecurity http) throws Exception {
    http.
        anonymous().disable()
        .authorizeRequests()
        .antMatchers("/products/**").access("hasRole('USER')")
        .and().exceptionHandling().accessDeniedHandler(new OAuth2AccessDeniedHandler());
  }
}
```

The preceding class is annotated with the @EnableResourceServer annotation. It is used for OAuth2 resource servers and it enables a Spring Security filter that authenticates requests via an incoming OAuth2 token.

In our case, the resource application is an application which provides REST APIs to perform CRUD operations. But you need to pass the access token to call the REST API of the resource server.

Let's configure the Spring Security in the resource application using the following security configuration file:

```
package com.dineshonjava.prodos.security;

import org.springframework.beans.factory.annotation.Autowired;
import org.springframework.boot.autoconfigure.security.oauth2.resource.
ResourceServerProperties;
import org.springframework.context.annotation.Bean;
import org.springframework.context.annotation.Configuration;
import org.springframework.security.authentication.AuthenticationManager;
import org.springframework.security.config.annotation.authentication.builders.
AuthenticationManagerBuilder;
import org.springframework.security.config.annotation.web.builders.HttpSecurity;
import org.springframework.security.config.annotation.web.configuration.EnableWebSecurity;
import org.springframework.security.config.annotation.web.configuration.
WebSecurityConfigurerAdapter;
import org.springframework.security.config.http.SessionCreationPolicy;
import org.springframework.security.oauth2.config.annotation.web.configuration.
EnableResourceServer;
import org.springframework.security.web.authentication.www.BasicAuthenticationFilter;


@Configuration
@EnableResourceServer
@EnableWebSecurity
public class ResourceServerSecurityConfig extends WebSecurityConfigurerAdapter {

  @Autowired
  ResourceServerProperties resourceServerProperties;

  @Bean
   @Override
   public AuthenticationManager authenticationManagerBean() throws Exception {
```

```
    return super.authenticationManagerBean();
}


@Override
protected void configure(HttpSecurity http) throws Exception {
 http
 .authorizeRequests()
  .anyRequest().authenticated()
 .and()
  .addFilterBefore(new OAuth2AuthenticationFilter(), BasicAuthenticationFilter.class)
  .csrf().disable()
  .httpBasic().disable()
  .sessionManagement().sessionCreationPolicy(SessionCreationPolicy.STATELESS);
}


@Autowired
public void configureGlobal(AuthenticationManagerBuilder auth) throws Exception {
  auth.authenticationProvider(new OAuth2AuthenticationProvider(resourceServerProperties));
 }
}
```

As you can see in the preceding configuration file, we used a custom OAuth2AuthenticationFilter file to resolve the access token passed by the client application. Let's see the code of the custom filter:

```
package com.dineshonjava.prodos.security;

import java.io.IOException;
import javax.servlet.FilterChain;
import javax.servlet.ServletException;
import javax.servlet.ServletRequest;
import javax.servlet.ServletResponse;
import javax.servlet.http.HttpServletRequest;
import org.springframework.security.core.Authentication;
import org.springframework.security.core.context.SecurityContextHolder;
import org.springframework.util.StringUtils;
import org.springframework.web.filter.GenericFilterBean;
```

```
public class OAuth2AuthenticationFilter extends GenericFilterBean {

  private static final String AUTHORIZATION = "Authorization";
  private static final String PREFIX = "Bearer";
  private static final String EMPTY = "";

  @Override
  public void doFilter(ServletRequest request, ServletResponse response, FilterChain filterChain)
   throws IOException, ServletException {

  String accessToken = ((HttpServletRequest) request).getHeader(AUTHORIZATION);
  if (accessToken != null && accessToken.startsWith(PREFIX)) {
    accessToken= accessToken.replace(PREFIX, EMPTY).trim();
  }
  if(!StringUtils.isEmpty(accessToken)) {
    Authentication auth = new OAuth2AuthenticationToken(accessToken);
    SecurityContextHolder.getContext().setAuthentication(auth);
  }
  filterChain.doFilter(request, response);
  }
}
```

The previous filter will be applied before calling the actual controller class, and this filter resolves the Authentication object from the access token using the OAuth2AuthenticationToken class. We will also create a custom authentication provider to provide the authentication using the access token, and this class will call the authorization server to validate the access token.

We will define the user info URI in the resource server application configuration file as shown in the following code:

```
# *******OAuth Config*******

security.oauth2.resource.user-info-uri=http://localhost:8282/prodos_auth_srvr/user
```

Here, we are not going to discuss each class of the resource server application. You can find the complete source code of the Resource Server application from GitHub at https://github.com/dineshonjava/bpb-spring-boot-reactjs.

Let's test our OAuth2 application to secure our REST APIs. First, run the authorization server application. Then, generate the tokens. We will use the Postman and make a POST request at http://localhost:8282/prodos_auth_srvr/oauth/token. Let's take a look at the following screenshot:

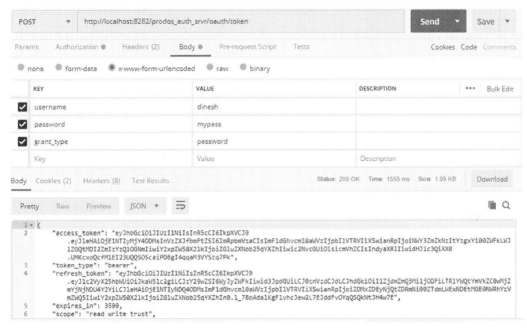

Figure 5.16: Generating tokens

As you can see in the preceding screenshot, we selected basic Auth and provided the username and password as dineshonjava and encoded the secret client key. Also, we provided the other parameters such as the username, password, and grant type. After sending the POST request, this will result in access_token, token_type, refresh_token, expiry, and so on.

Now, you can use the generated access token to consume the protected REST API on the resource server application as shown in the following screenshot:

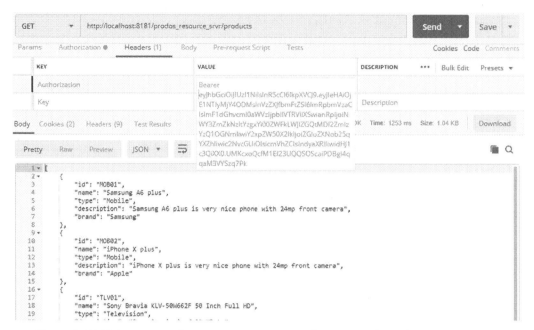

Figure 5.17: Using access tokens to consume protect the resource from the Resource Server

As you can see in the preceding screenshot, we used the generated access token with a GET request to the resource server to fetch a protected resource. We set the access token in the header as a Bearer token.

Implementing the client-server application

We will now implement a **Prodos Client-Server** application. This application will consume REST APIs hosted at the resource server application. The client application will send the access token to access the protected resource end points. Let's see the following project structure for the client server application:

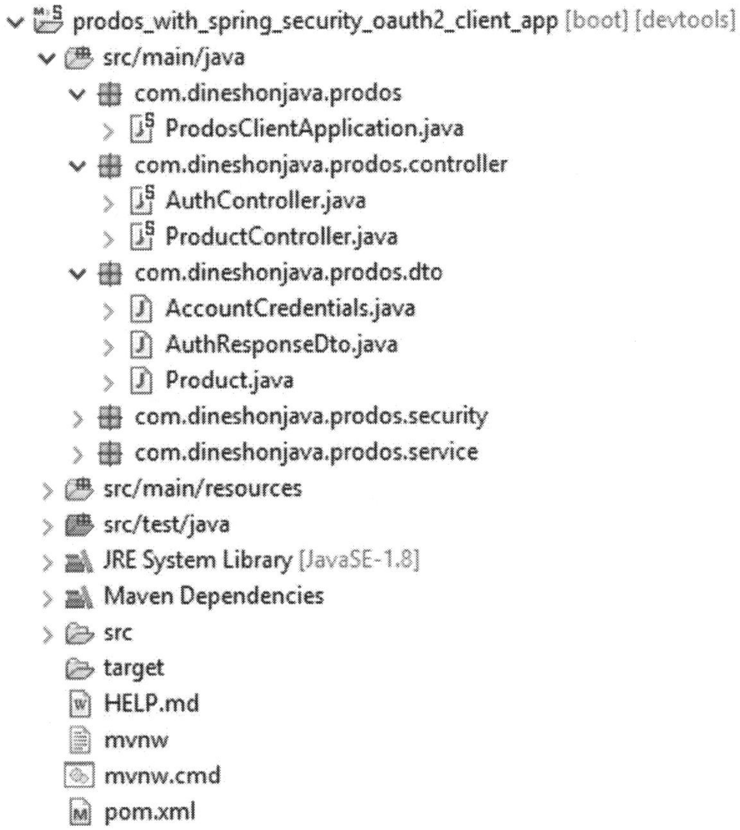

```
∨ 🗂 prodos_with_spring_security_oauth2_client_app [boot] [devtools]
   ∨ 📁 src/main/java
      ∨ ⊞ com.dineshonjava.prodos
         > 🗐 ProdosClientApplication.java
      ∨ ⊞ com.dineshonjava.prodos.controller
         > 🗐 AuthController.java
         > 🗐 ProductController.java
      ∨ ⊞ com.dineshonjava.prodos.dto
         > 🗐 AccountCredentials.java
         > 🗐 AuthResponseDto.java
         > 🗐 Product.java
      > ⊞ com.dineshonjava.prodos.security
      > ⊞ com.dineshonjava.prodos.service
   > 📁 src/main/resources
   > 📁 src/test/java
   > 📚 JRE System Library [JavaSE-1.8]
   > 📚 Maven Dependencies
   > 📂 src
     📂 target
     📄 HELP.md
     📄 mvnw
     📄 mvnw.cmd
     📄 pom.xml
```

Figure 5.18: The client application structure

Let's see the application configuration file of the client application:

server.servlet.context-path=/prodosapp
server.port=9000

spring.thymeleaf.cache=false

*******OAuth Config*******
security.oauth2.client.access-token-uri=http://localhost:8282/prodos_auth_srvr/oauth/token
security.oauth2.client.user-authorization-uri=http://localhost:8282/prodos_auth_srvr/oauth/authorize
security.oauth2.client.client-id=dineshonjava
security.oauth2.client.client-secret=dineshonjava

As you can see, we configured the access token URI and user authorization URI. The client application will provide the username and password to the Auth server application to get the access token and this token is used to pass the resource server to get the protected resource.

Let's see the following controller class that is responsible to get the access token from the Auth server:

package com.dineshonjava.prodos.controller;

import org.springframework.beans.factory.annotation.Autowired;

import org.springframework.ui.ModelMap;

import org.springframework.web.bind.annotation.GetMapping;

import org.springframework.web.bind.annotation.RequestParam;

import org.springframework.web.bind.annotation.RestController;

import com.dineshonjava.prodos.service.AuthService;

@RestController
public class AuthController {

  @Autowired
  AuthService authService;

  @GetMapping(value = "/prodos-auth")
  public String getAccessToken(@RequestParam String username, @RequestParam String password, ModelMap model) {
    String accessToken = null;
    accessToken = authService.generateAccessToken(username, password);
    return accessToken;
  }
}

As you can see in the preceding code, the controller class has the Autowired dependency with the AuthService class as shown in the following code:

package com.dineshonjava.prodos.service;

import java.io.IOException;

import java.util.HashMap;

import java.util.Map;

import org.slf4j.Logger;

```
import org.slf4j.LoggerFactory;
import org.springframework.beans.factory.annotation.Autowired;
import org.springframework.beans.factory.annotation.Value;
import org.springframework.stereotype.Service;
import org.springframework.util.StringUtils;

import com.dineshonjava.prodos.dto.AuthResponseDto;
import com.fasterxml.jackson.databind.ObjectMapper;

@Service
public class AuthService {
  private static final Logger logger = LoggerFactory.getLogger(AuthService.class);

  @Autowired
  private RestCallService restCallService;

  @Value("${security.oauth2.client.access-token-uri}")
  private String ACCESS_TOKEN_API_DOMAIN_URI;

  @Value("${security.oauth2.client.client-id}")
  private String ACCESS_TOKEN_API_CLIENT_ID;

  @Value("${security.oauth2.client.client-secret}")
  private String ACCESS_TOKEN_API_CLIENT_SECRET;

  public String generateAccessToken(String username, String password) {
   String response = null;
   Map<String, String> params = new HashMap<String, String>();

   params.put("username", username);
   params.put("password", password);
   params.put("grant_type", "password");

   String auth = ACCESS_TOKEN_API_CLIENT_ID+":"+ACCESS_TOKEN_API_CLIENT_SECRET;

   try {
     response = restCallService.restTemplatePost(ACCESS_TOKEN_API_DOMAIN_URI, params,
auth);
```

```
} catch (Exception e) {
  logger.error("Exception while calling access token API:{} ", e.getMessage());
}

if (!StringUtils.isEmpty(response)) {
  ObjectMapper mapper = new ObjectMapper();
  try {
    AuthResponseDto authResponseDto = mapper.readValue(response, AuthResponseDto.class);

    response = authResponseDto.getAccess_token();
  } catch (IOException e) {
    e.printStackTrace();
  }
}
return response;
}
}
```

The preceding AuthService class is responsible to get the tokens generated by the Auth server. We are not going to explain all the classes of the client application in this book. You can find the complete source code for the client application from GitHub at https://github.com/dineshonjava/bpb-spring-boot-reactjs.

Now, run the client application and access the homepage of the client application in the browser. It will render a login page. You need to provide credentials here:

Figure 5.19: The client application login page

Let's provide appropriate credentials and then you will be redirected to the homepage as shown in the following screenshot:

Figure 5.20: The client application login page

Now, the client application has the access token generated by the Auth server application. Let's make a call to the resource server by clicking on the **Access all Products** link as shown in the following screenshot:

Welcome to Prodos Application, a Product Management Tool

Listed Products with Prodos

Name	Type	Brand	Description	Edit	Delete	View
Samsung A6 plus	Mobile	Samsung	Samsung A6 plus is very nice phone with 24mp front camera	Edit	Delete	View
iPhone X plus	Mobile	Apple	iPhone X plus is very nice phone with 24mp front camera	Edit	Delete	View
Sony Bravia KLV-50W662F 50 Inch Full HD	Television	Sony	Sony Bravia is full HD tv	Edit	Delete	View
Canon EOS 1500D Digital SLR Camera	DSLR Camera	Canon	Best DSLR camera in the market	Edit	Delete	View
JBL Cinema 510 5.1 with Powered Subwoofer	Home Theater Speaker	JBL	This sound system is suitable for the Home Theater	Edit	Delete	View

Figure 5.21: The client application login page

In the preceding screenshot, the page rendered all the products fetched from the resource server application. Let's see the following source code for a method that will be used to fetch the protected resource from the resource server:

```
public String findAllProducts(ModelMap model) {
    String accessToken = authService.generateAccessToken("dinesh", "mypass");
    HttpHeaders headers = new HttpHeaders();
    headers.setContentType(MediaType.APPLICATION_JSON);
    headers.set("Authorization", "Bearer " + accessToken);
    HttpEntity<String> entity = new HttpEntity<>("parameters", headers);
     List<Product>  products = restTemplate.exchange(BASE_URL+"/products", HttpMethod.GET,
entity, List.class).getBody();
    model.put("products", products);
    return "products";
 }
```

As you can see in the preceding source code, first we used AuthService to receive an access token for a given user (username: dinesh and password: mypass). We set this token to the Header as the Bearer token. Then, we made a call to the resource server using the exchange() method of the RestTemplate object.

Finally, we can get the product list as a resource from the resource server. In this chapter, we created the applications to secure your REST APIs. But OAuth2 is one of most widely used authentication mechanisms. Even Spring Security provides an exhaustive support to the other authentication mechanism.

Conclusion

In this chapter, we discussed the Spring Security auto-configuration in our RESTful application. We implemented the HTTP basic authentication in our PRODOS RESTful application. But the HTTP basic authentication is not appropriate for the production application and a large number of users.

We also implemented Spring Security with the JWT token mechanism. We secured our REST APIs with Spring Security and the JWT authentication, which is a lightweight authentication method suitable for our needs.

OAuth2 is the most widely used authentication mechanism to secure your REST APIs. In this chapter, we implemented OAuth2 and Spring Security with the JWT. We created three separate applications such as **Prodos OAuth Server**, **Prodos Resource Server**, and **Prodos Client-Server** application.

In the next *Chapter 6: Testing Spring Boot Application*, we will discuss how to test our REST services using Spring Boot.

Questions

1. What is Spring Security?

2. What is the delegating filter proxy?

3. What is the security filter chain?

4. How to use in-memory user store configuration?

5. How to use the JDBC user store configuration?

6. How to use an LDAP user store configuration?

7. How to create the custom user details service configuration?

8. What is password encoding?

9. What is the security context?

10. How is a principal defined?

11. What are authentication and authorization? Which should come first?

12. How to use JWT?

13. What is OAuth2?

CHAPTER 6

Testing a Spring Boot Application

Once you have created the product, then testing of the product is also an important part. Testing and test cases are a crucial part for your application; test cases do not only verify your code but also make sure that your application works as per your expectations. In this chapter, we will explore testing modules of Spring Boot and we will learn how to test a Spring Boot application using the unit testing and integration testing. You will learn to unit test Spring Boot services and also learn to mock Spring Boot services.

Spring Boot does not provide any specific module to write unit tests for an application. Spring Boot provides the integration testing module for your application because the Spring framework does bean wiring between the application components in your Spring application. You can use this module to write integration tests to test whether each component of your Spring application is properly configured and created. But for the unit test cases, you can use the JUnit library in your application.

In this chapter, we will start by adding a testing module to your Spring application (the PRODOS application as we have used throughout all chapters) and this module enables an application context for your testing environment. In this chapter, we will discuss the following topics:

- Testing in Spring Boot
- Creating unit tests
- Creating integration tests
    - o   Testing the controllers
    - o   Testing auto-configured data JPA repository

      o   Testing authentication controllers

- Loading test configurations
- Activating profiles for a test class

Testing in Spring Boot

The Spring framework provides us with a separate module for testing the Spring application, that is, Spring test. This module provides the testing runner class that helps to load a Spring application context in JUnit-based application tests. But with Spring Boot, it is very easy to add the testing framework, by default; Spring Boot enables the testing framework.

Let's take a look at your pom.xml file. The Spring Boot test starter can be added to your application pom.xml file as shown in the following code:

```
<dependency>
 <groupId>org.springframework.boot</groupId>
 <artifactId>spring-boot-starter-test</artifactId>
 <scope>test</scope>
</dependency>
```

The preceding Maven dependency adds the Spring Boot test starter to your application. It provides us with a lot of handy libraries for testing such as JUnit, Mockito, AssertJ, and more. Also, the Spring Boot Initializr creates a separate source folder as the names test and adds an initial testing application class to this source folder, as shown in the following screenshot:

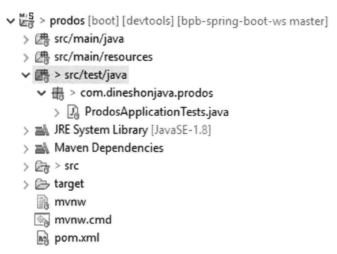

Figure 6.1: Test Sorce folder created in the Spring Boot Application

In the preceding screenshot, the src/test/java source folder is created and you can see a ProdosApplicationTests test class. The following code is created by default:

```
package com.dineshonjava.prodos;

import org.junit.Test;
import org.junit.runner.RunWith;
import org.springframework.boot.test.context.SpringBootTest;
import org.springframework.test.context.junit4.SpringRunner;

@RunWith(SpringRunner.class)
@SpringBootTest
public class ProdosApplicationTests {

  @Test
  public void contextLoads() {
  }
}
```

As you can see, the previous generated test class is annotated with the @SpringBootTest annotation. This annotation enables the Spring test modules in your application. The @SpringBootTest annotation provides the following features:

- It uses SpringBootContextLoader as the default ContextLoader.
- This annotation automatically searches for the configuration files annotated with the @SpringBootConfiguration annotation.
- It also allows you to customize the Environment properties using the properties attribute.
- This annotation allows you to customize different webEnvironment modes such as the ability to start a fully running web server by listening on a defined or random port.
- In the REST consumer applications, this annotation registers a TestRestTemplate and/or WebTestClient bean for use in web tests.

If your test is @Transactional, by default, the Spring Boot test framework rolls back all the transactions at the end of each test method. And the Spring Boot test framework frame uses an in-memory database such as H2, HSQL, and so on.

Testing is an important part of software development. The Spring Initializr gives you a test class to get started with. Let's start with the unit testing of the application.

Creating unit tests

Unit tests are very important for your application. Unit testing tests one unit of functionality and the unit test does not require any external dependencies. You can simply create stubs or mock objects for external classes because external dependencies are not available since we are testing a unit.

So, in unit testing, you can use the fake object or stub implementation of the original object to resolve the external dependencies. The external dependencies cannot be a show stopper for unit testing. There are many frameworks available that provide mocking objects such as Mockito, jMock, and EasyMock. Let's see the following diagram related to the external dependencies in the unit testing of a controller class:

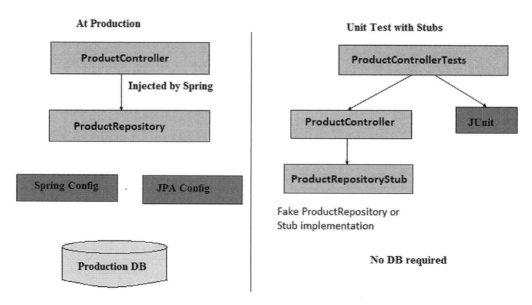

Figure 6.2: Stub implementation of ProductRespository in unit testing

In the preceding diagram, you can see both modes of your application, the production mode and unit test mode. In the production mode, the Spring framework injects all the required external or internal dependencies with the controller class using the Spring configuration class. But in the unit testing mode, the Spring framework does not play any role. Here, we create a stub object of the product repository that is provided to the controller class. The stub object of the ProductRespository class does not make any connection to the database. The stub object has own dummy data for testing.

In this example, I want to create a unit test for the ProductController class and test two methods, findProductById() and findAllProducts().

The findProductById() method will return the product object associated product ID and findAllProducts() will return the list of products.

Let's create the ProductController class and test this class with unit testing:

```
package com.dineshonjava.prodos.controller;

import java.util.ArrayList;
import java.util.List;
import org.springframework.http.MediaType;
import org.springframework.web.bind.annotation.GetMapping;
import org.springframework.web.bind.annotation.PathVariable;
import org.springframework.web.bind.annotation.RestController;
import com.dineshonjava.prodos.domain.Product;
import com.dineshonjava.prodos.repository.ProductRepository;

@RestController
public class ProductController {

  private ProductRepository productRepository;

  public ProductController(ProductRepository productRepository) {
    super();
    this.productRepository = productRepository;
  }

  @GetMapping(value = "/products", produces = {MediaType.APPLICATION_JSON_VALUE})
  public List<Product> findAll(){
    List<Product> products = new ArrayList<>();
    productRepository.findAll().forEach(i -> products.add(i));
    return products;
  }

  @GetMapping(value = "/products/{id}", produces = {MediaType.APPLICATION_JSON_VALUE})
  public Product findProductById(@PathVariable String id){
    return productRepository.findById(id).isPresent() ? productRepository.findById(id).get() : null;
  }
}
```

The preceding ProductController class has a dependency on the ProductRepoistory implementation. Let's now create a stub implementation of the ProductRepository class for unit testing the ProductController class:

```
public class StubProductRepository implements ProductRepository {

  ...
  @Override
  public Account findProductById(String id) {
    return new Product("MOB301", "POCO", "Mobile", "Xiomi Smart Phone with 24MP front camera", "Xiomi");
  }

  @Override
  public List<Account> findAll() {
    List<Account> products = new ArrayList<>();

    products.add(new Product("MOB302", "OPPO F6", "Mobile", "OPPO Smart Phone with 24MP front camera", "OPPO"));
    products.add(new Product("MOB303", "VIVO V15", "Mobile", "VIVO Smart Phone with 24MP front camera", "VIVO"));

    return products;
  }
  ...
}
```

The StubProductRepository class is a stub implementation of ProductRepository, by implementing methods with dummy data without calling the actual database. Let's take a look at the following diagram that explains the two implementations of ProductRepository:

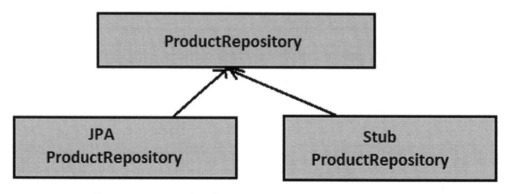

Figure 6.3: JPA and Stub implementation of ProductRepository

In the preceding diagram, you can see two implementations of the ProductRepository class available in the application, that is, JpaProductRepository and StubProductRepository. The StubProductRepository is used for unit testing without integrating the database dependency. Let's take a look at the following ProductControllerTests unit test class using the stub repository:

```
com.dineshonjava.prodos

import static org.junit.Assert.assertFalse;
import static org.junit.Assert.assertTrue;
import org.junit.Before;
import org.junit.Test;
import com.dineshonjava.prodos.repository.StubProductRepository;


public class ProductControllerTests {

  ProductController productController;

  @Before
  public void setUp() {
    productController = new ProductController( new StubProductRepository() );
  }

  @Test
  public void testFindProductById() {
    assertTrue(productController.findProductById("MOB01").getType().equals("Mobile"));
  }

  @Test
  public void testFindAll() {
    assertFalse(productController.findAll().size() == 5);
  }
}
```

In the preceding test class of the controller, we have three methods. The setup() method creates an object of the ProductController class, and this method is annotated with the @Before annotation. That means JUnit will call this method before the test methods execute. The other two methods, testFindProductById() and testFindAll(), are annotated with the @Test annotation, which indicates that these are test methods.

We discussed how to write the unit tests for any class in your application. The unit tests are easy to implement and understand. The unit tests of stub classes are reusable. But any change in the interface will force you to make the same changes in the stub implementation of the same interface.

The Spring framework provides support to integration testing in your Spring application. Let us see how Spring provides support to integration testing in the next section.

Creating integration tests

In integration testing, we test the interactions of multiple components of the application working together. In contrast to unit testing, integration testing makes sure that all internal or external dependencies work fine. So, integration testing also ensures all components perform as per expectations, including all dependencies. The Spring framework provides support to resolve these dependencies, which is similar to the production application. Let us see the following diagram about the integration testing:

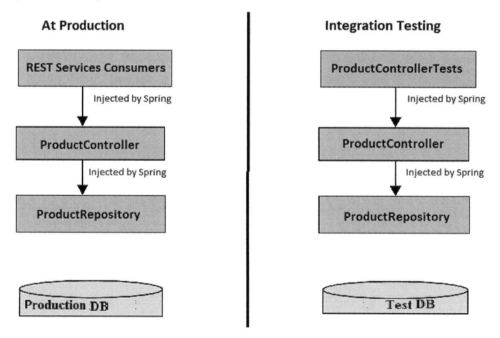

Figure 6.4: Components in integration testing

As you can see in the preceding diagram, ProductControllerTests is using the actual ProductRepository implementation instead of its stub or mock implementation we have used in the unit tests. Also, the AccountRepository class uses data from the database instead of using the dummy data we have used in unit testing.

Spring Boot provides a separate testing module (spring-test.jar) for integration testing and consists of several JUnit test-support classes. Spring has a central support class, which is SpringRunner. It caches a shared ApplicationContext across test methods.

Let's see the following class with integration testing.

Testing the controllers

Spring provides some powerful support for testing and makes it possible to test a web application easily. Let us start with a simple controller class with the single request handler method. So, we will write a test class for this controller class, and create a test method to perform an HTTP GET request for the root path / and expect successful results with the returned content that contains the phrase Hello World!!!. Let's take a look at the following testing class for the HomeController class:

```
package com.dineshonjava.prodos;


import static org.hamcrest.Matchers.containsString;
import static
org.springframework.test.web.servlet.request.MockMvcRequestBuilders.get;
import static
org.springframework.test.web.servlet.result.MockMvcResultMatchers.content;
import static
org.springframework.test.web.servlet.result.MockMvcResultMatchers.status;
import org.junit.Test;
import org.junit.runner.RunWith;
import org.springframework.beans.factory.annotation.Autowired;
import org.springframework.boot.test.autoconfigure.web.servlet.WebMvcTest;
import org.springframework.test.context.junit4.SpringRunner;
import org.springframework.test.web.servlet.MockMvc;


@RunWith(SpringRunner.class)
@WebMvcTest(HomeController.class)
public class HomeControllerTest {

  @Autowired
  private MockMvc mockMvc;

  @Test
  public void testHome() throws Exception {
```

```
  mockMvc.perform(get("/"))
  .andExpect(status().isOk())
  .andExpect(content().string(
    containsString("Hello World!!!")));
 }
}
```

Run the test case and check whether the STS JUnit tab tests were passed:

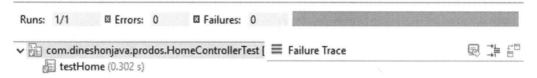

Figure 6.5: Showing successful test execution

Let's create the tests for your product controller as shown in the following code snippet:

```
package com.dineshonjava.prodos;

//imports

@RunWith(SpringRunner.class)
@WebMvcTest(ProductController.class)
public class ProductControllerTests {

  @Autowired
  private MockMvc mockMvc;

  @Autowired
  private ProductRepository productRepository;


  ...
  ...
}
```

The preceding test class, ProductControllerTests, is annotated with the @WebMvcTest annotation. We can use this annotation with @RunWith(SpringRunner.class) for the Spring MVC tests. This annotation can be used when you want to test only the Spring MVC components. We have passed the ProductController class as an argument of this annotation to expose the endpoints of ProductController.

The @WebMvcTest annotation disables all the auto-configuration of your application and enables only relevant configurations to MVC tests such as @Controller, @ControllerAdvice, @JsonComponent, and so on. Other than this, the classes annotated with @Component, @Service, or @Repository annotations will not be available in the application context.

By default, the @WebMvcTest annotation auto-configures Spring Security and MockMvc. You can use the @AutoConfigureMockMvc annotation to control MockMVC.

Let's add the first test case to test the /products/{ID} endpoint of the ProductController class:

```
@Test
public void testFindProduct() throws Exception {

  String expected = "{id: \"MOB01\",name: \"Samsung A6 plus\",type: \"Mobile\",description: "
    + "\"Samsung A6 plus is very nice phone with 24mp front camera\",brand: \"Samsung\"}";

  mockMvc.perform(get("/products/MOB01"))
    .andExpect(status().isOk())
    .andExpect(content().json(expected));
}
```

We will add another test case to create a new product to the database using the HTTP POST request to the /products endpoint:

```
@Test
public void testPostProduct() throws Exception {
    String newProduct = "{\"id\": \"MOB05\",\"name\": \"Samsung A6 plus\",\"type\": \"Mobile\",\"description\": "
    + "\"Samsung A6 plus is very nice phone with 24mp front camera\",\"brand\": \"Samsung\"}";
  mockMvc.perform(post("/products")
    .accept(MediaType.APPLICATION_JSON_VALUE)
    .content(newProduct)
    .contentType(MediaType.APPLICATION_JSON_VALUE))
  .andExpect(status().isCreated())
  .andExpect(content().json(newProduct));
}
```

We will also add another test case to the ProductControllerTests class to the /products/{ID} endpoint to test the update functionality using the HTTP PUT request, as shown in the following code snippet:

```
@Test
public void testPutProduct() throws Exception {
  String updatedProduct = "{\"id\": \"MOB03\",\"name\": \"Samsung A6 plus\",\"type\":
\"Mobile\",\"description\": "
    + "\"Samsung A6 plus is very nice phone with 24mp front camera\",\"brand\": \"Samsung\"}";
  mockMvc.perform(put("/products/MOB03")
    .accept(MediaType.APPLICATION_JSON_VALUE)
    .content(updatedProduct)
    .contentType(MediaType.APPLICATION_JSON_VALUE))
  .andExpect(status().isOk())
  .andExpect(content().json(updatedProduct));
}
```

Now, we will add another test case to the ProductControllerTests class to the /products/ {ID} endpoint to test the partial update functionality using the HTTP PATCH request:

```
@Test
public void testPatchProduct() throws Exception {

  String expected = "{id: \"MOB01\",name: \"Samsung A6 plus\",type: \"Mobile\",description: "
    + "\"Samsung A8 is very nice phone with 32mp front camera\",brand: \"Samsung\"}";

  String updatedProduct = "{\"id\": \"MOB01\",\"description\": "
    + "\"Samsung A8 is very nice phone with 32mp front camera\"}";

  mockMvc.perform(patch("/products/MOB01")
    .accept(MediaType.APPLICATION_JSON_VALUE)
    .content(updatedProduct)
    .contentType(MediaType.APPLICATION_JSON_VALUE))
  .andExpect(status().isOk())
  .andExpect(content().json(expected));
}
```

We will now add a test case to /products/{ID} endpoint to test how to delete a product of a given product ID using the HTTP DELETE request:

```
@Test
public void testDeleteProduct() throws Exception {

  mockMvc.perform(delete("/products/MOB01"))
```

```
     .andExpect(status().isNoContent());
}
```

Finally, we will run all the test cases and check whether tests were passed in the IDE JUnit tab as shown in the following screenshot:

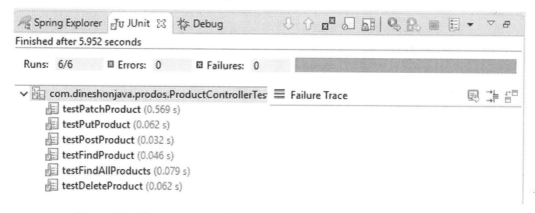

Figure 6.6: Showing successful tests execution for ProductControllerTests

We have now created the test cases for our controller class to verify REST API endpoints. Let us now create the test cases for the JPA repositories to test the CRUD functionalities of our application.

Testing auto-configured data JPA repository

The Spring Boot test module provides the @DataJpaTest annotation to test Spring Data JPA repositories. This annotation can be used with the @RunWith(SpringRunner.class) annotation for JPA tests. This annotation is basically used when you want to write the tests for the JPA components. This annotation enables only those configurations that are relevant to the JPA tests. The other configurations will be disabled, which means regular @Component beans are not loaded into the ApplicationContext object.

By default, tests annotated with @DataJpaTest will use an embedded in-memory database and this annotation scans for @Entity classes and configures Spring Data JPA repositories. You can use the @AutoConfigureTestDatabase annotation to override these settings.

If you want to use your application configuration with an embedded database for your test repositories, then you can use the @AutoConfigureTestDatabase annotation rather than @DataJpaTest with @SpringBootTest.

Let's create unit tests for our product repository to test the CRUD operations as shown in the following code snippet:

```
package com.dineshonjava.prodos;

import static org.assertj.core.api.Assertions.assertThat;
import org.junit.Test;
import org.junit.runner.RunWith;
import org.springframework.beans.factory.annotation.Autowired;
import org.springframework.boot.test.autoconfigure.orm.jpa.DataJpaTest;
import org.springframework.test.context.junit4.SpringRunner;
import com.dineshonjava.prodos.domain.Product;
import com.dineshonjava.prodos.repository.ProductRepository;

/**
 * @author Dinesh.Rajput
 *
 */

@RunWith(SpringRunner.class)
@DataJpaTest
public class ProductRepositoryTests {

  @Autowired
  private ProductRepository productRepository;


  ...

      ...
}
```

As you can see, we have created a new class called ProductRepositoryTests in the root test package. This test class is annotated with the @DataJpaTest annotation instead of the @SpringBootTest annotation. This class can be used when a test focuses only on JPA components.

Because of the @DataJpaTest annotation, the configurations related to the H2 database, Hibernate, and Spring Data will be available automatically for your JPA tests. This annotation enables SQL logging. And all JPA tests are transactional by default and roll back at the end of the test case.

In the previous test class for the JPA repository, let us add the first test case to test the creation of a new product to the database. A new product object is created and saved to the database using the save() method of the ProductRepository class. Then, we get the same object and check whether the product ID is not null if it is saved successfully:

```
@Test
public void testSaveProduct() {
  //TESTING: Create a new product
  productRepository.save(new Product("MOB301", "POCO", "Mobile", "Xiomi Smart Phone with
24MP front camera", "Xiomi"));
  Product product = productRepository.findById("MOB301").get();
  assertThat(product.getId()).isNotNull();


}
```

Let's add another test case to the ProductRepositoryTests class. We will fetch a product from the database with the given product ID and check if the returned product has the product ID:

```
@Test
public void testGetProduct() {
  //TESTING: Read a product with product id MOB01
  Product product = productRepository.findById("MOB01").get();
  assertThat(product.getId()).isNotNull();


}
```

In the last test case, we will get all the products from the database and check the size of the list of the product. The list size must be five because we have inserted five records to the H2 database at the start of the application. Also, we have called the deleteAll () method of the ProductRepository class. Then, we will check whether all cars are deleted from the database:

```
@Test
public void testDeleteProducts() {
  //TESTING: Delete all products
  assertThat(productRepository.findAll()).size().isEqualTo(5);
  productRepository.deleteAll();
  assertThat(productRepository.findAll()).isEmpty();


}
```

Finally, run all the test cases and click on the IDE JUnit tab to check whether the tests were passed, as shown in the following screenshot:

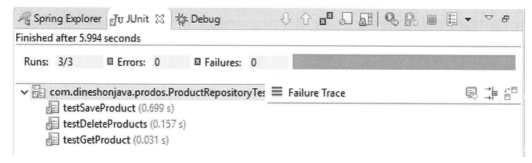

Figure 6.7: Showing successful execution of tests for the ProductRepositoryTests class

We have created the tests for the JPA Repository of our application. Let us now create the tests for the authentication functionality of our PRODOS application.

Testing authentication controller

Now, let us create tests for our AuthenticationController class in our PRODOS REST application. This test will verify our RESTful web service JWT authentication functionality. We are using MockMvc for testing this controller's endpoint (/auth/login). The MockMvc object provides a web environment without starting the server and you can perform the tests in the layer where Spring handles HTTP requests.

The MockMvc provides a real web environment, including all HTTP request methods so that you can use these HTTP methods according to your REST endpoint. In our case, we are using the HTTP POST request to /auth/login and set credentials to the request body.

Let's create the tests to perform two requests. The first request will be performed with the correct credentials and the second request will be performed with the incorrect credentials. The request will check whether the status is OK. The second request will check whether we get a 4XX HTTP error:

```
package com.dineshonjava.prodos;

import static org.springframework.test.web.servlet.request.MockMvcRequestBuilders.post;
import static org.springframework.test.web.servlet.result.MockMvcResultMatchers.status;
import org.junit.Test;
import org.junit.runner.RunWith;
import org.springframework.beans.factory.annotation.Autowired;
import org.springframework.boot.test.autoconfigure.web.servlet.WebMvcTest;
import org.springframework.boot.test.context.SpringBootTest;
```

```
import org.springframework.http.MediaType;
import org.springframework.test.context.junit4.SpringRunner;
import org.springframework.test.web.servlet.MockMvc;

/**
 * @author Dinesh.Rajput
 *
 */

@RunWith(SpringRunner.class)
@SpringBootTest
@WebMvcTest
public class AuthenticationControllerTests {

  @Autowired
  private MockMvc mockMvc;

  @Test
  public void testSignIn() throws Exception {

    //TESTING: Login with correct credentials
    this.mockMvc.perform(post("/auth/login")
      .content("{\"username\":\"dinesh\", \"password\":\"mypass\"}")
      .contentType(MediaType.APPLICATION_JSON_VALUE))
      .andExpect(status().isOk());

    //TESTING: Login with wrong credentials
    this.mockMvc.perform(post("/auth/login")
      .content("{\"username\":\"dinesh\", \"password\":\"mypasswrong\"}")
      .contentType(MediaType.APPLICATION_JSON_VALUE))
      .andExpect(status().is4xxClientError());
  }
}
```

Let's run the preceding tests with the correct and incorrect credentials. The following screenshot displays that the test passed:

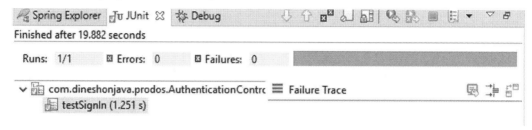

Figure 6.8: Showing successful execution of tests for the AuthenticationControllerTests class

As seen in the preceding screenshot, the green bar indicates that our tests are passed with the correct and incorrect credentials. We have implemented all tests for our PRODOS REST application.

Loading test configurations

The Spring test framework also allows you to load the separate configurations related to the testing environment Let's the @ContextConfiguration(classes=...) annotation. Also, you can use inner configuration classes inside the test classes for segregating the testing configurations.

But in case of Spring Boot, often you do not need to use the @ContextConfiguration annotation and inner configuration classes, you can use the @*Test annotations of Spring Boot to search your primary test configuration automatically. You can still use the @TestConfiguration annotation to customize the primary test configuration for your application.

Note: The Spring framework shares the application context between the tests in your application by caching the application contexts.

Activating profiles for a test class

The Spring Boot test module also allows you to set the active profiles by using the @ActiveProfiles annotation inside the test class. This annotation activates the profiles for the testing environment only. Spring beans and configurations will be available according to the active profiles in your application at the execution time of tests. Let's take a look at the following example:

@RunWith(SpringRunner.class)

@SpringBootTest

@ActiveProfiles({ "prod", "dev" })

```
public class ProdosApplicationTests {

  ...

}
```

In the preceding configuration, we have used two profiles, prod and dev. So, the beans that are related to either prod or dev will be available in the test application context.

Conclusion

Testing is one of the major parts of the software development lifecycle. As a developer, we must write unit tests in our application. The unit testing tests a class in isolation without any external dependencies. In this chapter, we created the unit tests for our application using the stub or mock object.

We implemented the integration test in our application. Integration testing ensures the working of components and its interaction with each other. Spring provides good support for integration testing for your application.

In the next *Chapter 7: Getting Started with React JS*, we will discuss the React JS framework for the front end application.

Questions

1. What is a unit test?
2. What is integration testing?
3. How to load testing configurations?
4. Write tests for Spring Data JPA.
5. What is mocking or a stub object?
6. How to activate profiles for a test class?

CHAPTER 7

Getting Started with React JS

Up till now, we have discussed about Spring Boot and its essential keys features. We have also created the backend using Spring Boot 2.2. In first chapter, we learned about Spring Boot and how to create the Spring Boot application. In *Chapter 2: Customizing Auto-Configuration*, we customized the auto-configuration provided by Spring Boot.

In chapter 3, we configured the H2 and MariaDB database to the Spring Boot application. We also defined the CRUD functionalities for our PRODOS application. After that, in *Chapter 4: Creating REST APIs with Spring Boot 2.2*, we exposed REST APIs in the PRODOS application to perform the CRUD operations using the REST endpoints by the client application. We have RestTemplate and Traverson as the REST clients in our PRODOS client application.

In *Chapter 5: Securing REST APIs*, we secured our REST APIs using Spring Security, OAuth2, and JWT. We also have created test cases to test our application's controllers, repositories, and authentication in *Chapter 6: Testing Spring Boot Application*.

The created client application has used Thymeleaf as front-end technology. But Thymeleaf is not in the scope of this book. Now, we will discuss React JS as a front-end technology and we will configure it for our PRODOS front-end application. In this chapter, we will explore how to set up React JS in your machine for the front-end application development. In this chapter, we will discuss the following topics:

- Introducing React
  - Features of React JS
  - Advantages of React JS

    o   Limitations of React JS

 • Setting up the environment for React JS

    o   Installing NodeJS and NPM

    o   Installing Visual Studio Code Editor

 • Creating a React application

    o   Using **webpack** and **babel**

    o   Using the **create-react-app** command

Let's discuss these topics in detail.

Introducing React

React developed by Facebook is one of the most popular front-end development technologies based on JavaScript libraries. You can use React JS for your front-end application development and to create mobile and web applications. You can create the reusable front-end UI components and build composable user interfaces using React JS. React does not use the typical original DOM but instead uses its own virtual react DOM. The virtual react DOM rendering is faster than the original DOM object. Let us see the React official documentation about the React JS technology.

According to React's official documentation,

React is a declarative, efficient, and flexible JavaScript library for building user interfaces. It lets you compose complex UIs from small and isolated pieces of code called components.

For the front-end application user interface, we can divide the user interface into multiple small UI visuals, and for each UI visual, you can create a React component because in React, the components are basic building blocks. These UI components are reusable. You can reuse them for a similar type of visuals in your front-end application. And also these are independent UI components for your front-end application.

We will discuss more about React JS but before that, let's discuss the React features.

Features of React JS

React is a component-based JavaScript library and it has the following features:

Declarative behaviour

You can create a very interactive and dynamic user interface for your mobile or website application using React. It creates a simple and small view component for each state of data in your application. React updates the view components efficiently where your data changes. This is the declarative behaviour of React and it makes your application code more readable and reusable.

Virtual DOM object

It is another very important feature of React. It creates a virtual DOM object for every DOM object in your front-end application. A virtual DOM object is just a virtual copy of the original DOM object. Data binding is very fast as compared with the original DOM because in the virtual DOM object, there is nothing that gets drawn on the screen.

Event handling model

As React creates its own virtual DOM object, similarly it also creates its own event system which is fully compatible with the W3C object model. Its event model wraps all the browsers' native events. The React event model provides the cross-browser interface to implement a native event. So, it reduces the incompatible event errors. It also has a pool of event objects to reduce the memory overhead and increase performance.

JSX

It is one of the best React JS features. JSX stands for JavaScript and XML. It is not an HTML but it looks like HTML. JSX is used to create React components and the components are the building blocks of the React UI.

Component-based approach

React provides a component-based approach for the front-end UI implementation. In React, everything is a component. A web page view (or UIs) will be created using several small components. In the front-end application, each part of the view will be associated with a self-contained module known as a component. Components in React will be reusable for a similar type of visuals and you can easily render a rich amount of data without impacting the performance of the front-end application due to the component logic is written in JavaScript.

React native

It is another face of the React library. It is another type of custom renderer for React like React DOM on the websites. It uses native components instead of the React web components.

We have just discussed the important features of React. Let us see some advantages and limitations of React in the next section.

Advantages of React JS

These are the following advantages of using React in your front-end application:

Apps performance

React uses the virtual DOM object and it is a JavaScript object. It improves the performance of the front-end application because rendering in the virtual DOM is faster than the regular DOM.

Code reusability

React uses the components-based approach to render the UI and a component is a small part of visuals. These components can be reused in the same type of visual.

Code readability

A web page is split into multiple components and a component is a self-contained module used to render a particular visual. It increases code readability. Finally, components and data patterns improve readability, which helps to maintain larger apps.

Across platforms

React can be used on the client side as well as server side with other frameworks.

There are many more advantages of React in the front-end application development which we are not going to discuss all here. Let us take a look at some limitations of React in the front-end application development in the next section.

Limitations of React JS

The following are the limitations of React in the front-end application development:

- React provides support to only the view layer of the application. You still have to use other tools to get a complete application.

- It uses inline styles and templates.

- In a large application, too many smaller components can create overload to manage them and also increase boilerplate.

- State change and rendering UI somehow depend on the render() method. So, we have to give special attention to the React front-end application to call render() properly.

We have discussed React features, advantages and limitations. Now, let's go ahead and set up the environment for React and install other useful tools.

Setting up the environment for React JS

In this section, we will explore some important tools to help us in the front-end application development. Also, we will set up the environment for these tools in your system. Here, I am using the Windows-based system, but I will discuss how to set up these tools in either Linux or Windows.

Installing Node.js and NPM

The Node.js is a platform that works at the server side. It is an open source technology based on the JavaScript server-side environment. It is available for multiple platforms such as Windows, macOS, and Linux.

If you want to use React as a front-end technology for your front-end application, then you need to install the Node.js platform, which is needed for the React JS development.

You can download the Node.js installation package from https://nodejs.org/en/ download/ to your machine. You can download the latest version of Node.js for your operating system. Here, I have downloaded the Node.js MSI installer for Windows 10 operating system.

Let's execute the downloaded installer as shown in the following installation wizard and leave the default settings unchanged:

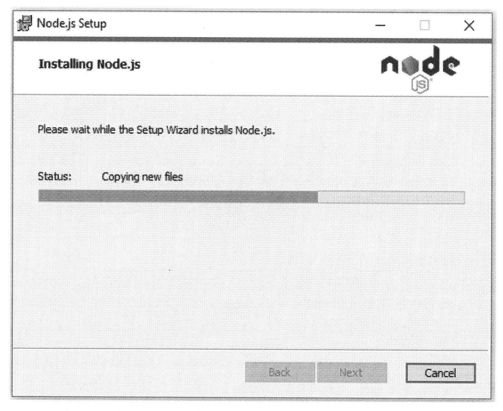

Figure 7.1: Node.js installation in Windows 10 OS

After successfully installing Node.js, we can verify that our Node.js was installed fully on your PC. Let us open PowerShell or whichever Terminal of OS you are using and run the following commands:

node -v

npm -v

The following screenshot displays the output for the preceding commands in PowerShell:

Figure 7.2: Verifying Node.js installation in Windows 10 OS

In the preceding screenshot, it shows the version of Node.js and npm. There is no need to install NPM separately as it is installed with the Node.js installation. NPM is a package manager for JavaScript.

After successfully installing Node.js and NPM, let us now install React in Node.js using NPM. But before moving ahead, let us install an Editor for the React application. Here, I am using Visual Studio Code (VS Code). Let us install Visual Studio Code.

Installing the Visual Studio Code Editor

It is an open source code editor. You can not only use it for React but also use it for other multiple programming languages. You can download it from https:// code.visualstudio.com/download. There are several options available to download according to your operating systems such as Windows, macOS, and Linux.

But I have downloaded the MSI installer for the Windows operating system. Let's install it with its default settings.

The following screenshot displays a complete workbench of the VS Code with a lot of options. You can use these options in your application development.

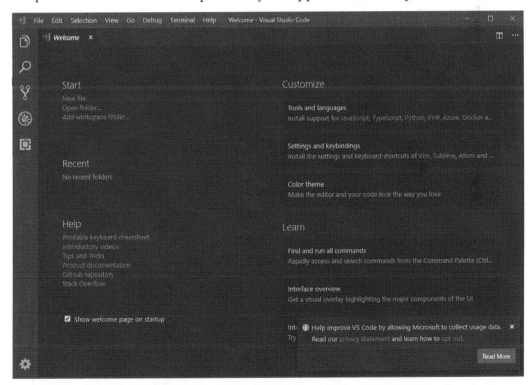

Figure 7.3: Open workbench of the VS Code Editor in Windows 10 OS

We have installed a supportive environment for the React application development in our machine. Now let us now create a React application and see how to run a React application.

Creating a React application

You can create a React application using the following two ways:

- Using webpack and babel
- Using the create-react-app command

Let's start with the first way to create a React application.

Using webpack and babel

Webpack is a module bundler used to manage modules and it loads modules to the React application. It creates a single bundle by taking the modules inside it after compiling.

Babel is JavaScript compiler used to compile the source code to others. It allows you to use the new ES6 feature in your React application.

Let's create a React application using them.

First, we will create a root application directory such as prodos_react_app:

```
PS F:\personal data\book\Full-stack-development-spring-boot-2-react> mkdir prodos_react_
app
```

**PS F:\personal data\book\Full-stack-development-spring-boot-2-react> cd prodos_react_
app**

Let's use the npm init command in PowerShell to generate the package.json file:

PS F:\personal data\book\Full-stack-development-spring-boot-2-react> npm init -y

We have used the -y option in the preceding command to skip asking information about the module such as package name, description, author, and so on, as shown in the following screenshot :

```
PS F:\personal data\book\Full-stack-development-spring-boot-2-react\prodos_react_app> npm init -y
Wrote to F:\personal data\book\Full-stack-development-spring-boot-2-react\prodos_react_app\package.json:

{
  "name": "prodos_react_app",
  "version": "1.0.0",
  "description": "",
  "main": "index.js",
  "scripts": {
    "test": "echo \"Error: no test specified\" && exit 1"
  },
  "keywords": [],
  "author": "",
  "license": "ISC"
}
```

Figure 7.4: Executing the npm init -y command

Now, let's install React and react-dom in the React application directory using the following command:

PS F:\personal data\book\Full-stack-development-spring-boot-2-react> npm install react react-dom --save

The following screenshot displays the output after executing the preceding command:

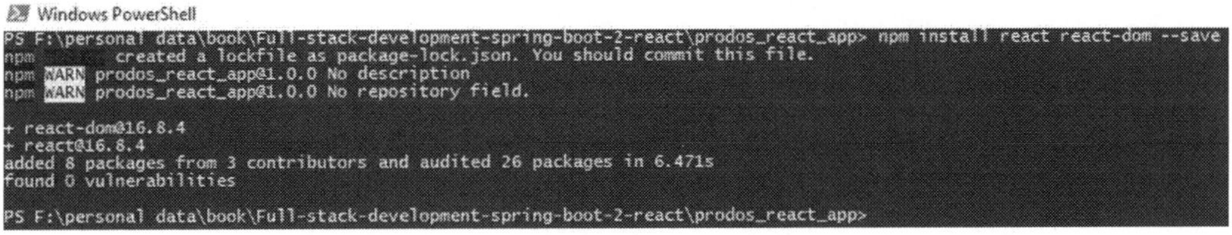

Figure 7.5: Installing React and react-dom

We will now install webpack, webpack-dev-server, and webpack-cli to generate a bundler using the following commands:

PS F:\personal data\book\Full-stack-development-spring-boot-2-react> npm install webpack --save

PS F:\personal data\book\Full-stack-development-spring-boot-2-react> npm install webpack-dev-server --save

PS F:\personal data\book\Full-stack-development-spring-boot-2-react> npm install webpack-cli --save

The following screenshot displays the output after executing the preceding command:

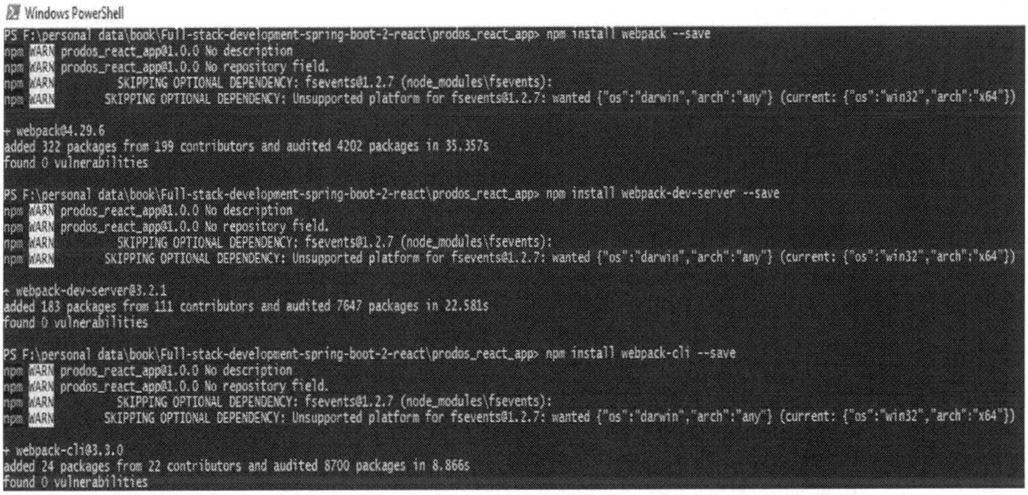

Figure 7.6: Installing webpack, webpack-dev-server and webpack-cli

Now, we will install the babel compiler in your React application using the following commands:

PS F:\personal data\book\Full-stack-development-spring-boot-2-react> npm install babel-core --save-dev

PS F:\personal data\book\Full-stack-development-spring-boot-2-react> npm install babel-loader --save-dev

PS F:\personal data\book\Full-stack-development-spring-boot-2-react> npm install babel-preset-env --save-dev

PS F:\personal data\book\Full-stack-development-spring-boot-2-react> npm install babel-preset-react --save-dev

PS F:\personal data\book\Full-stack-development-spring-boot-2-react> npm install html-webpack-plugin --save-dev

The following screenshot displays the output after executing the preceding commands:

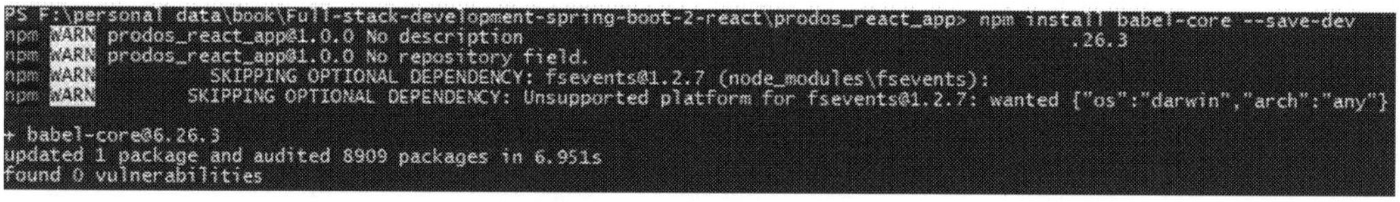

Figure 7.7: Installing babel

Let's create the required files for the React application. The file names we require are index.html, App.js, main.js, webpack.config.js, and .babelrc. After creating these files, we will edit the webpack.config.js file and set the compiler, server, and loader as shown in the following code snippet:

```
const path = require('path');
const HtmlWebpackPlugin = require('html-webpack-plugin');

module.exports = {
  entry: './main.js',
  output: {
  path: path.join(__dirname, '/bundle'),
  filename: 'index_bundle.js'
  },
  devServer: {
  inline: true,
  port: 8383
  },
  module: {
```

```
  rules: [
   {
   test: /\.jsx?$/,
   exclude: /node_modules/,
   loader: 'babel-loader',
   query: {
     presets: ['es2015', 'react']
   }
   }
  ]
  },
  plugins:[
  new HtmlWebpackPlugin({
   template: './index.html'
  })
  ]
}
```

As you can see in the following screenshot, application files are created after all the commands get executed:

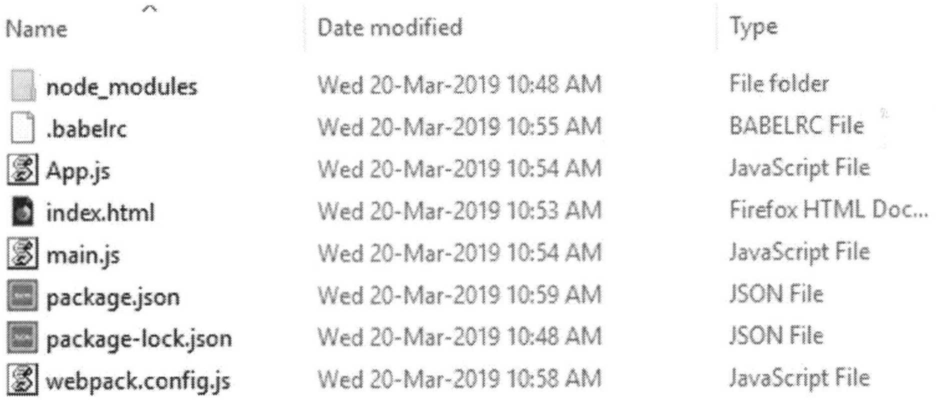

Name	Date modified	Type
node_modules	Wed 20-Mar-2019 10:48 AM	File folder
.babelrc	Wed 20-Mar-2019 10:55 AM	BABELRC File
App.js	Wed 20-Mar-2019 10:54 AM	JavaScript File
index.html	Wed 20-Mar-2019 10:53 AM	Firefox HTML Doc...
main.js	Wed 20-Mar-2019 10:54 AM	JavaScript File
package.json	Wed 20-Mar-2019 10:59 AM	JSON File
package-lock.json	Wed 20-Mar-2019 10:48 AM	JSON File
webpack.config.js	Wed 20-Mar-2019 10:58 AM	JavaScript File

Figure 7.8: Generated files under the React application

Let's edit the package.json file as shown in the following code:

```
{
  "name": "prodos_react_app",
  "version": "1.0.0",
  "description": "",
  "main": "index.js",
```

```
"scripts": {
  "test": "echo \"Error: no test specified\" && exit 1"
},
"keywords": [],
"author": "",
"license": "ISC",
"dependencies": {
  "react": "^16.8.4",
  "react-dom": "^16.8.4",
  "webpack": "^4.29.6",
  "webpack-cli": "^3.3.0",
  "webpack-dev-server": "^3.2.1"
},
"devDependencies": {
  "babel-core": "^6.26.3",
  "babel-loader": "^8.0.5",
  "babel-preset-env": "^1.7.0",
  "babel-preset-react": "^6.24.1",
  "html-webpack-plugin": "^3.2.0"
  }
}
```

We will delete the highlighted text from the preceding code because we do not have any test that can be executed for our React application as of now. And now we will add the following lines inside the script in place of the deleted line:

```
"start": "webpack-dev-server --mode development --open --hot",
```

```
"build": "webpack --mode production"
```

Now, we will edit the index.html file as shown in the following code:

```
<!DOCTYPE html>
<html lang = "en">
  <head>
    <meta charset = "UTF-8">
    <title>Welcome to PRODOS React Application</title>
  </head>
  <body>
    <div id = "prodos-app"></div>
    <script src = 'index_bundle.js'></script>
```

```
</body>
</html>
```

The preceding file will be the home page of the PRODOS front-end application, and now we can edit the App.js file and add the following code inside this file:

```
import React, { Component } from 'react';
class App extends Component{
 render(){
  return(
   <div>
    <h1>Welcome to the PRODOS frontend application using the React</h1>
   </div>
  );
 }
}
export default App;
```

Let's edit the mail application file, that is, main.js and add the following script code inside this file:

```
import React from 'react';
import ReactDOM from 'react-dom';
import App from './App.js';


ReactDOM.render(<App />, document.getElementById('prodos-app'));
```

In the preceding file, we have imported some files that are needed in our React application. You can import other files as per your requirements in the application.

Finally, let's add the following script to the.babelrc file before running the application:

```
{
 "presets":["env", "react"]
}
```

Let's run the React application by executing the following command in PowerShell.

PS F:\personal data\book\Full-stack-development-spring-boot-2-react\prodos_react_app> npm start

This will open the web browser and you can navigate to http://localhost:8383/ as shown in the following screenshot:

Welcome to the PRODOS frontend application using the React

Figure 7.9: Running the React application

We have created and installed the React application using webpack and babel. We have another simple and easy option to create a React application. Let's see how to create the React application using the create-react-app command in the next section.

Using the create-react-app command

In this section, we will create a React application using Facebook's create-react-app (https://github.com/facebook/create-react-app). We need to follow the given steps to create a React application using the create-react-app command:

1. Install the create-react-app starter using the following command:

   PS F:\personal data\book\Full-stack-development-spring-boot-2-react> npm install -g create-react-app

2. Open PowerShell and run the following command:

   PS F:\personal data\book\Full-stack-development-spring-boot-2-react> create-react-app prodos-front-app

The preceding command installs the create-react-app starter and this starter will be used to develop the React application. The following screenshot displays the output after running the application:

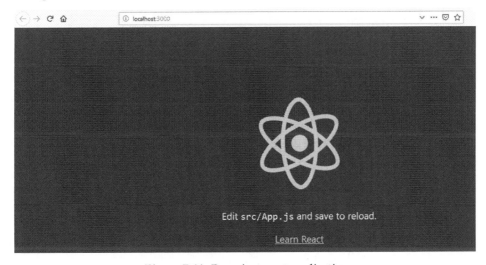

```
PS F:\personal data\book\Full-stack-development-spring-boot-2-react> create-react-app prodos_front_app
Creating a new React app in F:\personal data\book\Full-stack-development-spring-boot-2-react\prodos_front_app.

Installing packages. This might take a couple of minutes.
Installing react, react-dom, and react-scripts...

+ react-dom@16.8.4
+ react-scripts@2.1.8
+ react@16.8.4
added 1839 packages from 718 contributors and audited 36232 packages in 191.752s
found 63 low severity vulnerabilities
  run 'npm audit fix' to fix them, or 'npm audit' for details

Initialized a git repository.

Success! Created prodos_front_app at F:\personal data\book\Full-stack-development-spring-boot-2-react\prodos_front_app
Inside that directory, you can run several commands:

  npm start
    Starts the development server.

  npm run build
    Bundles the app into static files for production.

  npm test
    Starts the test runner.

  npm run eject
    Removes this tool and copies build dependencies, configuration files
    and scripts into the app directory. If you do this, you can't go back!

We suggest that you begin by typing:

  cd prodos_front_app
  npm start

Happy hacking!
PS F:\personal data\book\Full-stack-development-spring-boot-2-react>
```

Figure 7.10: Creating a React application using the create-react-app command

The preceding screenshot displays some important commands to help you build and run the React application.

3. Go inside the application folder using following command:

cd prodos_front_app

4. Start the React application using the following command:

npm start

Now, the application is running and it will open in the browser as shown in the following screenshot:

Edit src/App.js and save to reload.

Learn React

Figure 7.11: Running react application

The preceding screenshot displays the default page created by the create-react-app command. Let us modify the default generated file of our React application.

Open the generated React application using the VS Code editor by selecting **File** | **Open** folder. You can see the following application structure in the VS Code:

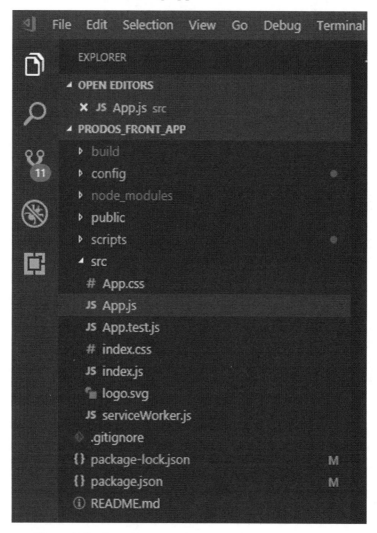

Figure 7.12: Open React PRODOS application in VS Code

Now, open the App.js file from the src folder in the code editor and edit the code as shown in the following code:

```
import React, { Component } from 'react';
import logo from './logo.svg';
import './App.css';

class App extends Component {
  render() {
   return (
    <div className="App">
     <header className="App-header">
      <img src={logo} className="App-logo" alt="logo" />
      <p>
       Edit <code>src/App.js</code> and save to reload.
      </p>
      Welcome to PRODOS application with React
     </header>
    </div>
   );
  }
}

export default App;
```

Now, let's refresh the browser. You should be able to immediately see the changes made in the App.js file as shown in the following screenshot:

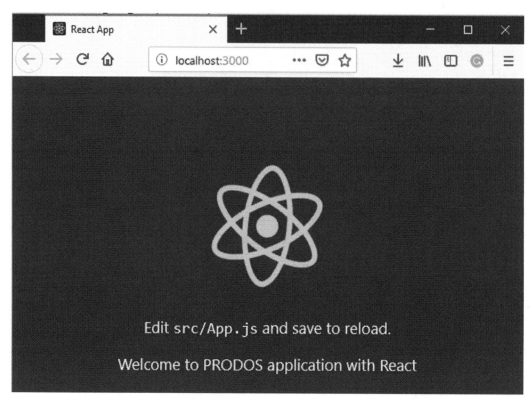

Figure 7.13: Modifying the home page of the generated React application

Now, let's change the logo of our React application. To do this, just add the logo.jpg file to the src folder of the application and make changes to the App.js file accordingly as shown in the following code snippet:

```
import React, { Component } from 'react';
import logo from './logo.jpg';
import './App.css';

class App extends Component {
 render() {
  return (
   <div className="App">
    <header className="App-header">
     <img src={logo} className="App-logo" alt="logo" />
     Welcome to PRODOS application with React
    </header>
   </div>
  );
```

```
  }
}
```

export default App;

These changes are automatically reflected in the browser as shown in the following screenshot:

Figure 7.14: Changed logo and styles of the React application

Conclusion

In this chapter, we discussed how to set up the environment for the React application. We also configured other supporting tools such as the VS Code editor for the React application development.

We installed Node.js for running the React application. We created the React application for our PRODOS front-end application and also created the front-end application using webpack and babel. We also used the create-react-app starter kit to create our first React JS application.

Finally, we run the React application and modified it. Here, we only created the React application and application structure. In the next chapter, we will discuss some more details about the React components.

In the next *Chapter 8: Creating ReactJS Components,* we will discuss how to create React components and JSX.

Questions

1. What is React?

2. What are advantages of using React?

3. What are limitations of using React?

4. How is React useful as a front-end technology?

5. What is Node.js?

6. How to create a React front-end application?

CHAPTER 8

Creating React JS Components

In the previous chapter, we set up the React JS environment of the front-end application development. We installed Node.js and the VS code editor. In this chapter, we will discuss how to create React JS components and how to manage the React JS component lifecycle. We will also see how to use props and state in components.

JSX is used by React for templating. In this chapter, we will cover the following topics and create the examples:

- React JSX
    - o JSX and styling
    - o Adding JavaScript expressions
    - o Using custom attributes tags
- React components
    - o Data flow in React components
    - o Event flow in React components
- Creating React components for our front-end application
    - o Using multiple React components
    - o Using properties (props) in React components

> o Using state in React components
>
> o Creating Header and Footer components to the Prodos front-end application

- Handling lists with React

- Handling events with React

- Handling forms with React

  > o Using input text fields in form with React components

- The React component lifecycle

Let us discuss each topic in detail.

React JSX

JSX is another way of writing the JavaScript code. JSX means JavaScript and XML tags. It is used to declare the UI component in your React application. JSX is not mandatory to use with your React application but it provides a lot of benefits as the following:

- It makes development easier and faster to write templates because JSX looks like a regular HTML.

- JSX provides a very clean way to declare your UI component.

- JSX is also type-safe because its code is compiled with JavaScript. And most of the errors can be caught at the compilation time.

- JSX has faster rendering.

The JSX code gets created in the UI component and this code is transpiled and converted to small and lightweight objects and these objects are used to represent UI elements for your front-end application. Let's take a look at the following code, that is, a JSX code:

```
import React from 'react';


class ProdosApp extends React.Component {
 render() {
  return (
   <h1>Welcome, hello there PRODOS.</h1>
  );
 }
}
```

export default ProdosApp;

In the preceding JSX file, you can save it as Prodos.jsx. This JSX file has some code very similar to the HTML file, but it is not a regular HTML file. We need to take care when working with React applications using JSX. Let us run the NPM server and access the prodos.html file, which is using the Prodos.jsx file. After starting the NPM server using the npm start command, navigate to the http://localhost:3000/prodos.html as shown in the following screenshot:

Welcome, hello there PRODOS.

Figure 8.1: The Prodos React front-end application

Using the container for nested elements

In React, we need to use a container for more elements. This container wraps all nested elements. If you do not use any container, then the web page will not display any content. You can use <div> as a wrapper for <h1>, <h2> and <p> elements as shown in the following example:

```
import React from 'react';

class ProdosApp extends React.Component {
 render() {
  return (
  <div>
   <h1>Welcome, hello there PRODOS.</h1>
   <h2>Product List</h2>
   <p>This is the product list</p>
  </div>
  );
 }
}


export default ProdosApp;
```

Let's navigate to the same web page http://localhost:3000/prodos.html as shown in the following screenshot:

Welcome, hello there PRODOS.

Product List

This is the product list

Figure 8.2: JSX with nested elements

HTML tags in lowercase

In JSX, HTML tags must be in lowercase such as div, span, and h1. HTML tags in uppercase such as <H1> are invalid.

Using the custom attribute in an HTML tag

You can also use the custom attribute with HTML tags in the JSX file using data-prefix. Let's take a look at the following example:

```
import React from 'react';

class ProdosApp extends React.Component {
  render() {
    return (
    <div>
      <h1>Welcome, hello there PRODOS.</h1>
      <h2>Product List</h2>
      <p data-customAttribute="myvalue">This is the product list</p>
    </div>
    );
  }
}
```

export default ProdosApp;

Using Style in the JSX code

You can also use styles with the HTML tags. Let's take a look at the following code with the styling in the JSX code:

```
import React from 'react';

class ProdosApp extends React.Component {
  render() {
   var prodosStyle = {
    fontSize: 35,
    color: '#FFA000'
   }

   return (
   <div>
    <h1>Welcome, hello there PRODOS.</h1>
    <h2 style={prodosStyle}>Product List</h2>
    <p>This is the product list</p>
   </div>
   );
  }
}

export default ProdosApp;
```

In the preceding JSX code, we have defined prodosStyle CSS and after that, we have used it with the <h2> element. React recommends that you use an inline style with the JSX code. After adding the styles, the output will look as the following screenshot:

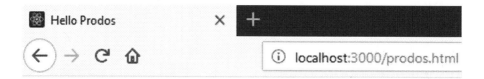

Welcome, hello there PRODOS.

Product List

This is the product list

Figure 8.3: JSX with styles

Adding JavaScript expressions in JSX

You can also use the JavaScript expression with the JSX code by wrapping it with curly brackets {}. Let's take a look at the following JSX code:

```
import React from 'react';

class ProdosApp extends React.Component {
 render() {
  return (
  <div>
   <h1>Welcome, hello there PRODOS.</h1>
   <p>{2+4}</p>
  </div>
  );
 }
}

export default ProdosApp;
```

There are a lot of things we can discuss with the JSX file, but we will discuss other things about JSX later in this chapter. First, we will discuss about React components and how we can use JSX to create React components.

React components

Creating a front-end application with React is all about the creation of the component based on your application user interface. These components are nothing but small pieces of the visuals of your web page, the home page or product details page. Using React, you can compose complex UIs from small and isolated pieces of code, and these pieces of code are known as components.

The components are basic building blocks of the React library. In React, a user interface is created using a number of components. These components are composed together as per requirements in a user interface. And each component can be reused and has a different role such a form, button, popup, and more.

These components talk to each other in a React application. Let us create a mock user interface for our PRODOS front-end application:

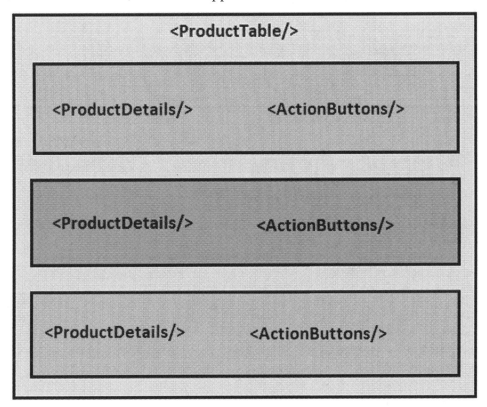

Figure 8.4: The PRODOS mock user interface with React components.

In the preceding diagram, we created a mock user interface using the components <ProductTable/>, <ProductDetails/>, <ActionButtons/>, and so on. We need to create these React components and combine them together to create a PRODOS application user interface.

Data flow in the React components

As you can see in the following diagram, the React components have a parent-child relationship and parent components provide data to their children. And data supplied to a child component by its parent is referred to as properties or props for short.

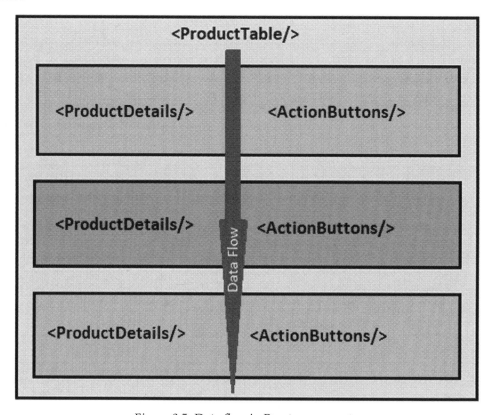

Figure 8.5: Data flow in React components

As you can see in the preceding diagram, data is flowing in one direction only. So, we need to take care of how the data moves in the application and check which data should be in which part of the application of the unidirectional data flow. The debugging is much easier and it also makes the maintenance of the application simple and easy.

The event or action flows in the React components are as simple as the data flow in the React application. Let us discuss this in the following section.

Event flow in the React components

Similar to the data flow in the React components, the action or event flow in the React components is unidirectional but the action or event flow is a child to parent as shown in the following diagram:

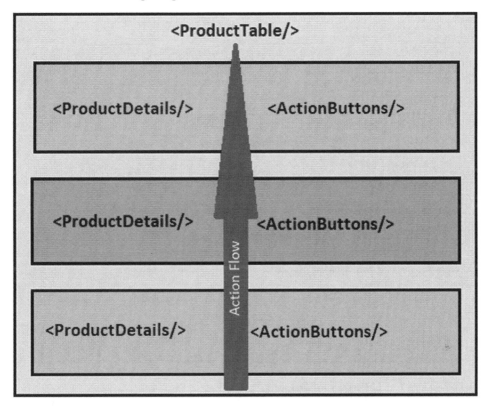

Figure 8.6: Action or Event flow in React components

As you can see in the preceding diagram, the actions tend to flow upwards but data flows downwards in React components. For example, when a user types in the text box, data is entered in the text box as the child on a form but this data is owned by its parent. As you can see in the following diagram, where we write the username in the username input box, it directly reflects the parent component:

Figure 8.7: Action flow in React components Child to Parent

In the preceding diagram, as we type in the username input box, it reflects the parent login box. The event generated in the child component propagates to the parent components in the React application.

Let's move on to the next section and create the components for our PRODOS front-end application.

Creating React components for the PRODOS front-end application

Let's create the React components for our PRODOS front-end application using JSX. Before we create the components, we first need to understand one of the web pages of our application. The web page in a React application is nothing but the composition of several React components as shown in the following screenshot:

Name	Type	Brand	Description	Edit	Delete	View
Samsung A6 plus	Mobile	Samsung	Samsung A6 plus is very nice phone with 24mp front camera	Edit	Delete	View
iPhone X plus	Mobile	Apple	iPhone X plus is very nice phone with 24mp front camera	Edit	Delete	View
Sony Bravia KLV-50W662F 50 Inch Full HD	Television	Sony	Sony Bravia is full HD tv	Edit	Delete	View
Canon EOS 1500D Digital SLR Camera	DSLR Camera	Canon	Best DSLR camera in the market	Edit	Delete	View
JBL Cinema 510 5.1 with Powered Subwoofer	Home Theater Speaker	JBL	This sound system is suitable for the Home Theater	Edit	Delete	View

Figure 8.8: A PRODOS web page

As you can see in the preceding screenshot, the user interface of the product list is split into components. There is an application root component, a table component, and a table row component.

The React components in the preceding screenshot are arranged in a tree-like structure (aka a visual hierarchy) as shown in the following diagram. You can also observe that the dataflow is from the parent component to the child component.

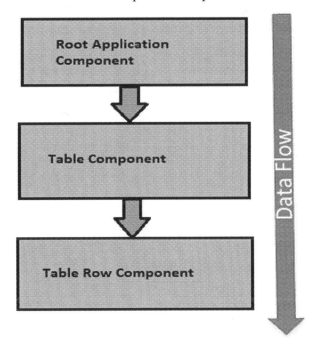

Figure 8.9: A tree hierarchy of React components

The React components can be defined using the traditional JavaScript methods or using the ES6 JavaScript class. Let's see the following JavaScript function:

// Using JavaScript function
```
const HelloProdos = function(props) {
 return (
 <h1>Welcome, hello there PRODOS.</h1>
 );
}
```

The preceding JavaScript code does the following things:

- The preceding code creates an anonymous JavaScript function and it assigns it to a constant as HelloProdos.

- This JavaScript function has only one statement, return.

- This statement returns the JSX code to represent a view using the HTML <h1> tag.

- This JSX h1 element contains the string Welcome, hello there PRODOS.

In the preceding code, we created a HelloProdos component using the JavaScript function. Now, let's create the same component using the ES6 JavaScript class as shown in the following code:

```
// Using ES6 JavaScript class
class HelloProdos extends React.Component {
 render() {
  return (
   <h1>Welcome, hello there PRODOS.</h1>
  );
 }
}
```

In the preceding code, the React.Component is implemented using the HelloProdos class and this class contains the required render() method. This method displays and updates the rendered output of the component. The name of the user-defined component should start with a capital letter.

Here, we created a very simple React component using the JavaScript function and ES6 JavaScript class. We will then create our application related to the React component, but before that, we will see how to display a React component in a browser.

We need to render the React component to the web browser to display it and rendering the React component is another aspect in React. So, a React component can be rendered in the following two ways:

- We can use a React component inside the JSX code of another React component.

- We can use a React component to render by passing it to ReactDOM.

In the following code, we are using a React component that we created in the preceding section:

```
ReactDOM.render(
 <HelloProdos />,
 document.getElementById("content")
);
```

In the preceding code, we are using the ReactDOM.render() method to display the React component. The ReactDOM object is part of the standard React libraries and its render() method takes a React component and an element from the HTML document with the document ID as its content. But you could have a question in your mind – from where are we getting the HTML document with the ID content.

Let's see the following code with the HTML and React component together:

```
<!DOCTYPE html>
<html lang="en">
<head>
 <meta charset="utf-8" />
 <title>Hello Prodos</title>

 <script src="https://unpkg.com/react@15/dist/react.js"></script>
 <script src="https://unpkg.com/react-dom@15/dist/react-dom.js"></script>
 <script src="https://unpkg.com/babel-standalone/babel.min.js"></script>

 <script type="text/babel">
 class HelloProdos extends React.Component {
  render() {
   return (h1>Welcome, hello there PRODOS.</h1>);
  }
 }

 ReactDOM.render(
  <HelloProdos />,
  document.getElementById("content")
 );
 </script>

</head>

 <body>
  <div id="content"></div>
 </body>
</html>
```

As you can see in the preceding code, we used an HTML div element with id= "content". In this div element, the React component HelloProdos will be rendered. We will save this file and open it in the browser as shown in the following screenshot:

Welcome, hello there PRODOS.

Figure 8.10: A rendered React component

Using multiple React components

If you have multiple React components in a web page, then all React components must be wrapped in an enclosing tag:

```
<div>
 <Prodos1Component />
 <Prodos2Component />
</div>
```

Suppose if you do not enclose the preceding two React components, then you will see an error *"JSX elements must be wrapped in an enclosing tag."* If you wrap the React component using a single HTML div, then the JSX compiler will compile it successfully.

If one React component uses another React component inside, then we do not need to enclose the HTML div element:

```
<Prodos1Component>
   <Prodos2Component />
</Prodos1Component>
```

That means the React components must be returned as a single element in the JSX. Now, we will see how to pass the properties to the React components.

Using properties (props) in React components

In this section, we will see how to pass the properties to the React components. We already discussed that React data flows downwards. Let's see the following code:

```
<!DOCTYPE html>
<html lang="en">
<head>
 <meta charset="utf-8" />
 <title>Hello Prodos</title>
```

```
<script src="https://unpkg.com/react@15/dist/react.js"></script>
<script src="https://unpkg.com/react-dom@15/dist/react-dom.js"></script>
<script src="https://unpkg.com/babel-standalone/babel.min.js"></script>

<script type="text/babel">
class HelloProdos extends React.Component {
        render() {
  return (
   <h1>{this.props.greeting}.</h1>
  );
        }
      }

ReactDOM.render(
  <HelloProdos greeting="Welcome, hello there PRODOS" />,
  document.getElementById("content")
 );
 </script>

</head>

 <body>
  <div id="content"></div>
 </body>
</html>
```

In the preceding code, we are using a React component with an attribute greeting with the value Welcome, hello there PRODOS. In JSX, this attribute is very similar to the HTML attribute. And the value of this attribute is passed as the property (props object) to React. This props object is passed from a parent to a child component. And props are immutable objects so these cannot be changed by the child components.

Let's take a look at another example of using props in the React component:

```
class ProductList extends React.Component {
  render() {
   return (
    <div>
     <h1>Product List for {this.props.name}</h1>
     <ul>
```

```
            <li>Samsung A6 Plus</li>
            <li>iPhone X Plus</li>
            <li>Vivo V15 Pro</li>
          </ul>
        </div>
      );
    }
  }
```

We can use the following React component in your JSX code:

```
<ProductList name="Mobile" />
```

We have used props in the React components. Now we will see how to use the state in the React components in the next section.

Using state in React components

In the React components, the data comes from the state. We need to create stateful components in our front-end application where the data should be rendered and not create an unnecessary stateful component to reduce the complexity of the React application. In the following sample code, we will how to create a stateful component in React using the ES6 syntax:

```
import React from 'react';

class ProdosApp extends React.Component {
  constructor(props) {
    super(props);

    this.state = {
      product1: "Samsung A6 Plus",
      product2: "iPhone X Plus",
      product3: "Vivo V15 Pro"
    }
  }
  render() {
    return (
      <div>
    <h1>Product List for {this.props.name}</h1>
    <ul>
```

```
    <li>{this.state.product1}</li>
    <li>{this.state.product2}</li>
    <li>{this.state.product3}</li>
  </ul>
    </div>
  );
 }
}
export default ProdosApp;
```

As you can see in the preceding code, we initialized a state with some values in the constructor of the React component. This React component is stateful because it is using the state to carry the data to the child components. In the following code, we will see how to use this stateful React component:

```
import React from 'react';
import ReactDOM from 'react-dom';
import ProdosApp from './ProdosApp;


ReactDOM.render(<ProdosApp />, document.getElementById(content));
```

The following screenshot displays the output of the code:

Product List for Mobile

- Samsung A6 Plus
- iPhone X Plus
- Vivo V15 Pro

Figure 8.11: A stateful React component

As you can see in the preceding screenshot, we rendered data using the state in the React components. Currently, we have used hardcoded data in the constructor of this stateful React component. In the next chapter, we will fetch this data using the REST API.

We saw how to use the state with React components, now we will see how to use the state and props together with React components. In the following example, we will see how to combine the props and state in your front-end React-based application:

```
import React from 'react';

class ProdosApp extends React.Component {
  constructor(props) {
    super(props);
    this.state = {
      product1: "Samsung A6 Plus",
      product2: "iPhone X Plus",
      product3: "Vivo V15 Pro"
    }
  }
  render() {
    return (
      <div>
      <h1>Product List for {this.props.name}</h1>
      <ul>
        <li><Product1 product1Prop = {this.state.product1}/></li>
        <li><Product2 product2Prop = {this.state.product2}/></li>
        <li><Product3 product3Prop = {this.state.product3}/></li>
      </ul>
      </div>
    );
  }
}
class Product1 extends React.Component {
  render() {
    return (
      <div>
        <h1>{this.props.product1Prop}</h1>
      </div>
    );
  }
}
class Product2 extends React.Component {
  render() {
    return (
```

```
      <div>
        <h1>{this.props.product2Prop}</h1>
      </div>
    );
  }
}
class Product3 extends React.Component {
  render() {
    return (
      <div>
        <h1>{this.props.product3Prop}</h1>
      </div>
    );
  }
}


export default ProdosApp;
```

In the preceding code, we combined props and state with the React component s in a React-based front-end application. We set the state in our parent component and passed it down the component tree using props. Inside the render function, we set product1Prop, product2Prop, and product3Prop used in child components.

Creating Header and Footer components to the Prodos front-end application

In this section, we will provide more shape to our PRODOS front-end application. We will add the header and footer to our front-end application. We will create a header React component for our React application as shown in the following code snippet:

```
import React, { Component } from 'react';
import logo from './logo.jpg';
import './App.css';


class ProdosHeader extends Component {
render() {
 return (
  <div>
  <table className="App-Header">
   <tr >
```

```
    <td >
      <img alt="prodos logo" src={logo} height="150px;"/>
    </td>
    <td >
      <h2>Welcome to Prodos Application, a Product Management Tool</h2>
    </td>
    </tr>
   </table>
   </div>
  );
}
}
```

export default ProdosHeader

You can see that we created a **ProdosHeader** component for our React application. This is a stateless component and let's create a footer React component for our PRODOS React application as shown in the following code:

import React, { Component } from 'react';
import './App.css';

```
class ProdosFooter extends Component {
   render() {
    return (
      <div>
       <table className="App-Footer">
        <tr>
         <td><b> PRODOS a Product Management Tool &copy; <a href="https://www.
dineshonjava.com/" target="_blank"> Dinesh on Java </a></b></td>
        </tr>
       </table>
      </div>
    );
  }
}
```

export default ProdosFooter

We created a **ProdosFooter** React component for our React application. Now, we will use these React components (ProdosHeader and ProdosFooter) in the Prodos front-end application. Let's see the following code using the header and footer:

```
import React, { Component } from 'react';
import ProdosHeader from './ProdosHeader';
import ProdosFooter from './ProdosFooter';

class ProdosApp extends Component {
 constructor(props) {
  super(props);

  this.state = {
  product1: "Samsung A6 Plus",
  product2: "iPhone X Plus",
  product3: "Vivo V15 Pro"
  }
 }
 render() {
 return (
 <div>
  <ProdosHeader/>
  <h1>Product List for {this.props.name}</h1>
  <ul>
  <li>{this.state.product1}</li>
  <li>{this.state.product2}</li>
  <li>{this.state.product3}</li>
  </ul>
  <br/>
  <ProdosFooter/>
 </div>
 );
 }
}

export default ProdosApp
```

As you can see in the preceding JSX code, we used <ProdosHeader/> and <ProdosFooter/> React components in our ProdosApp React component of our Prodos front-end application. Let's refresh the browser and see the following output displayed in the screenshot:

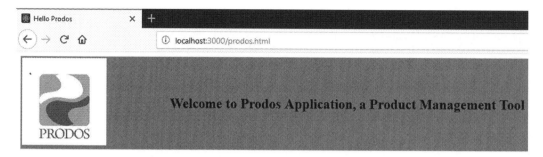

Figure 8.12: Added ProdosHeader and ProdosFooter React components

In the preceding screenshot, we added the header and footer UI components in our React application. Up till now, we have a product list in our application, so now we will create a React component for our content in the tabular format as discussed earlier.

Handling lists with React and creating a table React component for our Prodos React application

In this section, we will create a content section in a tabular format. We will render data using a list. We have a data list which contains some product details. We will render this list in a table in the middle section of the web page of the Prodos application. But before we implement a table React component, we will see how to handle a list with React application.

For list handling, we introduce a new JavaScript method, map(), which is handy when you need to manipulate a list. The map() method creates a new array with the results of calling a function to each element in the original array.

Let's see the following array of strings and array of list of products and render these in the ul element:

```
import React, { Component } from 'react';
import ProdosHeader from './ProdosHeader';
import ProdosFooter from './ProdosFooter';

class ProdosApp extends Component {
  render() {
  const products = ["Samsung A6 Plus", "iPhone X Plus", "Vivo V15 Pro"];

return (
 <div>
  <ProdosHeader/>
  <h1>Product List for {this.props.name}</h1>
  <ul>
  {products.map((number, index) => <li key={index}> {number}</li>)}
  </ul>
  <br/>
  <ProdosFooter/>
 </div>
 );
 }
}


export default ProdosApp
```

In the preceding code, we rendered an array of the strings using the map() function of JavaScript. Let's see the following output:

Figure 8.13: Rendering a product list using the array

Now, we will move one step ahead and use the data as an array of objects, and we can present this data using the table format. An array of objects is also rendered in the same way as stated earlier, but here we will map the array to the table row and render the data in the table format. Let's see the following code:

```
import React, { Component } from 'react';
import ProdosTableRow from './ProdosTableRow';
import './App.css';

class ProdosTable extends Component {
  constructor(props) {
    super(props);
    this.state = {
     products: [
       {
         name: "Samsung A6 plus",
         type: "Mobile",
         description: "Samsung A6 plus is very nice phone with 24mp front camera",
         brand: "Samsung"
       },
       {
         name: "Sony Bravia KLV-50W662F 50 Inch Full HD",
```

```
        type: "Television",
        description: "Sony Bravia is full HD tv",
        brand: "Sony"
      },
      {
        name: "Canon EOS 1500D Digital SLR Camera",
        type: "DSLR Camera",
        description: "Best DSLR camera in the market",
        brand: "Canon"
      }
    ]
  };
}

render() {
  return (
  <div>
    <h1 className= "Prodos">Product List for {this.props.name}</h1>
    <table border="1">
      <thead>
        <tr>
          <th>Name</th>
          <th>Type</th>
          <th>Brand</th>
          <th>Description</th>
          <th>Edit</th>
          <th>Delete</th>
          <th>View</th>
        </tr>
      </thead>
      <tbody>
        {this.state.products.map((productDetails, i) => <ProdosTableRow key = {i}
          product = {productDetails} />)}
      </tbody>
    </table>

  </div>
  );
```

```
    }
  }
```

```
  export default ProdosTable
```

In the preceding code, we are using the list of objects and this list of objects we have initiated in the constructor using the state. This list of the objects should be presented in the table format. So, we are creating a ProdosTable component. The ProdosTable component is using the ProdosTableRow component. Let's see the following code for the ProdosTableRow component:

```
import React, { Component } from 'react';
```

```
class ProdosTableRow extends Component {
```

```
render() {
  return (
  <tr>
    <td>{this.props.product.name}</td>
    <td>{this.props.product.type}</td>
    <td>{this.props.product.brand}</td>
    <td>{this.props.product.description}</td>
    <td><a href="#">Edit</a></td>
    <td><a href="#">Delete</a></td>
    <td><a href="#">View</a></td>
  </tr>
  );
}
}
```

```
export default ProdosTableRow
```

We will use the ProdosTable component inside the ProdosApp component as shown in the following code:

```
import React, { Component } from 'react';
import ProdosHeader from './ProdosHeader';
import ProdosForm from './ProdosForm';
import ProdosTable from './ProdosTable';
import ProdosFooter from './ProdosFooter';
```

```
class ProdosApp extends Component {

  render() {
   return (
   <div>
    <ProdosHeader/><br/>
    <ProdosForm />
    <ProdosTable name="Electronic Items"/> <br/>
    <ProdosFooter/>
   </div>
   );
  }
}
export default ProdosApp
```

As you can see in the preceding JSX code for the ProdosApp component, we used three React components such as <ProdosHeader/>, <ProdosTable/>, and <ProdosFooter/>. We will navigate to the browser and refresh the page. The output will be as shown in the following screenshot:

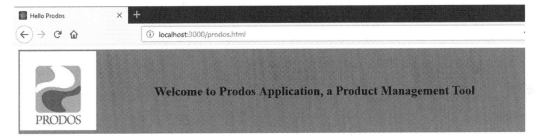

Figure 8.14: Rendering the product list in the table format

In the preceding screenshot, we added a list of product details in the table format. Till now, we have discussed how to handle a list of data with the React components. Now, let's move on to another section and see how to handle an event with the React components.

Handling events with React

The event in the React component is very similar to the event in the DOM elements of HTML. As we know that event names and style names are used in camelCase in React. Let's see the following code where we are adding a simple event listener to the links we have in the previous table of the products (Edit, Delete, and View). We will simply display an alert message when you click on the link:

```
import React, { Component } from 'react';


class ProdosTableRow extends Component {
linkClicked = () => {
 alert('Link clicked');
}


render() {
 return (
  <tr>
   <td>{this.props.product.name}</td>
   <td>{this.props.product.type}</td>
   <td>{this.props.product.brand}</td>
   <td>{this.props.product.description}</td>
   <td><a href="#" onClick={this.linkClicked} >Edit</a></td>
   <td><a href="#" onClick={this.linkClicked} >Delete</a></td>
   <td><a href="#" onClick={this.linkClicked} >View</a></td>
  </tr>
 );
}
}


export default ProdosTableRow
```

Let's run the application and see the following output when we click on any links in the rendered table:

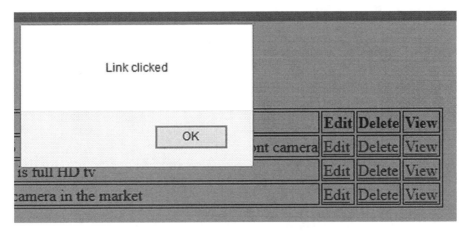

Figure 8.15: The event displays an alert message after clicking on any links.

As you can see in the preceding screenshot, when we click on any links from Edit, Delete, and View, an event onClink is generated and an alert message is displayed. Let's move on to the next section and see how to handle a form in React.

Handling forms with React

In React, the form handling is a little bit different from the traditional HTML form handling. In HTML, the form will navigate to the next web page after form is submitted. But in React, we need to avoid navigating to the next page after submitting the form.

In React, you can't stop the default behaviour by returning false from the event handler method. But you can use the preventDefault() method to prevent the default behaviour of the browser. Let's see the following JSX code where we are using a form and we need to prevent the form submission:

```
import React, { Component } from 'react';

class ProdosForm extends Component {

  handleSubmit(event) {
   alert('Prodos Form submitted');
   // Prevents default behavior
   event.preventDefault();
  }
  render() {
   return (
    <form onSubmit={this.handleSubmit}>
```

```
    <input type="submit" value="Submit" />
  </form>
  );
 }
}
```

export default ProdosForm

We created a simple form using only one submit button. When we submit this form, it will call the handleSubmit() handler function. This handler function displays an alert message and prevents the default behaviour of the browser as shown in the following screenshot:

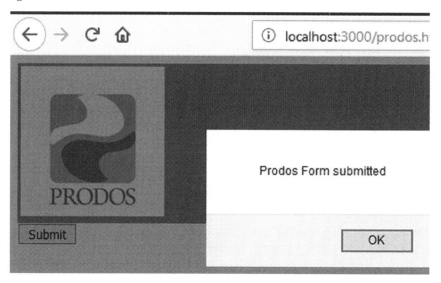

Figure 8.16: Event displays an alert message after submitting the form

Let's add some text fields to the form.

Using input text fields in form with React component

Let us see the following code. I have added a text field to the form and the submit button:

import React, { Component } from 'react';

class ProdosForm extends React.Component {
  constructor(props) {

```
super(props);
this.setState({data: 'type data in text field...'})
};


// Save input box value to state when it has been changed
textChanged = (event) => {
this.setState({data: event.target.value});
};


handleSubmit = (event) => {
alert("Data Typed: "+ this.state.data);
event.preventDefault();
}


render() {
return (
<form onSubmit={this.handleSubmit}>
  <input type="text" onChange={this.textChanged} value={this.state.data}/>
  <input type="submit" value="Submit"/>
</form>
);
}
}
```

export default ProdosForm

In the preceding code, we initialized a state in the constructor of the ProdosForm React component and then we defined two functions, textChanged() and handleSubmit(). The textChanged() function will be called when we type in the text field inside the form. This textChanged() function will update the value of the state. And the handleSubmit() button will submit the form and display an alert popup with the updated state value as shown in the following screenshot:

Figure 8.17: Adding a text field in the form and the
event displays an alert message after submitting a form

As you can see in the preceding screenshot, we typed in the text field and this typed text submits the updated value of data using the state of the React component. The alert message displays the updated value we have typed in the text field in the form at the time of submitting the form.

Adding multiple input text fields in the form

We have added only one text field but typically there are more text fields required in the form. In our Prodos front-end application, we need to create an application form to create a product. This form has more than one field such as Product ID, Product name, brand, type, and description. Let us see the following code which is a complete form to create a product:

```
import React, { Component } from 'react';

class ProdosForm extends Component {
 constructor(props) {
 super(props);
 this.state = {id: '', name: '', brand: '',type: '', description: ''};
 };


 inputChanged = (event) => {
 this.setState({[event.target.name]: event.target.value});
```

```
};

handleSubmit = (event) => {
alert("Hello " +this.state.id +" | "+this.state.name);
event.preventDefault();
}


  render() {
  return (
   <form onSubmit={this.handleSubmit}>
   <table>
    <tr>
    <td>ID: </td>
    <td><input type="text" name="id" onChange={this.inputChanged} value={this.state.id}/></
td>
    </tr>
    <tr>
    <td>Name: </td>
    <td><input type="text" name="name" onChange={this.inputChanged} value={this.state.
name}/></td>
    </tr>
    <tr>
    <td>Brand: </td>
    <td><input type="text" name="brand" onChange={this.inputChanged} value={this.state.
brand}/></td>
    </tr>
    <tr>
    <td>Type: </td>
    <td><input type="text" name="type" onChange={this.inputChanged} value={this.state.
type}/></td>
    </tr>
    <tr>
    <td>Description: </td>
    <td><input type="text" name="description" onChange={this.inputChanged} value={this.state.
description}/></td>
    </tr>
    <tr>
    <td></td>
```

```
    <td><input type="submit" name="Create Product" value="Create Product"/></td>
    </tr>
    </table>
  </form>
 );
 }
}
```

export default ProdosForm

In the preceding code, we created a proper form for our Prodos application to create a product. This form has five text fields and each field will generate an event at the time of input of any text. We have defined a inputChanged() handler. If the input field that triggers the handler is the product ID field, then event.target.name is the ID and the typed value will be saved to a state called ID. In this way, we can handle all input fields with the one change handler.

Let's navigate to the browser and see the updated output as shown in the following screenshot:

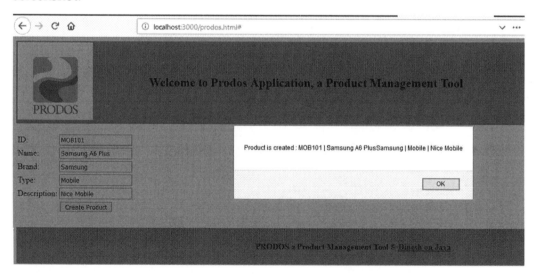

Figure 8.18: Adding multiple text fields in the form to create a product.

We discussed and created the React components for our front-end application. We will now see the React component lifecycle methods in the next section.

The React component lifecycle

There are several React component lifecycle methods provided by the React libraries. You can override these methods according to your application. In the React component lifecycle, these methods are executed in the specific phase. Let us see the following React component lifecycle methods:

- componentWillMount(): This method will be executed before rendering either on the server side or on the client side.

- componentDidMount(): This is a useful method in the mounting phase. This method will be executed after it has been mounted. This method can be used to fetch data from the REST APIs. That means it is suitable where AJAX requests and DOM or state updates should occur. We can also use this method for integration with other JavaScript frameworks.

- componentWillReceiveProps(): This method will be called as soon as the props are updated before another render is called.

- shouldComponentUpdate(): This method will either return a true or false value. This method is used to determine whether a React component is updated or not. This method returns true by default. You can override it if you do not need to render after the state or props are updated and you can return a false value.

- componentWillUpdate(): This method will be executed just before rendering.

- componentDidUpdate(): This method will be executed just after rendering.

- componentWillUnmount(): This method will be executed after a React component is unmounted from the DOM.

- constructor(): This method is like a constructor and it will be executed on the mounting phase of the component lifecycle.

- render(): This method will be executed when the created component is inserted into the DOM. That means it will be called on the mounting phase of the component lifecycle.

As you can see in the preceding list of the React component lifecycle methods, the names of the methods are self-descriptive and you can guess what they are going to be executed.

Let's see the following JSX code. We are initializing the this.state.product to Samsung A6 plus and at the time of mounting, we will change this value to iPhone X:

```
class ProdosApp extends React.Component {
  constructor(props) {
    super(props);
    this.state = {product: 'Samsung A6 plus'}
```

```
}

componentDidMount() {
  this.setState({product: 'iPhone X'});
}

render() {
  return <h1>Hello Prodos, let's present a Product {this.state.user}</h1>;
}
}
```

Similarly, you can test other React component lifecycle methods.

Conclusion

In this chapter, we learned a lot of things related to the React libraries. Still, there are more you can learn about React, but in this chapter, we discussed all the related things that are required for our Prodos front-end application.

We created several React components which we are going to use to build our front-end application. We discussed the basic of JSX, React components, props, and state. We learned how to handle a list and how to iterate a list using the React component and also learned about the stateful and stateless React components. We learned how to handle events in React and how to handle a form in the React-based front-end application.

In the next *Chapter 9: Consuming the REST API with React JS Application*, we will discuss how to consume the created REST services using the React front-end application.

Questions

1. What is JSX?

2. What is a React component?

3. How to create a React component using JSX?

4. How to provide styling to React components?

5. Explain data flow in React components.

6. Explain event flow in React components.

7. How to use multiple React components within a View?

8. What is a stateless React component?

9.   What is a stateful React component?

10.   How to handle a list in a React component?

11.   How to handle an event in a React component?

12.   How to handle a form in a React Components?

13.   What are all React component life cycle methods?

14.   Which method is suitable for making a REST call in life cycle of React components?

## CHAPTER 9

Consuming REST API with React

In the previous chapter, we discussed React and its basic features such as JSX, React components, state, props, and how to create a stateless and stateful React component. We created our Prodos front-end application using React. And we rendered various React components to design a front-end application.

We worked with the events handling with React and iterated a list in the React component to display a list of data in the table format. We also created a form to create a product using the Prodos front-end application. But whatever we rendered that was hardcoded in the application. But in an actual live project, hard coding kills the application. So in this chapter, we will consume REST APIs with the React JS application we created in the previous chapter.

This chapter will provide a quick overview of consuming the REST API using the React application. You will learn how to consume REST APIs using the React front-end application.

In this chapter, we will discuss the following topics:

- Using REST services in a React application
- Using the REST services with the Fetch API
  - o Fetching data using the Fetch API
  - o Posting data using the Fetch API
  - o Editing data using the Fetch API
  - o Deleting data using the Fetch API

- Using third-party React components

Using REST services in a React application

In previous chapters, we created a Prodos backend application. It provides REST APIs to fetch data for the React-based front-end application. In the Prodos backend application, we implemented security as well to access the REST APIs with basic authentication and JWT token-based security.

But as of now, we will not use Spring security, so we have to disable Spring security in the Prodos backend application. We will enable it later in this chapter. We will use the Prodos application REST APIs with Spring security. Let's run the Prodos backend application and access the list of products listed with the Prodos application:

http://localhost:8080/api/products

This preceding REST API will return a list of the products in the JSON format as shown in the following screenshot:

```
←  →  C  ⌂   ⓘ localhost:8080/api/products

{
-  _embedded: {
  -  products: [
    -  {
          name: "Samsung A6 plus",
          type: "Mobile",
          description: "Samsung A6 plus is very nice phone with 24mp front camera",
          brand: "Samsung",
      -  _links: {
        -  self: {
              href: "http://localhost:8080/api/products/MOB01"
          },
        -  product: {
              href: "http://localhost:8080/api/products/MOB01"
          }
        }
      },
    -  {
          name: "iPhone X plus",
          type: "Mobile",
          description: "iPhone X plus is very nice phone with 24mp front camera",
          brand: "Apple",
      -  _links: {
        -  self: {
              href: "http://localhost:8080/api/products/MOB02"
          },
        -  product: {
              href: "http://localhost:8080/api/products/MOB02"
          }
        }
      },
    -  {
          name: "Sony Bravia KLV-50W662F 50 Inch Full HD",
          type: "Television",
          description: "Sony Bravia is full HD tv",
          brand: "Sony",
      -  _links: {
```

Fig 9.1: REST API response

As you can see in the preceding screenshot, the REST API http://localhost:8080/api/products has returned the product list as a resource in the JSON format. In our front-end application, we will use this REST API and render this product list in the web browser. We will discuss how to fetch the REST APIs using React JS in the next section.

Using the REST services with the Fetch API

In the React front-end application, you can use the Fetch API to make a web request to the API server. The Fetch API supports the API and it is very straightforward to use in the React front-end application. The Fetch API has a fetch() method and this method is used to call a remote resource using a REST API. The fetch() method has one mandatory argument that is the path URI of the resource you want to fetch in your React front-end application.

Let's method and this REST API returns a JSON response:

```
//define fetch() method to make a server call in the React
fetch('http://yourapi.com')
  .then(response => response.json())
  .then(responseData => console.log(responseData));
  .catch(error => console.error(error))
```

In the preceding code, we are using the fetch() method which returns a promise that contains the response. Now, we can use the json() method to parse the JSON body from the response.

We can also make an HTTP call with the POST method using the fetch() method of the Fetch API, but in this case, you need to pass another argument to the fetch() method of the Fetch API. The second argument is the object where we can define multiple request settings such as HTTP methods, headers, content type, mode, and more. Let's see the following code:

```
//define fetch() method to make a server call with POST method in the React

fetch('http://yourapi.com',
{
  method: 'POST'
})
.then(response => response.json())
.then(responseData => console.log(responseData))
.catch(error => console.error(error));
```

In the preceding code, we defined only the HTTP POST method as the second argument in the fetch() method of the Fetch API. Let's move ahead and see how to define other important attributes to make a web request.

Now, we will add headers inside the second argument. Let's see the following fetch() code which contains the 'Content-Type' : 'application/json' header:

```
//define fetch() method to make a server call with POST method and by setting content type as application/json in the React
fetch('http://yourapi.com',
{
  method: 'POST',
  headers:{
    'Content-Type': 'application/json'
  }
})
.then(response => response.json())
.then(responseData => console.log(responseData))
.catch(error => console.error(error));
```

Now, if we want to send data to the server, then we have to send this data using the JSON-encoded inside the request body as shown in the following code:

```
//define fetch() method to make a server call with POST method and by setting content type as application/json with request body data in the React

fetch('http://yourapi.com',
{
  method: 'POST',
  headers:{
    'Content-Type': 'application/json'
  },
  body: JSON.stringify(data)
}
.then(response => response.json())
.then(responseData => console.log(responseData))
.catch(error => console.error(error));
```

In the preceding code, we are sending the data using the request body in the JSON format. We have set a header as the content type application/json. Let's implement the Fetch API in our Prodos front-end application.

Fetching data using the Fetch API

As we created the ProdosTable.js file for the ProdosTable React component, let us open the ProdosTable.js file and see the code that we created to render, which will be fetched from the REST API http://localhost:8080/api/products:

```
import React, { Component } from 'react';

class ProdosTable extends Component {
 render() {
  return (
  <div>
  <h1>Product List</h1>
  //Products will be rendered here
  </div>
  );
 }
}
```

```
export default ProdosTable;
```

You can see the code for the ProdosTable component which is stateful because it will render a product list which will be fetched from the backend Prodos application.

But before rendering the product list, we need to add the constructor and define one array type state variable that will be used as a state for the products that were fetched from the REST API (http://localhost:8080/api/products). Let's see the following code that needs to be added to the ProdosTable React component:

```
constructor(props) {
 super(props);
 //Define array type state with default with an empty array
 this.state = {
  products: [

  ]
 };
}
```

In the preceding code, we defined a state as products. Initially, this array is an empty array, but you can assign some default values in case of fallback as shown in the following code:

```
constructor(props) {
 super(props);
 //Define array type state with default with some products in array
 this.state = {
  products: [
  {
    name: "Samsung A6 plus",
    type: "Mobile",
    description: "Samsung A6 plus is very nice phone with 24mp front camera",
    brand: "Samsung"
  },
  {
    name: "Sony Bravia KLV-50W662F 50 Inch Full HD",
    type: "Television",
    description: "Sony Bravia is full HD tv",
    brand: "Sony"
  },
  {
    name: "Canon EOS 1500D Digital SLR Camera",
    type: "DSLR Camera",
    description: "Best DSLR camera in the market",
    brand: "Canon"
  }
  ]
 };
}
```

In the preceding code, we added some products to an array. These products will be rendered if the REST API does not return any response due to some errors at the server end or anything else. But it is not recommended for each application; you can use it according to your business application.

Now, it is time to add the fetch() method to call a REST API to fetch a product list from the server instead of rendering the hardcoded default product list. As we discussed in the lifecycle methods of the React component, we need to add the componentDidMount() lifecycle method to execute the fetch() method of the Fetch API. Let us see the following code that needs to be added to the ProdosTable React component:

```
componentDidMount() {
 fetch('http://localhost:8080/api/products')
```

```
.then((response) => response.json())
.then((responseData) => {
 this.setState({
 products: responseData._embedded.products,
 });
 })
 .catch(err => console.error(err));
}
```

In the preceding code, we are fetching the products from the REST API, that is, http://localhost:8080/api/products. The Fetch API internally uses promise, so the REST API returns data in the JSON format. We are using the then() method of promise. In this method, we have assigned the response to the responseData object. Finally, we used then() to set a state with a products array type.

The REST API returns a product list as shown in the following code:

```
{
 _embedded: {
  products: [
   {

   },
   {

   },
   ..
   ..
  ]
 }
}
```

You can see the JSON format that is returned by the REST API, so we need to assign a product array (_embedded.products) to the state. That is why we initialized our state:

```
this.setState({
 products: responseData._embedded.products,
});
```

We wrote a code to fetch a product list from the server using a REST API. Now, we need to use the map function to transform the product list objects into table rows in the render() method. And we also need to add the table element as shown in the following code:

```
render() {
 return (
 <div>
 <h1>Product List</h1>
 <table border="1">
  <thead>
   <tr>
    <th>Name</th>
    <th>Type</th>
    <th>Brand</th>
    <th>Description</th>
    <th>Edit</th>
    <th>Delete</th>
    <th>View</th>
   </tr>
  </thead>
  <tbody>
{this.state.products.map((productDetails, i) => <ProdosTableRow key = {i}
     product = {productDetails} />)}
  </tbody>
 </table>

 </div>
 );
}
```

In the preceding code, we rendered a product list using a table. We defined a table element of the HTML and also defined a table head for a table using the <thead> element. But the interesting thing inside the table body is using the <tbody> element. In the <tbody> element, we are using another React component, ProdosTableRow. This ProdosTableRow component will create the table rows. Let's see the following code for the ProdosTableRow React component:

```
import React, { Component } from 'react';

class ProdosTableRow extends Component {
 render() {
  return (
```

```
      <tr>
       <td>{this.props.product.name}</td>
       <td>{this.props.product.type}</td>
       <td>{this.props.product.brand}</td>
       <td>{this.props.product.description}</td>
       <td><a href="#">Edit</a></td>
       <td><a href="#">Delete</a></td>
       <td><a href="#">View</a></td>
      </tr>
    );
  }
}
```

```
export default ProdosTableRow;
```

Here is the complete code to render a product list:

```
import React, { Component } from 'react';
import ProdosTableRow from './ProdosTableRow';
import './App.css';


class ProdosTable extends Component {
   constructor(props) {
      super(props);
      this.state = {
       products: [
         {
          name: "Samsung A6 plus",
          type: "Mobile",
          description: "Samsung A6 plus is very nice phone with 24mp front camera",
          brand: "Samsung"
         },
         {
          name: "Sony Bravia KLV-50W662F 50 Inch Full HD",
          type: "Television",
          description: "Sony Bravia is full HD tv",
          brand: "Sony"
         },
         {
          name: "Canon EOS 1500D Digital SLR Camera",
```

```
        type: "DSLR Camera",
        description: "Best DSLR camera in the market",
        brand: "Canon"
      }
    ]
  };
}

componentDidMount() {
  fetch('http://localhost:8080/api/products', {mode: 'cors'})
  .then((response) => response.json())
  .then((responseData) => {
  this.setState({
    products: responseData._embedded.products,
    });
  })
  .catch(err => console.error(err));
}

  render() {
   return (
   <div>
     <h1 className= "Prodos">Product List for {this.props.name}</h1>
     <table border="1">
       <thead>
         <tr>
           <th>Name</th>
           <th>Type</th>
           <th>Brand</th>
           <th>Description</th>
           <th>Edit</th>
           <th>Delete</th>
           <th>View</th>
         </tr>
       </thead>
       <tbody>
         {this.state.products.map((productDetails, i) => <ProdosTableRow key = {i}
           product = {productDetails} />)}
```

```
        </tbody>
      </table>

    </div>
    );
  }
}

  export default ProdosTable;
```

Now, if you start the React app with the npm start command, you will see the following list page:

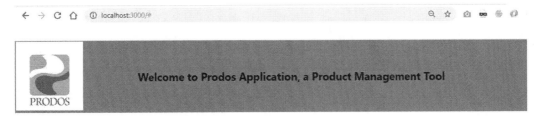

Figure 9.2: *Rendering a product list fetched from a REST API.*

As you can see in the preceding screenshot, our front-end application rendered a product list that is fetched from the REST API.

Posting data using the Fetch API

In the previous section, we fetched a list of products and rendered it using the React component. Now in this section, we will create a new product and send it to the server using the REST API and React component.

We will create a React component that is a file called ProdosForm.js and write the component code for this file as shown in the following code:

```
import React, { Component } from 'react';
```

```
class ProdosForm extends Component {
  render() {
   return (
    <div>
      //Add product form
    </div>
    );
  }
 }
```

export default ProdosForm;

Now, we will add a state that contains all the product-related fields and these fields will be passed to the server using the REST API:

import React, { Component } from 'react';

```
class ProdosForm extends Component {
  constructor(props) {
     super(props);
     this.state = {id: '', name: '', brand: '',type: '', description: ''};
  };

  render() {
   return (
    <div>
      //Add product form
    </div>
    );
  }
 }
```

export default ProdosForm;

As you can see, we added a state for product-related fields, and now we will add an HTML form that contains the input fields needed to collect the product data. All input fields should have the name attribute with a value that is the same as the name of the state the value will be saved to. Input fields also have the onChange handler, which saves the value to the state by invoking the inputChanged() function:

```
import React, { Component } from 'react';

class ProdosForm extends Component {
  constructor(props) {
    super(props);
    this.state = {id: '', name: '', brand: '',type: '', description: ''};
  };

  inputChanged = (event) => {
    this.setState({[event.target.name]: event.target.value});
  };


  render() {
   return (
    <div>
     <form onSubmit={this.handleSubmit}>
   <table>
   <tr>
    <td>ID: </td>
    <td><input type="text" name="id" onChange={this.inputChanged} value={this.state.id}/></td>
   </tr>
   <tr>
    <td>Name: </td>
    <td><input type="text" name="name" onChange={this.inputChanged} value={this.state.name}/></td>
   </tr>
   <tr>
    <td>Brand: </td>
    <td><input type="text" name="brand" onChange={this.inputChanged} value={this.state.brand}/></td>
   </tr>
   <tr>
    <td>Type: </td>
    <td><input type="text" name="type" onChange={this.inputChanged} value={this.state.type}/></td>
   </tr>
   <tr>
```

```
    <td>Description: </td>
    <td><input type="text" name="description" onChange={this.inputChanged} value={this.state.
description}/></td>
  </tr>
  <tr>
  <td></td>
  <td><input type="submit" name="Create Product" value="Create Product"/></td>
  </tr>
  </table>
</form>

  </div>
  );
 }
}
```

```
export default ProdosForm;
```

As you can see in the HTML form in the React component, we called a handleSubmit() function while submitting the form using onSubmit function. Let us implement the handleSubmit() function to the ProdosForm.js file that will send the POST request to the backend prodos/products endpoint. The request will include the new product object inside the body and the 'Content-Type': 'application/json' header. The header is needed because the product object is converted to the JSON format using the JSON. stringify() method:

```
import React, { Component } from 'react';

class ProdosForm extends Component {
  constructor(props) {
    super(props);
    this.state = {id: ", name: ", brand: ",type: ", description: "};
  };

  inputChanged = (event) => {
    this.setState({[event.target.name]: event.target.value});
  };

handleSubmit = (event) => {
  event.preventDefault();
```

```
    var newProduct = {id: this.state.id, name: this.state.name, brand: this.state.brand,
      type: this.state.type, description: this.state.description};

  const myHeaders = new Headers({
      'Content-Type': 'application/json',
      'Accept': 'application/json'
    });

    // Add new product
    fetch('http://localhost:8181/prodos/products',
    {
      method: 'POST', mode: 'no-cors', body: JSON.stringify(newProduct),
      headers:myHeaders,
    })
    .then(response => console.log('Success:', JSON.stringify(response)))
  .catch(error => console.error('Error:', error));
};

    render() {
     return (
      <div>
       <form onSubmit={this.handleSubmit}>
     <table>
     <tr>
      <td>ID: </td>
      <td><input type="text" name="id" onChange={this.inputChanged} value={this.state.id}/></
     td>
      </tr>
      <tr>
      <td>Name: </td>
      <td><input type="text" name="name" onChange={this.inputChanged} value={this.state.
     name}/></td>
      </tr>
      <tr>
      <td>Brand: </td>
      <td><input type="text" name="brand" onChange={this.inputChanged} value={this.state.
     brand}/></td>
      </tr>
```

```
  <tr>
   <td>Type: </td>
   <td><input type="text" name="type" onChange={this.inputChanged} value={this.state.
type}/></td>
  </tr>
  <tr>
   <td>Description: </td>
   <td><input type="text" name="description" onChange={this.inputChanged} value={this.state.
description}/></td>
  </tr>
  <tr>
   <td></td>
   <td><input type="submit" name="Create Product" value="Create Product"/></td>
  </tr>
  </table>
 </form>

   </div>
  );
 }
}


export default ProdosForm;
```

Now, we added a React component to our front-end Prodos application to add a new product. We will start the front-end application as shown in the following screenshot:

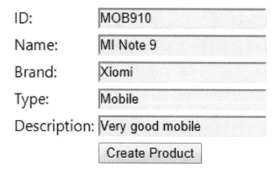

Figure 9.3: Rendering a Product Form to add a new product

As we have added a product form in the HTML web page, let us add a new product by clicking on the Create Product button. In the following screenshot, you can see a new product being added to the product list:

Product List for Electronic Items

Name	Type	Brand	Description	Edit	Delete	View
Samsung A6 plus	Mobile	Samsung	Samsung A6 plus is very nice phone with 24mp front camera	Edit	Delete	View
iPhone X plus	Mobile	Apple	iPhone X plus is very nice phone with 24mp front camera	Edit	Delete	View
Sony Bravia KLV-50W662F 50 Inch Full HD	Television	Sony	Sony Bravia is full HD tv	Edit	Delete	View
Canon EOS 1500D Digital SLR Camera	DSLR Camera	Canon	Best DSLR camera in the market	Edit	Delete	View
JBL Cinema 510 5.1 with Powered Subwoofer	Home Theater Speaker	JBL	This sound system is suitable for the Home Theater	Edit	Delete	View
MI Note 9	Mobile	Xiomi	Very good mobile	Edit	Delete	View

Figure 9.4: A new product is added to the product list.

In the preceding screenshot of the product list, the last product added a new product using the React component and REST API POST http://localhost:8181/prodos/ products. We saw how to add a new product using the REST API with the React-based front-end application. Now, we will see how to edit the information for an existing product.

Editing data using the Fetch API

To update the product data, we need to send a PUT HTTP request to the http:// localhost:8181/prodos/products/{productId} URL. You need to send the updated product object at the time calling this REST API. The HTTP PUT request contains the updated product data either inside the form data or request body.

The product form structure is similar to the add product functionality. Here is the code that needs to be added to update the product data in the server:

```
handleUpdate = (event) => {
  event.preventDefault();
  var updatedProduct = {id: this.state.id, name: this.state.name, brand: this.state.brand,
      type: this.state.type, description: this.state.description};

  const myHeaders = new Headers({
      'Content-Type': 'application/json',
      'Accept': 'application/json'
  });

  //Update a product
  fetch('http://localhost:8181/prodos/products/'+this.state.id,
  {
    method: 'PUT', mode: 'no-cors', body: JSON.stringify(updatedProduct),
    headers:myHeaders,
```

```
})
  .then(response => console.log('Success Updated:', JSON.stringify(response)))
  .catch(error => console.error('Error:', error));
};
```

The preceding code is needed to update the product data. We will update the description of the newly added product in the earlier section with the product ID (MOB910). We will update this product with a new description of the product. Let's see the following screenshot to update the product data:

ID:	MOB910
Name:	MI Note 9
Brand:	Xiomi
Type:	Mobile
Description:	Very good mobile with 32MP

Update Product

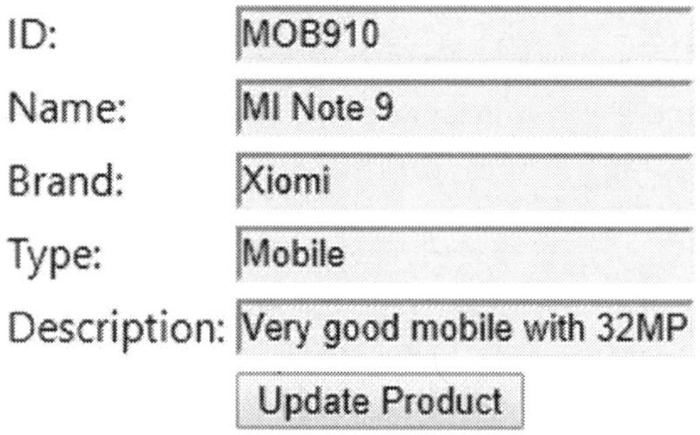

Figure 9.5: Rendering a Product Form to update the product data

As you can see in the preceding screenshot, we updated a product with the product ID (MOB910), which was created in the previous section. In this product, we are only updating the product description. Click on the Update Product button and see the following updated product list:

Name	Type	Brand	Description	Edit	Delete	View
Samsung A6 plus	Mobile	Samsung	Samsung A6 plus is very nice phone with 24mp front camera	Edit	Delete	View
iPhone X plus	Mobile	Apple	iPhone X plus is very nice phone with 24mp front camera	Edit	Delete	View
Sony Bravia KLV-50W662F 50 Inch Full HD	Television	Sony	Sony Bravia is full HD tv	Edit	Delete	View
Canon EOS 1500D Digital SLR Camera	DSLR Camera	Canon	Best DSLR camera in the market	Edit	Delete	View
JBL Cinema 510 5.1 with Powered Subwoofer	Home Theater Speaker	JBL	This sound system is suitable for the Home Theater	Edit	Delete	View
MI Note 9	Mobile	Xiomi	Very good mobile with 32MP front camera	Edit	Delete	View

Figure 9.6: A product is updated into the product list

In the preceding screenshot, you can see the updated description of the product with the product ID (MOB910). Now, we can add the delete functionality in our Prodos front-end application.

Deleting data using the Fetch API

Now, we will implement the delete functionality in our Prodos application. Products can be deleted from the database by sending the DELETE HTTP request to the REST API http://localhost:8181/prodos/products/{productId}. In the product list, we have a link to delete a product; we can implement the handleDeleteClick() function as shown in the following code:

```
handleDeleteClick = (id) => {
// Delete the product
fetch('http://localhost:8181/prodos/products/'+id,
{
method: 'DELETE',
})
.then(response => console.log('Success Deleted:', JSON.stringify(response)))
.catch(error => console.error('Error:', error));
};
```

We added the preceding code to the ProdosTableRow.js file, and one more change is required to call this method when anyone clicks on the delete link in the table list:

```
import React, { Component } from 'react';

class ProdosTableRow extends Component {
 handleDeleteClick = (id) => {
  // Delete the product
  fetch('http://localhost:8181/prodos/products/'+id,
  {
  method: 'DELETE',
  })
  .then(response => console.log('Successful Deleted:'))
  .catch(error => console.error('Error:', error));
 };
 render() {
  return (
   <tr>
    <td>{this.props.product.name}</td>
    <td>{this.props.product.type}</td>
    <td>{this.props.product.brand}</td>
    <td>{this.props.product.description}</td>
    <td><a href="#">Edit</a></td>
    <td><a href="#" onClick={()=>{this.handleDeleteClick(this.props.product.id)}} >Delete</a></
```

```
td>
    <td><a href="#">View</a></td>
  </tr>
 );
 }
}
```

export default ProdosTableRow;

We need to click on the delete link in the product list and the product will be deleted. Then, refresh the product list again to see the updated product list as shown in the following screenshot:

Product List for Electronic Items

Name	Type	Brand	Description	Edit	Delete	View
Canon EOS 1500D Digital SLR Camera	DSLR Camera	Canon	Best DSLR camera in the market	Edit	Delete	View
JBL Cinema 510 5.1 with Powered Subwoofer	Home Theater Speaker	JBL	This sound system is suitable for the Home Theater	Edit	Delete	View
MI Note 9	Mobile	Xiomi	Very good mobile with 32MP front camera	Edit	Delete	View

Figure 9.7: An updated product after deleting some products.

You can see the updated product list. We deleted some products by clicking on the delete link corresponding to each row of the table. We implemented the CRUD functionality using React and the REST API. In the next section, we will explore some third-party React components, and we will use them in our Prodos front-end application to beautify our UI.

Using third-party React components in our application

In this section, we will use third-party React components to make an interactive UI. First, we will use the React Table component instead of a traditional HTML table.

Using the ReactTable

Earlier, we have used the HTML table and rendered the product list in the web page. Now, we will use the ReactTable component. It is a featured React component and provides a lot of interactive UI features such as pagination, sorting, filtering, and more.

We will install the ReactTable component in our Prodos front-end application by using the following command.

npm install react-table --save

Now, let us update the code of the ProdosTable.js file:

```
import React, { Component } from 'react';
import ReactTable from "react-table";
import {API_SERVER_URL} from './constants.js'
import 'react-table/react-table.css';
import './App.css';

class ProdosTable extends Component {
  constructor(props) {
    super(props);
    this.state = {
     products: [

     ]
    };
  }
  componentDidMount() {
   fetch(API_SERVER_URL+'/prodos/products', {mode: 'cors'})
   .then((response) => response.json())
   .then((responseData) => {
   this.setState({
    products: responseData.products,
    });
   })
   .catch(err => console.error(err));
  }
  render() {
   const columns = [{
    Header: 'Name',
    accessor: 'name'
    }, {
    Header: 'Type',
    accessor: 'type',
    }, {
    Header: 'Brand',
    accessor: 'brand',
    }, {
    Header: 'Description',
```

```
    accessor: 'description',
   },]
  return (
  <div>
   <h1 className= "Prodos">Product List for {this.props.name}</h1>
   <ReactTable data={this.state.products} columns={columns} filterable={true}/>
   </div>
   );
  }
 }
export default ProdosTable;
```

In the updated code of the ProdosTable.js file, we removed the traditional HTML table rendering code, and we are using the ReactTable react component here. Also, we are using the API_SERVER_URL variable exported from the constants.js file. The code for fetching the products from the server is very similar to the earlier code.

In the render() method, we defined the columns of the table where an accessor is the field of the car object and the header is the text of the header. We also enabled filtering by setting the filterable prop of the table to true.

We will start the development server using the npm start command and navigate to the http://localhost:3000/. Now, the list page looks like the following screenshot:

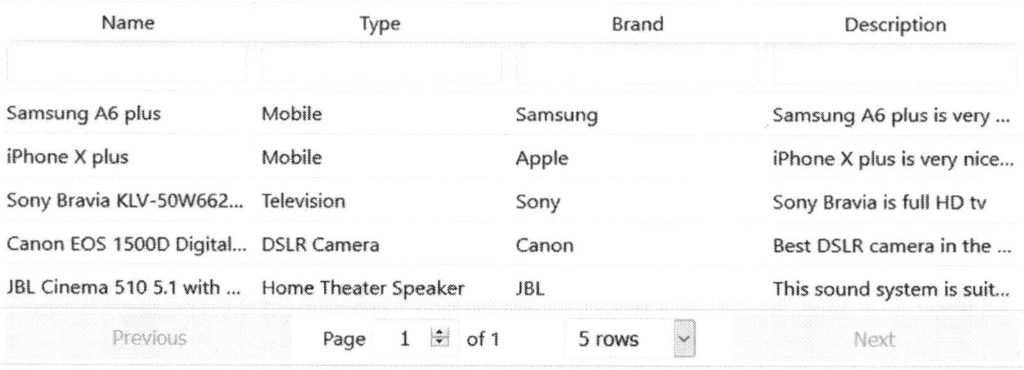

Name	Type	Brand	Description
Samsung A6 plus	Mobile	Samsung	Samsung A6 plus is very ...
iPhone X plus	Mobile	Apple	iPhone X plus is very nice...
Sony Bravia KLV-50W662...	Television	Sony	Sony Bravia is full HD tv
Canon EOS 1500D Digital...	DSLR Camera	Canon	Best DSLR camera in the ...
JBL Cinema 510 5.1 with ...	Home Theater Speaker	JBL	This sound system is suit...
Previous	Page 1 ⊕ of 1	5 rows ⌄	Next

Figure 9.8: Using the ReactTable React component

You can see the updated table, which renders the product list using the ReactTable react component.

Using React Skylight

Now, let us update the add product form using the React Skylight React component. First, we will install it using the following command:

npm install react-skylight --save

Let's now update the code of the ProdosForm.js file as shown in the following code snippet:

```
import React, { Component } from 'react';
import SkyLight from 'react-skylight';

class ProdosForm extends Component {
  constructor(props) {
   super(props);
   this.state = {id: '', name: '', brand: '',type: '', description: ''};
  };
  inputChanged = (event) => {
   this.setState({[event.target.name]: event.target.value});
  };
  handleSubmit = (event) => {
   // code for handle submit button, similar to the previous code
  };
  // Cancel and close modal form
  cancelSubmit = (event) => {
   event.preventDefault();
   this.refs.addDialog.hide();
  }

  render() {
   return (
    <div>
     <SkyLight hideOnOverlayClicked ref="addDialog">
     <form onSubmit={this.handleUpdate} id="product-form">
          //Input fields here, similar to the previous code
     </form>
     </SkyLight>
     <div>
       <button style={{'margin': '10px'}} onClick={() => this.refs.addDialog.show()}>New
Product</button>
```

```
      </div>
    </div>
  );
 }
}
export default ProdosForm;
```

As you can see in the preceding updated code of ProdosForm.js file, we used the ReactSkylight modal form component with buttons and the input fields that are needed to collect the product data.

Let's add this ProdosForm.js file to the ProdosTable.js file by importing using the following command:

```
import ProdosForm from './ProdosForm.js'
```

Let's add the ProdosFrom component to the render() method and pass the addProduct and fetchProducts functions as props to the ProdosForm component that allows us to call these functions from the ProdosForm component. Now, the return statement of the ProdosTable.js file should look like the following code:

```
<div>
 <h1 className= "Prodos">Product List for {this.props.name}</h1>
 <ReactTable data={this.state.products} columns={columns} filterable={true} pageSize={5}/>
 <ProdosForm addProduct={this.addProduct} fetchProducts={this.fetchProducts}/>
</div>
```

Refresh the web browser and see the following updated UI:

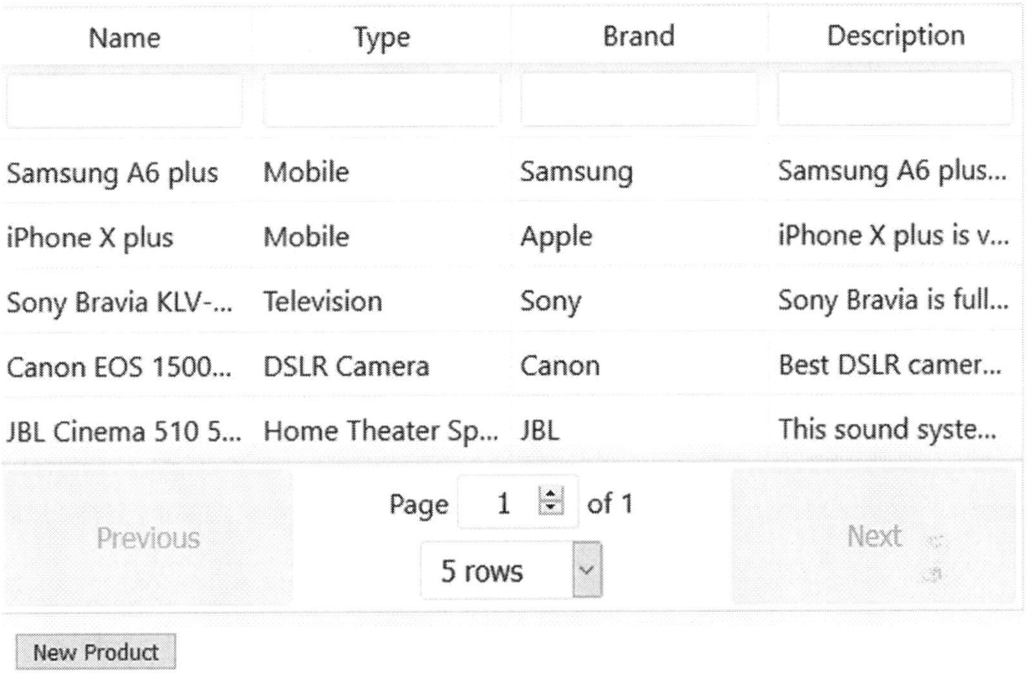

Name	Type	Brand	Description
Samsung A6 plus	Mobile	Samsung	Samsung A6 plus...
iPhone X plus	Mobile	Apple	iPhone X plus is v...
Sony Bravia KLV-...	Television	Sony	Sony Bravia is full...
Canon EOS 1500...	DSLR Camera	Canon	Best DSLR camer...
JBL Cinema 510 5...	Home Theater Sp...	JBL	This sound syste...

Page 1 of 1

Previous   5 rows   Next

New Product

Figure 9.9: Adding the New Product button

As you can see in the preceding screenshot, there is a button named **New Product**. When you click on this button, it opens the modal form as shown in the following screenshot:

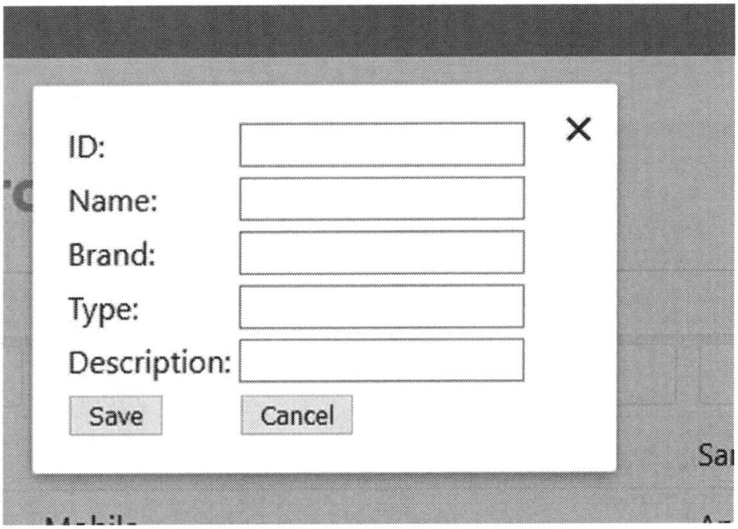

ID:
Name:
Brand:
Type:
Description:
Save   Cancel

Figure 9.10: Adding the New Product Form with the Skylight React Component

You can see the updated product form with the Skylight React component.

Using the Toast message React component

You can also use the React-toastify component to generate a feedback message for any deletion or creation of the product. Let us install the React-toastify component using the following command:

npm install react-toastify --save

Let's implement the toast messages with the delete functionality. We need to import ToastContainer, toast, and the style sheet to start using React-toastify. Let's add the following import code to the ProdosTable.js file:

```
import { ToastContainer, toast } from 'react-toastify';

import 'react-toastify/dist/ReactToastify.css';
```

In the preceding code, we imported the ToastContainer container toast from React-toastify. The ToastContainer container is the component for showing toast messages. We need to define ToastContainer inside the render() method as shown in the following code:

```
return (
 <div>
 <h1 className= "Prodos">Product List for {this.props.name}</h1>
 <ReactTable data={this.state.products} columns={columns} filterable={true} pageSize={5}/>
 <ProdosForm addProduct={this.addProduct} fetchProducts={this.fetchProducts}/>
 <ToastContainer autoClose={2000} />
 </div>
 );
```

As you can see in the preceding code, we defined the ToastContainer with the duration of the toast message in milliseconds using the autoClose prop.

Now, we can call the toast method at the time of deleting a product in the handleDeleteClick() function to display the toast message. We can also define the position for the toast message on our web page. Let's see the following code:

```
handleDeleteClick = (id) => {
  // Delete the product
  fetch(API_SERVER_URL+'/prodos/products/'+id,
  {
   method: 'DELETE',
  })
```

```
     .then(res => {
       toast.success("Product deleted", {
         position: toast.POSITION.BOTTOM_LEFT
       });
       this.fetchProducts();
     })
     .catch(err => {
       toast.error("Error when deleting", {
       position: toast.POSITION.BOTTOM_LEFT
       });
       console.error(err)
     })
};
```

In the preceding code, we defined two toast messages. The first message is the success message, which will be shown when deletion succeeds, and the second message is the error message, which will be shown in the case of an error.

Let's delete a product from the product list page; a toast message will be displayed on the screen, as shown in the following screenshot:

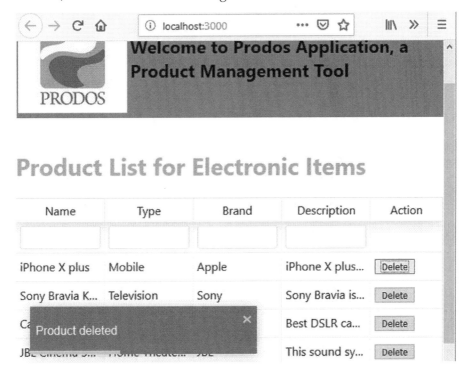

Figure 9.11: A toast message is shown when we delete a product.

We added the toast message after successful deletion; similarly, we can also use the delete confirmation message before we actually delete to avoid accidental deletion. Let us see in the next section.

Using the react-confirm-alert Component

Let's use the following command to install this React third-party component:

npm install react-confirm-alert --save

After successful installation, let us import this React component to the ProdosTable. js file:

import { confirmAlert } from 'react-confirm-alert';

import 'react-confirm-alert/src/react-confirm-alert.css'

Let's add a new deleteConfirm() function to the ProdosTable.js file. This function will be responsible to open the confirmation dialog. If you press YES, it will call the handleDeleteClick() function else the confirmation dialog box will be closed. Let's see the following code:

```
deleteConfirm = (id) => {
 confirmAlert({
   message: 'Are you sure to delete?',
   buttons: [
   {
    label: 'Yes',
    onClick: () => this.handleDeleteClick(id)
   },
   {
    label: 'No',
   }
   ]
 })
}
```

Now, we need to make some changes in the onClick() event of the delete button as shown in the following code:

```
render() {
 const columns = [{
 Header: 'Name',
 accessor: 'name'
```

```
}, {
Header: 'Type',
accessor: 'type',
}, {
Header: 'Brand',
accessor: 'brand',
}, {
Header: 'Description',
accessor: 'description',
},
{
  Header: 'Action',
  id: 'delbutton',
  sortable: false,
  filterable: false,
  width: 100,
  accessor: 'id',
  Cell: ({value}) => (<button onClick={()=>{this.deleteConfirm(value)}}>Delete</button>)
}]
  ...
}
```

Let's start the development server and refresh the browser and press the Delete button. You will see the confirmation dialog box as shown in the following screenshot:

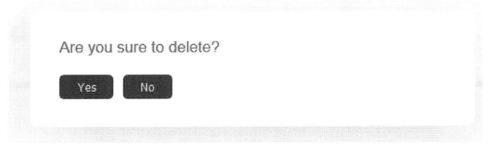

Figure 9.12: An alert confirmation message is shown when we delete a product.

In the preceding screenshot, there are two options YES or NO. If you press YES, the product will be deleted.

There are many more third-party React components available, which you can install in your application and import them to use accordingly. In this chapter, we discussed only those third-party React components that are needed for our Prodos front-end application.

Conclusion

In this chapter, we discussed how to consume REST APIs with the React-based front-end application. We used the fetch() method of the FETCH API to consume REST APIs. We implemented the CRUD functionalities using the REST APIs and React front-end application.

We also discussed the React third-party components to beautify our Prodos front-end application. We implemented some third-party React components such as ReactTable, skylight, toast messages, and alert confirmation messages, and more.

In the next *Chapter 10: Deploying and Containerizing Application*, we will discuss how to create the REST services using Spring Boot.

Questions

1. How to consume REST APIs?

2. How to test the REST API using Postman?

3. What are HTTP methods?

4. What is difference between POST and GET?

5. What is Fetch API in React?

6. How to set headers in React to make a REST call?

7. What are third-party react components and how to use them in our application?

CHAPTER 10

Deploying and Containerizing Applications

We created a Prodos front-end application using the React JS framework and also created a Prodos backend application using Spring Boot 2. We also implemented security in the Prodos backend application. In the previous chapter, the Prodos front-end application has consumed REST APIs provided by the Prodos backend application.

In this chapter, we will explain how to deploy our Prodos backend and front-end application to a server. There are several varieties of platforms available such as the **Platform as a Service (PaaS)**, **Amazon Web Service (AWS)**, Heroku, Pivotal Cloud Foundry, Google Cloud, Microsoft Azure, and Digital Ocean. We can use any one of them. We will use Heroku Cloud which supports multiple programming languages such as Java, Node.js, Scala, Clojure, Python, PHP, and Go.

In this chapter, we will also discuss how to use Docker containers in deployment. We will create a Docker image for our Prodos backend application and we will use this Docker image in the server.

In this chapter, we will cover the following topics:

- Deploying applications to the Cloud platform
    - o   Deploying the Spring Boot backend application
    - o   Deploying the React JS front-end application

- Introduction to containers
    - o Benefits of the container-oriented approach
    - o Drawbacks of the container-oriented approach
- Getting started with Docker
- Deploy using Docker containers
    - o Creating Dockerfile
    - o Creating a Docker image using a Maven plugin
    - o Creating a Docker image using the Docker build command

After reading this chapter, you will be able to understand how to deploy your backend and front-end application to the cloud server. You will also understand how to create a Docker image for your application.

Deploying applications to the Cloud platform

Nowadays, technologies are evolving in each area. Earlier, if you wanted to deploy your application to the server, then you needed at least a server. But, now, the cloud services make it very easy to deploy your application to the server in the cloud.

The cloud computing provides the **Platform as a Service** (**PaaS**) to provide the platform and infrastructure that are required to deploy your applications. So, you don't need to maintain any server or infrastructure for your application.

There are many platforms available such as Microsoft Azure, Google Cloud, AWS, Heroku, Cloud Foundry, and so on. You can use any one of them. But in this chapter, we will see how to deploy your front-end and backend application to the Heroku cloud platform.

Heroku is a cloud platform as a service supporting several programming languages. Heroku, one of the first cloud platforms, has been in development since June 2007, when it supported only the Ruby programming language, but now supports Java, Node.js, Scala, Clojure, Python, PHP, and Go. For this reason, Heroku is said to be a polyglot platform as it allows a developer to build, run and scale applications in a similar manner across all the languages. Heroku was acquired by Salesforce.com in 2010.

We are not going to discuss more about the Heroku platform. We will directly move on to the deployment of your applications using the Heroku platform.

Deploying the Spring Boot backend application

If you want to use your own application server, then you can easily deploy your Spring Boot-based backend application. You can generate an executable JAR file of your application using the following Maven command:

$ mvn clean install

The preceding command creates an executable JAR file for your Spring Boot backend application and runs the created JAR file using the Java command, java -jar prodos-backend.jar. Your application will run on the embedded Tomcat server.

If you don't want to use the embedded Tomcat server for your application, then you can use a separate application server. In this case, you need to create a WAR file instead of a JAR file of your Spring Boot backend application. To create a WAR file, you need to make the following change in the pom.xml file:

<packaging>war</packaging>

As you can see in the preceding code, we changed the packaging from JAR to WAR in the pom.xml file. We also need to add the following Maven dependency to avoid using the embedded Tomcat server:

```
<dependency>
  <groupId>org.springframework.boot</groupId>
  <artifactId>spring-boot-starter-tomcat</artifactId>
  <scope>provided</scope>
</dependency>
```

Along with these changes, one more change is required to be made inside the application class file as shown in the following code:

```
@SpringBootApplication
public class ProdosApplication extends SpringBootServletInitializer {

  @Override
  protected SpringApplicationBuilder configure(SpringApplicationBuilder application) {
    return application.sources(ProdosApplication.class);
  }

  public static void main(String[] args) throws Exception {
    SpringApplication.run(ProdosApplication.class, args);
  }
}
```

As you can see in the preceding code, we modified an application main class by extending SpringBootServletIntializer and overriding the configure method.

After making the above changes, build your application to create a WAR file. You can deploy this WAR file to any Tomcat server by copying the file to Tomcat's / webapps folder.

Furthermore, let us discuss how to deploy your Prodos backend application to the Heroku cloud platform instead of a local application server. Before using the Heroku platform, you need to create an account on the Heroku platform. Let us go to https:// www.heroku.com/ to create an account.

Let's follow the given steps for the deployment process with the Heroku cloud platform:

1. Create an account on Heroku https://www.heroku.com/ and after creating your account with Heroku, log in to the account and navigate to the dashboard. You can select **Create a new app** from the menu as shown in the following screenshot:

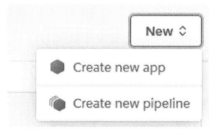

Fig 10.1: The Heroku dashboard to create a new app.

2. After clicking on **Create new app**, provide a name to your app and select a region as shown in the following screenshot:

Fig 10.2: Create a new app

3. In the preceding step, we provided our application name as prodosbackend to the Heroku cloud platform and clicked on the **Create app** button. After clicking on the **Create app** button, on the next screen, select a deployment method. There are several deployment methods available as shown in the following screenshot:

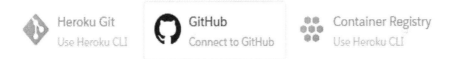

Fig 10.3: Application deployment methods

4. You can choose any one of them. We are using the GitHub option. First, you need to push your application to the GitHub repository and then you need to connect your Github repository to Heroku as shown in the following screenshot:

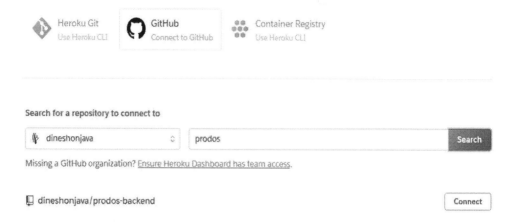

Fig 10.4: GitHub selected as a deployment method

5. In the preceding screenshot, we searched our application repository in GitHub by typing prodos. Finally, we got the prodos-backend application repository and let us connect by clicking on the **Connect** button.

6. After clicking on the connect button, the next screen will appear on the screen. In the next screen, you need to select the branch of your application repository from GitHub; we selected the **Master** branch as the default value. There are other two options available, manual and automatic deployment. The automatic option deploys your application if any change or new version is pushed to the connected GitHub repository. And in manual, we need to deploy it manually by selecting the branch. In our case, we are using the manual option of the deployment as shown in the following screenshot:

Enable automatic deploys from GitHub

Every push to the branch you specify here will deploy a new version of this app. **Deploys happen automatically:** be sure that this branch is always in a deployable state and any tests have passed before you push. Learn more.

Choose a branch to deploy

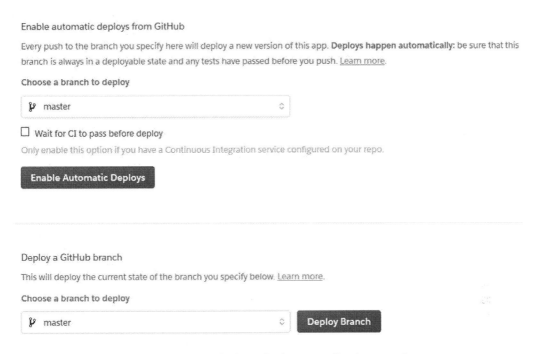

☐ Wait for CI to pass before deploy

Only enable this option if you have a Continuous Integration service configured on your repo.

Enable Automatic Deploys

Deploy a GitHub branch

This will deploy the current state of the branch you specify below. Learn more.

Choose a branch to deploy

Fig 10.5: Selecting the branch of your application repository

7. Click on the **Deploy Branch** button on the preceding screen. Now, the deployment has started and you can see a build log as shown in the following screenshot:

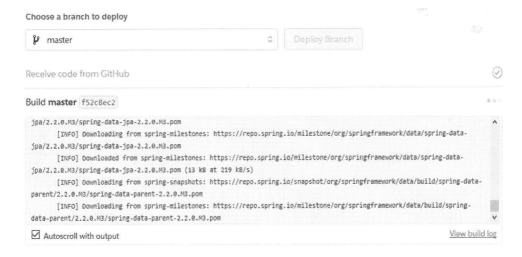

Fig 10.6: Build Logs

8. You can see the logs in the preceding screenshot which means our application is being deployed to the Heroku cloud platform. You will see the following message if your application was deployed successfully:

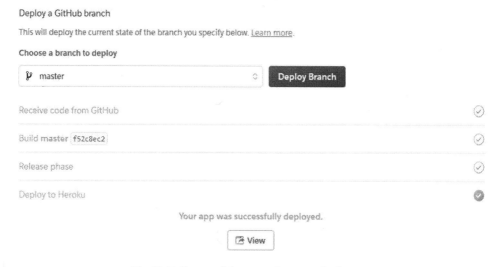

Deploy a GitHub branch

This will deploy the current state of the branch you specify below. Learn more.

Choose a branch to deploy

⨾ master

Deploy Branch

Receive code from GitHub

Build master f52c8ec2

Release phase

Deploy to Heroku

Your app was successfully deployed.

View

Fig 10.7: Successful screen for your deployment

9. As you can see in the preceding screenshot, your application has been deployed to the Heroku cloud server successfully. Now, we can verify it by clicking on the **View** button. The Heroku cloud server has exposed our backend application at https://prodosbackend.herokuapp.com/. Let's make a call to REST endpoint /prodos/products to test this deployment of our prodos backend application as shown in the following screenshot:

https://prodosbackend.herokuapp.com/prodos/products

```
products: [
  - {
        id: "MOB01",
        name: "Samsung A6 plus",
        type: "Mobile",
        description: "Samsung A6 plus is very nice phone with 24mp front camera",
        brand: "Samsung"
    },
  - {
        id: "MOB02",
        name: "iPhone X plus",
        type: "Mobile",
        description: "iPhone X plus is very nice phone with 24mp front camera",
        brand: "Apple"
    },
  - {
        id: "TLV01",
        name: "Sony Bravia KLV-50W662F 50 Inch Full HD",
        type: "Television",
        description: "Sony Bravia is full HD tv",
        brand: "Sony"
    },
```

Fig 10.8: REST API output

10. You can view the application logs by clicking on **View logs** from the **More** menu:

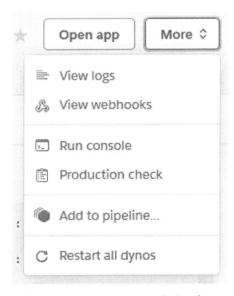

Fig 10.9: More options and View logs

We deployed our Prodos backend application to the Heroku cloud server. And we also verified this using a REST endpoint (/prodos/products). Now, it is time to deploy our Prodos front-end application to the Heroku cloud server.

Deploying the React JS front-end application

Now, we will deploy our Prodos front-end application to the Heroku cloud server. As we know that we have used the React JS for our front-end application. So, its deployment process is a little bit different from the process of the backend application deployment. In the backend application deployment, we used the Heroku web console to deploy our Prodos backend application.

But in this case, we will use the Heroku CLI to deploy our React front-end application to the Heroku cloud server. We will use the **Heroku Buildpack** for create-react-app from https://github.com/mars/create-react-app-buildpack. Let's follow the given steps to deploy the React JS front-end application:

1. First, let's install the Heroku CLI by downloading the installation package from https://devcenter.heroku.com/articles/heroku-cli. After the installation is complete, we can use the Heroku CLI from PowerShell or any other command prompt.

2. As we know, our front-end application uses the REST API server to make a REST call to fetch the product data. So, now we need to change our REST API server in the Prodos front-end application by setting API_SERVER_URL = 'https://prodosbackend.herokuapp.com/' in our constants.js file of the Prodos front-end application.

3. Now, we will commit our Prodos front-end application code to the GitHub local repository by running the following git commands:

   ```
   $ git init
   $ git add .
   $ git commit -m "your commit message"
   ```

4. Let's create a new Heroku application using the following command:

   ```
   $ heroku create prodosfrontend --buildpack https://github.com/mars/create-react-app-buildpack.git
   ```

   In the preceding command, we used prodosfrontend as a Heroku application name. It will ask for credentials to log in to Heroku as shown in the following screenshot:

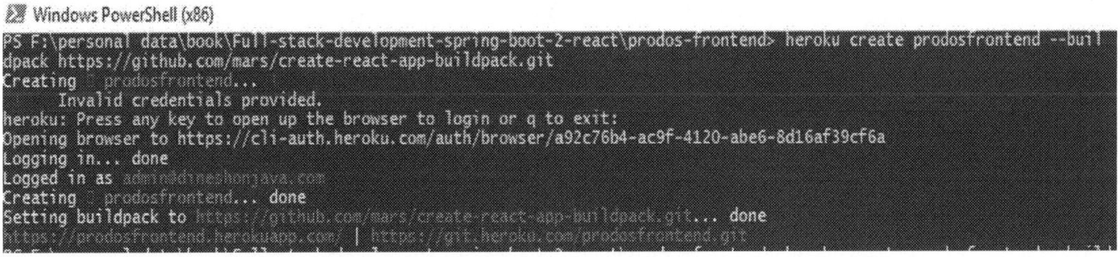

Fig 10.10: Creating a Heroku application using the CLI

As you can see in the preceding screenshot, a prodosfrontend application is created and a buildpack is set to https://github.com/mars/create-react-app-buildpack.git.

5. Now, let's deploy the created prodosfrontend application using the following command:

$ git push heroku master

After running the preceding command on PowerShell, the output will be as shown in the following screenshot:

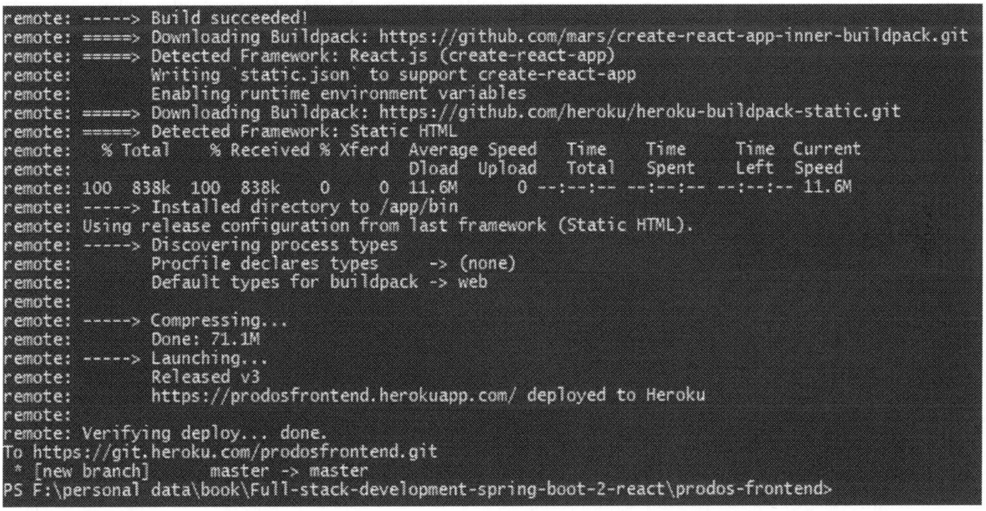

Fig 10.11: The Prodosfrontend application deployment using the Heroku CLI

As you can see in the preceding screenshot we successfully deployed the front-end application to the Heroku cloud server. Now, you can go to the Heroku dashboard and see that there are two applications that have been deployed to the Heroku cloud server, as shown in the following screenshot:

Fig 10.12: Heroku Dashboard

As you can see, both the applications, backend and frontend, are available now on the Heroku cloud server.

6. Now, navigate to your front-end application using the URL exposed by the Heroku cloud server as https://prodosfrontend.herokuapp.com/:

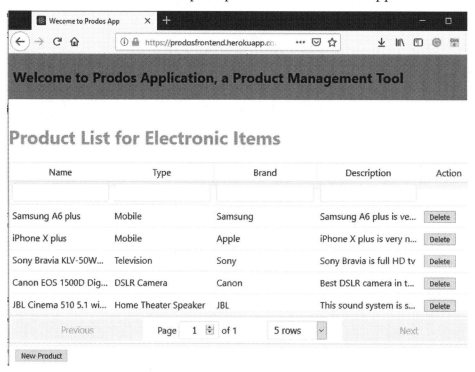

Fig 10.13: Prodos Frontend application

As you can see in the preceding screenshot, we opened a web page of the product list. The products are fetched from the Prodos backend application using the REST API.

We deployed our Prodos backend and frontend applications to the Heroku cloud server. We also verified both the applications. Now, in the next section, we will discuss how to use containers to deploy an application and how to create a container image to ship this image across the platform.

Introducing containers

With the advent of technology and the advancement that it has brought to the modern world, we are left astounded every day because of the heights it has reached and the potential heights it has yet to discover. But this has only been the association with the tangible aspects of our society.

If we dare delve into the advancements that are carrying the intricacy behind those tangible things, we cannot justify their presence by merely acknowledging them. Software is the concept relaying the advanced technologies we proudly brag about. One of these discoveries is known as **Docker** which uses containers.

These containers are the face of virtualizing applications. They deal with the successful running of an application while Docker manages to package that software into completion. It is a kind of storage unit that binds libraries, configuration files, binary code, and other dependencies together. They are referred to as the operating system virtualization though it may get you wondering about the virtual machines and their system of virtualization.

However, a container is very similar to the physical or virtual machine, but the concepts used by the container technology are different from the concepts used by the virtual machines. Let's see the following diagram about a VM:

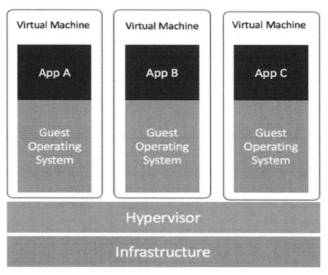

Fig 10.14: A VM architecture

As you can see in the preceding diagram, VMs have their own operating systems and use a hypervisor to share a common infrastructure. A Hypervisor is computer software that manages and shares the hardware among the VMs. Each application (**App A** or **App B** or **App C**) is deployed to a dedicated VM.

Unlike virtual machines, the containers don't have their own dedicated operating systems. The containers have a file system and you can access them over a network just like a VM. Let's see the following diagram about containers:

Containerized Applications

App A
Bins/Lib

App B
Bins/Lib

App C
Bins/Lib

Docker (Container Engine)

Host Operating System

Infrastructure

Fig 10.15: A container architecture

As you can see in the preceding diagram of the container architecture, each application (**App A**, **App B**, or **App C**) has its own bins and related libraries. The containers use the same host operating system. They share the resources of the operating system using the container engines such Docker. Containers share resources so they require fewer resources than virtual machines. The containers are running as an isolated process on the host operating system.

Let's see the following differences between the VMs and containers:

- A VM and container share the same interest, to isolate an application along with the dependent variables the application possesses. The point at which they differ is their host system; the VM utilizes the hyperservice system while containers are rendered towards a sharing system of kernels with other containers.

- Containers are initialized on the Linux system. Though the market is focusing on its expansion towards a broader area, they have been on a small scale for now. But they are steadily gaining momentum, expanding across different OS and offering the flexibility of work for developers.

Understanding how a container works

Let's dive a bit deeper to understand how a container works. Usually, if you are, say a Python developer, you would opt to create a virtual environment; a local collection of storage and memory allocated to the development of a particular application. What a virtual environment does is allocate RAM and memory of your laptop or PC, and allows you to seamlessly work while ensuring other applications are not disturbed. Furthermore, if you are someone who requires working on multiple versions of Python and developing various applications for each, then virtual environment is a neat way of achieving that. Creating multiple virtual environments can isolate the space for each of the applications, associating the respective version with each, respectively.

But where does a container come in this picture? A step ahead of the virtual environment is a container. The container-based approach allows you to package the entire application neatly into a single *container* and share it with other developers or users very easily. A single server hosts an engine for the container. On that engine, you can run multiple instances of the engine, which means you can have multiple container-based applications on your system which is a single host machine. Let's see the following image:

Container

Fig 10.16: A container

A single container is capable of hosting an entire web-based application or a service. For instance, for a host server on a Linux, if there exists the docker host, it is capable of running multiple applications and services, each encapsulated within its own container. Provided the machine itself has sufficient resources, to allow containers running in parallel, containerized applications can seamlessly work and/or provide a service from a single host machine.

On system-level architecture, what gives containers an edge is their ability to share the host resources, whereas separating the containers on the contents of each of the applications using it. However, virtual environments take a piece of the hardware each that they are running on, which may compromise performance to an extent. This makes the container lightweight in usage and highly portable across systems. However, the two technologies are not mutually exclusive. Where virtual environments have their own perks, it works in a complementary manner with containers, allowing developers with extended portability, scalability and manageable solutions for development.

An implementation of the container

Docker containers are Linux-based containerization, whereas Windows Server and Hyper V are container solutions offered by Microsoft for containerization. Some renowned container-based solutions include Docker, Kubernetes, Amazon ECS, Azure Container Service, and OpenStack Magnum.

Containerization is a cutting-edge approach to application development. Be it a desktop-based application or a web-hosted service or application, containers offer a lightweight, scalable and robust solution that is reliable, self-contained and efficient in terms of resource usage and management. Having expertise in containers is a considerably sought-after skill by employers and software firms. Therefore, learning about it is definitely rewarding.

Benefits of a container-oriented approach

With any advancement in the technological world, the researches that usually acquire more recognition are those with comparatively higher benefits. The discoveries that tend to be acknowledged among the common people are those that are offering an advantageous addition to the previous less-modern society. That is how it works, right?

Hence, ignoring the obvious confrontation of directing you to the tremendous benefits the containers could offer, we will cut to the chase. But, for those who are unaware of the term containers in the technological world, let me give you a quick review. Containers might remind you of the obvious storage trucks that roll around the street, right? I would call out the techs here to request them to not kill me for using this reference, but they do have a similar purpose.

Containers are an organized approach toward virtual operating systems. An attempt to sophisticatedly manage and run any kind of software or an application transitioned into a success. The amount of data that is signifying and vital in processing the software involved can be stored in a reliable single container which includes code, libraries, files for configuration, and more. It is just like a container for oil heading for its journey with a composed purpose to execute and process.

The traditional virtualization world has converted into a basic, simple but a far more diverse world that carries the necessity that it is supposed to offer accompanied with a touch of innovativeness. This was made possible through Docker that marked the importance of software development by establishing the final step of its initiation, packaging, and delivery of an application through the use of containers. But the thing I would like to jump onto is the numerous benefits that have entranced all the software geeks towards itself.

Let's see some of the benefits of the container-oriented approach:

Consistent

With the utilization of containers, you are freed from the obvious instability that exhibits with the use of inconsistent environment setups. Not only this but also the obstructions that arise with the inconsistency displayed in these setups can tire the individual involved, resulting in refusal from doing the task at hand. These unnecessary hindrances stress a man out and delay the progress that has been planned by the individual in accordance with his own daily schedule. This uncertainty will not be a part of your experience with containers. A container-oriented approach will eradicate such challenges and offer you a stable environment setup.

Faster processing

A container-oriented approach permits the exemplary work of a fast processor. You can introduce new containers into an ongoing task to establish a much diverse, intricate and creative display of software that has the subtlety of loops but provides a unique, friendly experience to the customer. Moreover, you can create new containers on your path to software completion and transfer that to a microservice as per your required necessities of the tasks in hand.

This kind of simplicity is not exhibited to the customer but is often directed to the manufacturer. But the real victory (apart from the simplicity is the key option, not offending anyone) is to conjure up complexity to integrate a simple experience for the customers. This is what the containers offer.

Portable

With this advanced setup, you are bound to be astounded by the various loopholes that assist in the provision of a modern yet simple software completion tool. Sometimes, the simple benefits are what any tool should offer for the client and all that he is looking for. This simple benefit in the case of software development is allocating the successful application in other environments. A container-oriented approach allows you to transfer your resources to be processed in other setups, which is accompanied with the fact that you can run and manage your successful application in any kind of stable setup.

Light weight

The utilization of a container-oriented program assists the user with ease in portability. The reason for such simplicity is the fact that the containers do not allow the storage of operating system images which eradicates any additional redundant storage problems to be encountered by the user and reduces the potential stress on the user. Moreover, the containers use fewer resources which minimize the compressing effect on the system. With smart working, only the application needs to be transitioned into the container which helps in the deliverance of a light weight program.

Efficient

The container-oriented approach sums up all the complexity into one efficient program that has the capability to promote and dignify the customer experience. With easy application development assistance, the need for experimenting can be rendered with the use of containers. This ensures a safe and effective tool to be utilized for software development because of what use is time when you are not able to manage it coherently? Hence, maximizing value and saving time can be covered with the sweet entrance of containers.

We discussed some key benefits of the container-oriented approach. Along with the benefits, this approach has also some drawbacks. Let's discuss them in the next section.

Drawbacks of a container-oriented approach

What is the point of promoting a product if you are not doing it honestly? With any kind of advancement, there is an obscured list of cons that are obviously made oblivious because that is how marketing goes. By ignoring the forms of marketing, we are here to offer you an honest review of the container-oriented approach.

Yes, there are benefits to this tool. There is always a list of pros and cons. It is how you envision it for your use makes the decision for your future plans. Like any other basic tool, there are numerous benefits accompanied by the use of a container-oriented approach and yes, they are effective for any client looking for packaging and processing of software. But there are certain drawbacks that tie the customer in fits of *'Whether I should be investing my time and money into the product?'*.

We are not here to mark your ability to opt for an indecisive dilemma. But there are things you should consider for comparison of products because studies have shown that people prefer comparing two or more choices before opting for the obvious choice. It is part of human nature. So, before you dive into a critical approach, make room for some honest cons that can assist you in directing yourself towards the heavy choice.

Let's see some of the following drawbacks of the container-oriented approach:

Impaired flexibility

There has been some research done regarding the tool that it only runs in Linux-based operating systems which refrains the user to minimize his expansion of work. Moreover, it has been found that not many applications are found to be running effectively within this system of work. A container-oriented approach focuses on the use of multiple containers to initialize the concept of compact software working in unison with these containers that may give an impression of a long chain to offer comprehensive efficiency. This system of work is enhanced by the use of microservice but is not compatible with other existing applications which restrict the user to experimenting.

Poor security

With many virtual machines, there is a coherent and enhanced system of security; the hypervisor that offers a high and quality level of isolation that the containers do not readily offer. The reason for such poor affiliation with a secure environment is the container's root access and sharing of a kernel operating system. This profound authorization level holds the accountability of a container to run which limits the efficacy insecurity. Furthermore, it provides an increased risk of embracing viruses and errors that accumulate within a container and work as a parasite in transition itself to other containers, eventually deteriorating the whole program.

Poor networking

Another issue that arose with the use of a container-oriented approach was the establishment of a proper networking channel. Many users have termed the use of containers as an art rather than a mere tool for enhancement in the scientific arena. The reason is that a proper channel would allow effective user experience inadequate networking but there are additional configuration challenges that need to be overcome when the problem of poor networking takes flight. With the obvious isolation and the issue with networking, comes the problem of deploying software efficiently. Hence, people are cornered with their choices majorly when they are stuck with the software hanging.

Lack of tools

There are a number of tools that are efficient with the proper management and processing of an application which is present with the approach of a container-oriented program. But these tools are limited in number. There are various virtual operating systems that offer far more tools in comparison with the containers and they are assisting in the provision of equal and increased enhancement in software development. Not to enunciate that whatever containers offer lack efficacy, but they are reduced to an amount that limits the expansive system of work that a user usually opts for, eventually minimizing the tasks that creativity could curve into with a container-oriented approach.

Dependencies

The use of a container-oriented approach calls out for other dependent tools which are often not acknowledged with the stability of such advanced software. Sharing with containers is not frowned upon as it can offer quality and with efficiency but there are certain dependencies that do not go well with containers. This additional baggage, if I may, decreases the chances of ease in portability which causes instability to be born within the system. Along with these faults, there is a potential for container-oriented approaches to be costly which may not be your ticket to downfall but offer you an expensive successful outcome.

We discussed the pros and cons of the container-oriented approach. Let's now look at a container implementation approach with Docker in the next section.

Getting started with Docker

To get started with something, you need to learn the purpose and background behind the concept. When talking about Docker, we need to rationalize what actually is the program we are talking about.

Docker is an open source containerization technology. We can use it to containerize your applications. It is based on the container-oriented approach and it is a software platform for containerization. In the software industry, the containerization is referred to as Dockerization due to the popularity of Docker. Docker is used to assist with creating, deploying, and running of applications using containers.

Docker allows you to package all different parts of an application such as binaries/libraries and dependencies in a container. We can also include other Docker images inside a Docker image as per the requirement of your application. The Docker image can be run isolated on any Linux machine. Docker is a software platform used to build, ship, and run light weight containers.

How do you start with Docker? Let us follow these simple steps:

Installing Docker

You can easily install Docker on your Linux machine. Docker is a kind of independent program that requires installation and is not necessarily built-in within computers for its successful installation.

Installing it is quite simple. You need to visit the official website for Docker and you will be able to view the installation page at the official page https://www.docker.com/get-started. This will lead you to the successful installation of the necessary tools, resources and the main Docker system that you are in need of. Follow the basic instructions that are mentioned in the system that will assist you in the setting up of Docker in your machine.

Installing Docker on Linux

Let's follow the given steps to install Docker on a Linux machine:

1. First, use the following command to update your apt packages index using the following command:

    $ sudo apt-get updates

2. Now, let's start the Docker-engine installation using the following command:

    $ sudo apt-get install docker-engine

3. The preceding command will install Docker on your Linux machine. Now, let's start the Docker daemon using the following command:

$ sudo service docker start

4. Now, verify the Docker installation in your Linux machine using the following command:

$ sudo docker run hello-world

After installing and running the preceding command of step 4, you can see if Docker is installed correctly as shown in the following screenshot. The $ sudo docker run hello-world will download the Hello World Docker image and run it in the container:

```
Windows PowerShell
PS F:\bpb-spring-boot-ws\prodos_with_spring_rest_api> docker run hello-world

Hello from Docker!
This message shows that your installation appears to be working correctly.

To generate this message, Docker took the following steps:
 1. The Docker client contacted the Docker daemon.
 2. The Docker daemon pulled the "hello-world" image from the Docker Hub.
    (amd64)
 3. The Docker daemon created a new container from that image which runs the
    executable that produces the output you are currently reading.
 4. The Docker daemon streamed that output to the Docker client, which sent it
    to your terminal.

To try something more ambitious, you can run an Ubuntu container with:
 $ docker run -it ubuntu bash

Share images, automate workflows, and more with a free Docker ID:
 https://hub.docker.com/

For more examples and ideas, visit:
 https://docs.docker.com/get-started/

PS F:\bpb-spring-boot-ws\prodos_with_spring_rest_api>
```

Fig 10.17: Docker on Linux machine

Installing Docker on Windows

We discussed how to install Docker on your Linux machine. If you don't have a Linux machine but you have Windows machine with Windows 10, then you can easily install Docker on your Windows machine by downloading it from https://download.docker.com/win/stable/Docker%20for%20Windows%20Installer.exe. It is available for Windows 10. You can also install Docker in the lower version of Windows that is for Windows by downloading Docker Toolbox from https://download.docker.com/win/stable/DockerToolbox.exe.

But here I am using Windows 10, so after downloading Docker from the website, let's install it by double clicking on .exe file of the Docker. Let's start Docker and run a simple Docker command.

Fig 10.18: Downloaded Docker .exe file in Windows 10 machine

Docker will be installed as shown in the following screenshot:

🐋 Installing Docker Desktop

Docker Desktop 2.0.0.3

Unpacking files...

```
Unpacking files : resources/docker.iso
Unpacking files : resources/docker-for-win.iso
Unpacking files : resources/ddvp.ico
Unpacking files : resources/config-options.json
Unpacking files : resources/concrt140.dll
Unpacking files : resources/componentsVersion.json
Unpacking files : resources/com.docker.proxy.exe
Unpacking files : resources/com.docker.localhost-forwarder.exe
Unpacking files : resources/com.docker.license.exe
Unpacking files : resources/com.docker.isowrap.exe
Unpacking files : resources/com.docker.diagnose.exe
Unpacking files : resources/CHANGELOG
Unpacking files : vcruntime140.dll
Unpacking files : vccorlib140.dll
Unpacking files : System.ValueTuple.dll
Unpacking files : System.Runtime.WindowsRuntime.UI.Xaml.dll
```

Fig 10.19: Docker installation on Windows 10 machine

After successful installing Docker on your Windows 10 machine, you can see that an icon of Docker is created at the desktop. Now, you can verify the installer Docker using the following command on the command prompt:

C:\Users\dinesh.rajput>docker --version

Let's see the following output of the preceding command:

Windows PowerShell

```
PS F:\bpb-spring-boot-ws\prodos_with_spring_rest_api> docker version
Client: Docker Engine - Community
 Version:           18.09.2
 API version:       1.39
 Go version:        go1.10.8
 Git commit:        6247962
 Built:             Sun Feb 10 04:12:31 2019
 OS/Arch:           windows/amd64
 Experimental:      false

Server: Docker Engine - Community
 Engine:
  Version:          18.09.2
  API version:      1.39 (minimum version 1.12)
  Go version:       go1.10.6
  Git commit:       6247962
  Built:            Sun Feb 10 04:13:06 2019
  OS/Arch:          linux/amd64
  Experimental:     false
PS F:\bpb-spring-boot-ws\prodos_with_spring_rest_api>
```

Fig 10.20: Verify Docker installation on Windows 10 machine

We successfully installed Docker on your machine, either Linux or Windows. Let's now learn how to deploy our application using the Docker container in the next section.

Deploy using the Docker container

In this section, we will create a Docker image for our Prodos backend application. We will see how to Dockerize a Spring Boot application (Prodos backend application) to run in an isolated environment.

Before creating a Dockerfile, we have to make a JAR for our Prodos backend application. As we know that the Spring Boot application is nothing but it just an executable JAR file. We can execute it with Java. The JAR file can be created with the following Maven command:

$ mvn clean install

You can also use this command via your Eclipse or STS IDE by running Maven goals by opening the **Run As | Maven Build**. You can type clean install into the **Goals** field and press the **Run** button as the following:

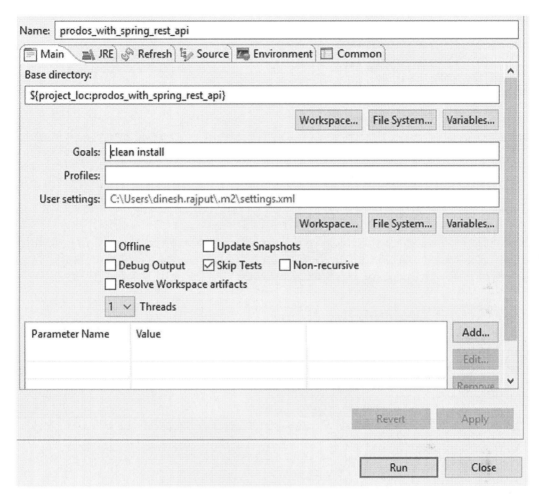

Fig 10.21: Creating a JAR file using STS IDE

After running this Maven command, it will create an executable JAR file for your Prodos backend application. You can see this JAR file inside the target folder of your application as shown in the following screenshot:

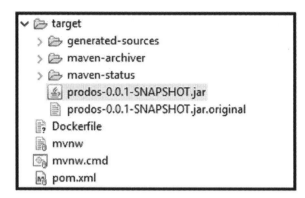

Fig 10.22: An executable JAR file created inside a target folder

Now, let's create a Docker image of your Prodos backend application. To achieve this, we need to create a build file that builds a file is known as Dockerfile in Docker. Let's create a Dockerfile in our Spring Boot application.

Writing Dockerfile

In the container-oriented approach, the Dockerfile is a build file. We need to define some commands and instructions that are required for your application. This file contains some steps to create a Docker build or container image, which can be used to run the application.

Dockerfile doesn't have any special extension; it is a simple text file used for a Docker build. You can automate the Docker image creation using Dockerfile. It has some commands that are very similar to the Linux commands. This means there is no special syntax or command required to create a Docker image.

Let's see the following Docker fine instructions which are used in our Prodos backend application:

```
#This is a Dockerfile for our Prodos backend application
# Use an official Java 8 runtime as a parent image
FROM Maven:3.5-jdk-8-alpine


VOLUME /tmp


#Set maintainer email id
MAINTAINER admin@dineshonjava.com


# Set the working directory to /app
WORKDIR /app
```

```
# Copy the current directory contents into the container at /app
ADD . /app

# Copy the current directory contents into the container at /app
ADD target/prodos-0.0.1-SNAPSHOT.jar prodos-backend.jar

# Make port 80 available to the world outside this container
EXPOSE 80

# Define environment variable
ENV JAVA_OPTS=""

# Run prodos-backend.jar when the container launches
ENTRYPOINT [ "sh", "-c", "java $JAVA_OPTS -
Djava.security.egd=file:/dev/./urandom -jar prodos-backend.jar" ]
```

You can see that I have created a Dockerfile for our Prodos backend application. This file is used to create a Docker image. We created this file inside the root directory of your application. Here are some important points to be considered at the time of writing Dockerfile:

1. The written commands in the Dockerfile are case-insensitive; you can use either capital case or lowercase.

2. Docker follows the top-to-bottom order to run instructions of Dockerfile. Each Dockerfile must have the first instruction as FROM in order to specify the base image.

3. In the preceding Dockerfile, a statement beginning with # is treated as a comment. Other instructions such as RUN, CMD, FROM, EXPOSE, and ENV can be used in our Dockerfile.

4. The next command is the person who is going to maintain this image. Here, you specify the MAINTAINER keyword and just mention the email ID.

5. You can use the WORKDIR command to set the working directory for any RUN, CMD, and COPY instruction that follows it in Dockerfile. If the working directory does not exist, it will be created by default. This command can be used multiple times in Dockerfile.

6. The ADD command is used to copy the current directory contents to the at / app container.

7. The EXPOSE command of Dockerfile is used to make port 80 available to the world outside this container.

8. The ENV command can be used to define the environment variables for our microservice application.

9. The last CMD command is used to execute the microservice application by the image.

We defined the Dockerfile for our Prodos backend application. Dockerfile defines Docker containers. We also created a Dockerfile inside the root directory of our Prodos backend application.

Creating a Docker image using the Maven plugin

You can use a Maven plugin to build Docker images. You need to add it to the pom. xml file of the application. This Maven plugin is developed by Spotify and can be found at https://github.com/spotify/docker-Maven-plugin. Let's see the following change need to be added to the pom.xml file to use the Docker Maven plugin:

```
<properties>
  ...
  <docker.image.prefix>doj</docker.image.prefix>
</properties>

<build>
  <plugins>
   <plugin>
    <groupId>com.spotify</groupId>
    <artifactId>dockerfile-Maven-plugin</artifactId>
    <version>1.3.4</version>
    <configuration>
     <repository>${docker.image.prefix}/${project.artifactId}</repository>
     <buildArgs>
      <JAR_FILE>target/${project.build.finalName}.jar</JAR_FILE>
     </buildArgs>
    </configuration>
   </plugin>
   ...
  </plugins>
</build>
```

In the preceding code, we configured a plugin that will be used to build a Docker image. This plugin has groupId com.spotify and artifactId dockerfile-Maven-plugin. We also provided a configuration; the repository will be used to provide a Docker image name and the name of the JAR file, exposing the Maven configuration as a build argument for Docker.

Let's see the following Maven command used to create a Docker image:

$mvn install dockerfile:build

Similarly, we can also use the Gradle plugin to build a Docker image. Let's see how to create a Docker image using the Docker commands.

Creating a Docker image using the Docker command

In this section, we will build a Docker image of our Spring Boot application using the Docker command. We have already created Dockerfile for our application, as shown in the following screenshot:

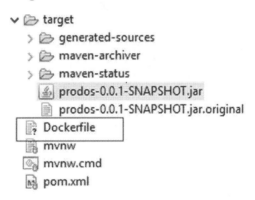

Fig 10.23: Dockerfile in the application root folder

As you can see, we created Dockerfile and placed it in the application root folder. Now, let's run the following command in the command prompt to build a Docker image:

$ docker build -t prodosbackend .

The preceding command creates a Docker image using the Dockerfile. The Docker image name will be prodosbackend. You can give any name to a Docker image. You need to provide a path of the Dockerfile for this command. In our case, you must have noticed that we mentioned "." at the end of the command, which means Dockerfile is located in the current working directory. And we have used the -t option to define a tag for a Docker image.

You can see the following after running the preceding command in the command prompt of your machine:

```
Windows PowerShell                                                    —   □   ×

PS F:\bpb-spring-boot-ws\prodos_with_spring_rest_api> docker build -t prodosbacken ^
Sending build context to Docker daemon   38.18MB
Step 1/9 : FROM openjdk:8-jdk-alpine
 ---> 3675b9f543c5
Step 2/9 : VOLUME /tmp
 ---> Using cache
 ---> 2dc11e30a309
Step 3/9 : MAINTAINER admin@dineshonjava.com
 ---> Using cache
 ---> 6e7dbf1cd21d
Step 4/9 : WORKDIR /app
 ---> Using cache
 ---> 2317248b5e46
Step 5/9 : ADD . /app
 ---> Using cache
 ---> 1ebcefabc493
Step 6/9 : ADD target/prodos-0.0.1-SNAPSHOT.jar prodos-backend.jar
 ---> Using cache
 ---> 0b763e86613c
Step 7/9 : EXPOSE 80
 ---> Using cache
 ---> 4c72f33714cf
Step 8/9 : ENV JAVA_OPTS=""
 ---> Using cache
 ---> e4e1939fd5d5
Step 9/9 : ENTRYPOINT [ "sh", "-c", "java $JAVA_OPTS -Djava.security.egd=file:/dev
 ---> Using cache
 ---> 18e5ed411b21
Successfully built 18e5ed411b21
Successfully tagged prodosbackend:latest
```

Fig 10.24: A Docker image creation using Dockerfile and Docker commands

As you can see in the preceding screenshot, a Docker image has been created successfully. Let's check a list of available Docker images in your machine using the following command:

$ docker image ls

You can see the following output of the preceding command:

```
Windows PowerShell

PS F:\bpb-spring-boot-ws\prodos_with_spring_rest_api> docker image ls
REPOSITORY          TAG             IMAGE ID            CREATED             SIZE
prodosbackend       latest          18e5ed411b21        6 hours ago         181MB
openjdk             8-jdk-alpine    3675b9f543c5        12 days ago         105MB
hello-world         latest          fce289e99eb9        3 months ago        1.84kB
PS F:\bpb-spring-boot-ws\prodos_with_spring_rest_api>
```

Fig 10.25: A list of Docker images

As we have created a Docker image for our Prodos backend application successfully, now you can run our application Docker image (prodosbackend) using the following command:

$ docker run -p 9000:8181 prodosbackend:latest

In the preceding command, we are using the port 9000 for the Docker container which binds with the application port 8181. After running the preceding command, the docker run command is used to run the container of the created prodosbackend Docker image as shown in the following screenshot:

Fig 10.26: A running Docker image

Now, we have run the Docker image of our application successfully. You can test the running prodosbackend application by accessing the URL http://localhost:9000/prodos/products. Let's see the following output image:

```
←  →  C  ⌂    ⓘ localhost:9000/prodos/products
{
  - products: [
    - {
          id: "MOB01",
          name: "Samsung A6 plus",
          type: "Mobile",
          description: "Samsung A6 plus is very nice phone with 24mp front camera",
          brand: "Samsung"
      },
    - {
          id: "MOB02",
          name: "iPhone X plus",
          type: "Mobile",
          description: "iPhone X plus is very nice phone with 24mp front camera",
          brand: "Apple"
      },
    - {
          id: "TLV01",
          name: "Sony Bravia KLV-50W662F 50 Inch Full HD",
          type: "Television",
          description: "Sony Bravia is full HD tv",
          brand: "Sony"
      },
```

Fig 10.27: The output of the Prodos backend application after running the Docker image.

In the preceding screenshot, you can see that API rendered data access from H2 DB. Now, we have Dockerized our Prodos backend application. And it is running as a Docker container. We can run this Docker image everywhere and on any platform.

Conclusion

We deployed our Prodos front-end and backend application to the Heroku cloud platform. You can use any PaaS platform to deploy the application such as AWS, Google Cloud, Microsoft Azure, Cloud Foundry, and so on.

We also discussed the role of the container-oriented approach for application deployment and how the container-oriented approach can be beneficiary in some aspects. We also discussed some drawbacks related to the container-oriented approach.

We used Docker as a container and installed it on our machine and created a Docker image using the Dockerfile with the Maven plugin or Docker build command. We ran our Prodos backend Docker image after creating it.

Questions

1. What is a PaaS platform and how does it help for our application deployment?

2. What are the benefits of PaaS?

3. What is the container-oriented approach?

4. What is a container in container-oriented approach?

5. How is a container different from a VM?

6. What is Docker?

7. What is Dockerfile?

8. How to create a Docker image for your application?

9. What are the benefits of the container oriented approach?

10. What are the drawbacks of the container-oriented approach?

Index

Manufactured by Amazon.ca
Bolton, ON